Indo-U.S. Civil Nuclear Deal

Indo-U.S. Civil Nuclear Deal

Volume–1

Edited by

Rahul Bhonsle
Ved Prakash
K.R. Gupta

ATLANTIC
PUBLISHERS & DISTRIBUTORS (P) LTD

Published by

ATLANTIC

PUBLISHERS & DISTRIBUTORS (P) LTD

B-2, Vishal Enclave, Opp. Rajouri Garden,
New Delhi-110027
Phones : 25413460, 25429987, 25466842

Sales Office
7/22, Ansari Road, Darya Ganj,
New Delhi–110002
Phones : 23273880, 23275880, 23280451
Fax : 91-11-23285873
web : www.atlanticbooks.com
e-mail : info@atlanticbooks.com

ISBN 81-269-0713-4 Vol. 1
ISBN 81-269-0714-2 Vol. 2
ISBN 81-269-0715-0 Set

Printed in India
at Nice Printing Press, Delhi

Preface

The Indo-U.S. Civil Nuclear Deal is seen as the most significant development giving implicit formal recognition to India's nuclear weapons status and a possible opening up of opportunities for it to become a global player in the field of nuclear energy. The wording in the July 18, 2005 joint statement between India and the U.S. provides an essence of the deal: India with its strong commitment to preventing WMD proliferation and as a responsible state with advanced nuclear technology, should acquire the same benefits and advantages, reciprocally assuming the same responsibilities and practices as other leading nations with advanced nuclear technology, such as the P-5.

Apart from non-proliferation, the U.S. President and the Indian Prime Minister have agreed on a large number of initiatives for economic prosperity, energy security, clean environment, knowledge partnership, global safety and security, deepening democracy and meeting international challenges. President Bush has called India in the 21st century as a natural partner of the United States. The successful transformation of the U.S.-India relationship is said to have a decisive and positive influence on the future international system as it evolves in this New Century.

The Indo-U.S. Civil Nuclear Deal is an attempt to create a delicate balance between the policies pursued by India, the Nuclear Suppliers Group as well as the nuclear non-proliferation watchdog, the International Atomic Energy Agency. It is a recognition of the fact that in a world facing severe energy crisis with escalating oil prices and rampant environmental pollution due to consumption of conventional sources of energy, it is illogical to deny clean fuel to India, which though a non-signatory to the Non-proliferation Treaty, has not violated any legal commitment and never encouraged proliferation of nuclear weapons.

Some experts view this deal as the United States' attempt to create a new global balance of power in order to counter the rising power of China. Others feel that the Deal is a discrimination in favor of India which would set an indefensible precedent as the U.S. struggles to curb the nuclear programs of countries like Iran and North Korea. Back home, there are many apprehensions that India will have to surrender some of its sovereign rights in order to receive new nuclear reactor units from abroad and fuel for new or existing reactors from the members of NPT. Some critics say the U.S. would not provide India with the state-of-the-art enrichment technology and equipment since its domestic law prohibits such a trade. On the other side, we have scientists, including no less a person than the former chairman of India's AEC, asserting publicly that India is so far ahead of the world in the fields of fast breeder reactors and nuclear reactor safety that they will come to us seeking help. Experts advocating the Indo-U.S. Civil Nuclear Deal hold that India should learn from China — perhaps their model of economic development. It is scouring all over the world, for energy to ensure its economic development. Look at the way it subjected itself to additional political conditionalities that Australia insisted upon for supplying uranium which China as an NPT-signatory could have resisted. That is pragmatism, demanded by long-term national interest. And what are the Indian 'patriots' doing? Fulminating at the trivialities: U.S.A. is changing goalposts, even when the final 123 Agreement is yet months away. In the same vein, they talk of India losing its autonomy in the nuclear decision-making on far-fetched reasoning. With such kind of facetious arguments, they may end up tying executive's hands, leaving it no space or flexibility to clinch the agreement in the final stages. Any bilateral agreement, by its very definition, is a function of give and take. If the U.S. has executed a near-u-turn in its non-proliferation policy to befriend India, the latter too must make some concessions somewhere, of course, without affecting its strategic interests. In international affairs, nothing comes free. Only beggars accept charity!

Chinese pragmatism deserves high praise. It has an over $200 billion annual trade deficit with the U.S., has invested $250 billion in the U.S. bonds and banks, and is a partner with U.S. in a number of international economic and technological arrangements. The critics of the Indo-U.S. Civil Nuclear Deal should expend their energy in convincing Indians to follow and emulate the Chinese pragmatism than on rustling up inane and venal arguments to oppose the Deal.

Indians must realise that power, economic and military, and especially the latter, is the currency of the international community. If India had not done what it did in 1998, the U.S.A. would not have offered it the strategic partnership. Weakness invites scorn, and at times, even aggression, even by a small neighbour. To wit, Pakistan attacked India in September 1965 because it was perceived to be 'weak' at that point of time. Indians must resolve that their country would never be perceived weak by any one or any nation in future.

As the Deal has to be approved not only by the legislative leg of the Washington power tripod but it must also clear hurdles in forty-five capitals in Europe, Asia and the Americas, which are tightly knit under the rubric of the Nuclear Suppliers Group (NSG), the action is not thus restricted within the U.S.

and India but spread worldwide and accordingly the reactions on the Deal are mixed.

The issue of the Indo-U.S. Civil Nuclear Deal is thus extremely complex involving national and international polity, nuclear non-proliferation, diplomacy as well as technicalities of the nuclear fuel cycle. This is also an important test case for both the United States as well as India to place their relationship in a new paradigm of collaborated acceleration rather than inconsistent progress in fits and starts. In the process, we will also be testing new waters of acceptance of India as a nuclear weapons state by the international community in general and the nations in our immediate neighborhood, China and Pakistan in particular. The present book in two Volumes thus attempts to provide a holistic perspective of the Indo-U.S. Civil Nuclear Deal in the context of international relations, economic as well as nuclear energy cooperation.

The book includes articles contributed by erudite experts in the field of international strategic affairs. It also consolidates in one source important documents relating to the Civil Nuclear Deal, e.g. speeches of the U.S. President, George W Bush, Indian Prime Minister, Mr Manmohan Singh, Senators, Congressmen, senior officials like Ms Condoleezza Rice, Nicholas Burns, Shyam Saran, the viewpoints of different countries, the Nuclear Suppliers Group and International Atomic Energy Agency Chief, ElBaradei. When different experts contribute papers on the same subject, some duplication becomes unavoidable. The Editors have not attempted to remove duplication with a view to provide the entire context in which the papers have been written by the authors.

The book is thus a Pone source primer on the Indo-U.S. Civil Nuclear Deal and will be found useful by students of strategic affairs and international relations. It will be helpful for Government executives, strategic analysts and parliamentarians, both of India and the United States. Common readers interested in current world affairs, Indo-U.S. relations and nuclear issues would also find the book interesting and useful.

Rahul Bhonsle
Ved Prakash
K.R. Gupta

Contents

Pages

VOLUME–2

U.S.-India 2005 Nuclear Accord

1

—U.N. Gupta

Significant development from the point of view of international diplomacy, international politics and energy augmentation for India is the accord and understanding reached between U.S. President Bush and Indian Prime Minister Manmohan Singh in July 2005. It is well-known that U.S. diplomacy is of bargaining advantages out of any international situation or transaction, it is always transitory and is neither charitable nor idealist in nature; U.S. has a concept of friendship based on mutual advantages or common interest that change with time. The notable point is that lately, U.S. has softened its attitude against India on civilian use of nuclear energy: away from the wider international restrictions of NPT, of Nuclear Suppliers Group and earlier U.S. unilateral sanctions. The reasons behind this softening of attitudes is also on realization of the situation that India has energy crunch and the U.S sanctions against India on its nuclear energy program are gradually proving meaningless, since other nations are willing to sell nuclear reactors under IAEA safeguards to India. India wants to go ahead for natural gas imports from Iran for meeting its fast growing energy crunch through an Iran-Pakistan-India natural gas pipeline in partnership with Pakistan. This might involve a dilution of U.S. close relationship with Pakistan. Further, the U.S. recognizes the reshuffling that has taken place on international diplomacy front. The U.S. policies in the Middle East are not paying any dividend; the lessons of unilateralism in Iraq war have reached embarrassing stagnation. Pakistan has not succeeded in capturing Osama bin Laden or in liquidating Al Qaeda and continues to be rigidly Islamic. Also,

China is fast becoming an economic giant and poses no immediate military threat to U.S. It is co-operating with U.S. in disarming and dismantling of nuclear weapons of North Korea as a common cause (2003-2005). India, on the other hand, is economically pro-West and is prospectively a good purchaser of arms and civil and military aircraft of U.S., French or British make alongwith military hardware. It has a counterbalancing presence against China in South Asia. Recognizing these recent changes in international diplomatic balance, freeing India from energy crunch appeared to be sensible to the U.S. As a preface to the change, in January 2004, a resolve for expanded cooperation between India and U.S. had taken place encompassing civilian nuclear activities, civilian space program and high technology trade including missile defence.[1] Then, as Next Steps in Strategic Partnership (NSSP) in April 2005, U.S. and India had signed the 10-year "New Framework for the U.S.-India Defence Relationship" (NFDR) agreement at ministerial level.[2] The NFDR aims at a broad range of joint military activities that include collaboration in multinational operations as might be 'in their common interest'. This NFDR is to strengthen the capabilities of the two militaries to promote security, defeat terrorism and enhance their capabilities to combat the proliferation of WMD in a cooperative perspective that was not perceived before.

U.S.-India Nuclear Pact

Following these steps in U.S. and India cooperation efforts, a turning point came with 18 July 2005 accord on civilian nuke cooperation, reached between U.S. President George W. Bush and Indian Prime Minister Manmohan Singh in Washington. The bilateral pact essentially contemplates the U.S. to resume under its laws[3] to be suitably amended, the supply of nuclear fuel and technology and reactors to India on various far-reaching conditions. The pact impliedly accepts India a nuclear power with the right of maintaining a minimum nuclear deterrence. India, on its part, is to unilaterally place its civilian nuclear reactors and nuclear materials to be acquired from U.S. within the purview of IAEA's new India specific guidelines; for this, India is to draw a wall of separation between its nuclear defensive deterrence program and nuclear energy producing reactor system. The U.S. has undertaken to make efforts or good offices to bring the other 44 States of Nuclear Suppliers Group also in line. It has been universally noticed by media and analysts that India is not a signatory of NPT, is both *de facto* nuclear power and *de jure* nuclear state on indigenous development efforts and its case is different from that of Pakistan, North Korea and Iran. The last two are NPT States and have developed or are developing nuclear weapons in violation of NPT while Pakistan is a confirmed proliferator of nuclear weapons and technology. The status of nuclear India is regarded to be unique. As United States Ambassador to India, David C. Mulford, has observed:

"India can truly be distinguished as a unique case and I say that because if you advance that unique case you can do so without violating or compromising *your own* commitment to non-proliferation. The U.S. commitment to non-proliferation and the international architecture is not going to change. And just because we want to find a special way to recognize India's unique position doesn't mean that we are giving up ours and undermining or moving away from it or even that we'll be any less intense in our following the non-proliferation regime."[4]

In essence, the Pact will allow India to acquire nuclear fuel and advanced reactors from the U.S. and other countries under the IAEA new India specific guidelines to meet the energy crunch. France, Russia and China follow NSG guidelines in the matter and not wider U.S. inhibitions that would now require some U.S. internal legislative changes. The States that come to do such trade with India do not violate their NPT obligations. This pact does not prevent India from obtaining natural gas additionally. An epilogue seems to have been expressed by U.S. in 2006, when it was observed that the prospect that India "could have civil nuclear energy is one that is welcomed not just by U.S. but also by the other countries of Nuclear Suppliers Group". The good argument taken is that U.S. couldn't have it both ways—telling carbon dependent countries like India that you can't engage in energy relations with a nation like "Iran, but by the way, access to civil nuclear (energy) is closed off to you"[5]

Details of the U.S.-India Nuclear Accord

The text of Indo-U.S. Joint Statement issued after the delegation-level meeting between the Prime Minister Dr. Manmohan Singh and the U.S. President Mr. George W. Bush, in Washington DC on July 18, 2005 noted the following:

"The Prime Minister's visit coincides with the completion of the Next Steps in Strategic Partnership (NSSP) initiative, launched in January 2004. The two leaders agree that this provides the basis for expanding bilateral activities and commerce in space, civil nuclear energy and dual-use technology."

Drawing a mutual vision for the U.S.-India relationship, the two leaders agreed on the concepts and mutual interest in "Economy", in "Energy and Environment", in "Democracy and Development", in "Non-Proliferation and Security" and for cooperation in the fields of "High-Technology and Space".

Further: "Building on the strengthened non-proliferation commitments undertaken in the NSSP" and "Recognizing the significance of civilian nuclear energy for meeting growing global energy demands in a cleaner and more efficient manner, the two leaders discussed India's plans to develop its civilian nuclear energy program" leading to the accord.

The Joint Statement recognized the strong commitment of India to preventing WMD proliferation as a responsible State. President Bush in the Joint Statement stated that India should acquire the same benefits and advantages of advanced nuclear technology as other such States. Continuing the Joint Statement records:

> The President told the Prime Minister that he would work to achieve full civil nuclear energy cooperation with India as it realizes its goals of promoting nuclear power and achieving energy security. The President would also seek agreement from Congress to adjust U.S. laws and policies, and the United States will work with friends and allies to adjust international regimes to enable full civil nuclear energy

cooperation and trade with India, including but not limited to expeditious consideration of fuel supplies for safeguarded nuclear reactors at Tarapur. In the meantime, the United States will encourage its partners to also consider this request expeditiously. India has expressed its interest in ITER and a willingness to contribute. The United States will consult with its partners considering India's participation. The United States will consult with the other participants in the Generation IV International Forum with a view toward India's inclusion.

"The Prime Minister conveyed that for his part, India would reciprocally agree that it would be ready to assume the same responsibilities and practices and acquire the same benefits and advantages as other leading countries with advanced nuclear technology, such as the United States. These responsibilities and practices consist of identifying and separating civilian and military nuclear facilities and programs in a phased manner and filing a declaration regarding its civilians facilities with the International Atomic Energy Agency (IAEA); taking a decision to place voluntarily its civilian nuclear facilities under IAEA safeguards; signing and adhering to an Additional Protocol with respect to civilian nuclear facilities; continuing India's unilateral moratorium on nuclear testing; working with the United States for the conclusion of a multilateral Fissile Material Cut-off Treaty; refraining from transfer of enrichment and reprocessing technologies to states that do not have them and supporting international efforts to limit their spread; and ensuring that the necessary steps have been taken to secure nuclear materials and technology through comprehensive export control legislation and through harmonization and adherence to Missile Technology Control Regime (MTCR) and Nuclear Suppliers Group (NSG) guidelines."

"The President welcomed the Prime Minister's assurance. The two leaders agreed to establish a working group to undertake on a phased basis in the months ahead the necessary actions mentioned above to fulfill these commitments. The President and the Prime Minister also agreed that they would review this progress when the President visits India in 2006."

"The two leaders also reiterated their commitment that their countries would play a leading role in international efforts to prevent the proliferation of weapons of mass destruction, including nuclear, chemical, biological and radiological weapons."

As already noted this Joint Statement amounted to an accord different from a treaty or agreement between two sovereign States. The U.S. is a member of NPT and so are the members of Nuclear Suppliers Group (NSG) but India is not a member of NPT and is a *de jure* nuclear State under international law. The Joint Statement noted through the two statements that U.S. will have to make internal constitutionally valid adjustments while India would be required to surrender some of its sovereign rights in order to receive new nuclear energy reactor units from abroad and fuel for new or existing reactors from the members of NPT.

The Prime Minister of India took into confidence the Parliament of India against the charges of sell-out of the sovereignty of the nation,[6] thus:

"I rise to inform this august House of the status of discussions with the United States on civil nuclear energy co-operation. Substantive aspects of this are reflected in the Joint Statement of July 18, 2005 that U.S. President Bush and I agreed upon during my visit to Washington DC last year. I would like to use this occasion to outline the context and core elements of the Joint Statement, before detailing the status of the ongoing negotiations."

"Hon'ble Members are aware that our effort to reach an understanding with the United States to enable civil nuclear energy cooperation was based on our need to overcome the growing energy deficit that confronts us.... While we have substantial reserves of coal, excessive dependence on coal-based energy has its own implications for our environment. Nuclear technology provides a plentiful and non-polluting source of power to meet our energy needs.... Our nuclear program is truly unique. Its uniqueness lies in the breadth of its overarching vision of India mastering a three-stage nuclear program using our vast thorium resources, and mastering more complex processes of the full nuclear fuel cycle...." Consequently, "our civilian and strategic programs are deeply intertwined across the expanse of the nuclear fuel cycle. Over the years, the maturation of our nuclear program, including the development of world-class thermal power reactors, has made it possible to contemplate some changes. These are worth considering if benefits include gaining unhindered access to nuclear material, equipment, technology and fuel from international sources...." However, "the Nuclear Suppliers Group (NSG), an informal group of 45 countries, largely determines international trade in nuclear material, equipment and technologies...." "The essence of what was agreed in Washington last July was a shared understanding of our growing energy needs. In recognition of our improved ties, the United States committed itself to a series of steps to enable bilateral and international cooperation in nuclear energy. These include adjusting domestic policies, and working with allies to adjust relevant international regimes. There was also a positive mention of possible fuel supply to the first two nuclear power reactors at Tarapur. The U.S. support was also indicated for India's inclusion as a full partner in the International Thermonuclear Experimental Research Project and the Generation IV International Forum."

The Prime Minister continued that the "Joint Statement offered the possibility of decades-old restrictions being set aside to create space for India's emergence as a full member of a new nuclear world order...."

"On our part, as Hon'ble Members may recall from my suo moto statement on July 29 last year, we committed ourselves to separating the civilian and strategic program. We have amply clarified our objective in pursuing full civil nuclear energy cooperation for our energy security and to reassure them of India's impeccable non-proliferation credentials."

"At the official level, we have constituted two groups comprising key functionaries concerned with strategic and nuclear matters. They included the Department of Atomic Energy, the Ministry of External Affairs, the Armed Forces and my Office. These two groups were respectively mandated to draw up an acceptable Separation Plan, and to negotiate on this basis. The directive given to both groups was to ensure that our strategic nuclear program is not compromised in any way, while striving to enlarge avenues for full civil nuclear energy cooperation with the international community."

"However, this was to be conditional upon, and reciprocal to, the United States fulfilling its side of the understanding...." "There have been discussions with other countries like Russia, U.K. and France as well. At the political level, I have maintained contact with President Chirac of France, President Putin of Russia, Prime Minister Blair of the U.K.... There have been discussions with other countries like Russia, U.K. and France as well. At the political level, I have maintained contact with President Chirac of France, President Putin of Russia, Prime Minister Blair of the U.K. I have also raised this subject with the Heads of State/Government of Norway, Republic of Korea, Netherlands, Czech Republic and Ireland—all members of the NSG. I also met President Bush in New York last September and discussed implementation of the July 18 statement...." "Hon'ble Members may be assured that in deciding the contours of a Separation Plan, we have taken into account our current and future strategic needs and programs after careful deliberation of all relevant factors, consistent with our Nuclear Doctrine. We are among very few countries to adhere to the doctrine of 'No first Use'. Our doctrine envisions a credible minimum nuclear deterrent to inflict unacceptable damage on an adversary indulging in a nuclear first strike. The facilities for this, and the required level of comfort in terms of our strategic resilience have thus been our criterion in drawing up a Separation Plan.... The Separation Plan that is being outlined is not only consistent with the imperatives of national security, it also protects our vital research and development interests. We have ensured that our three-stage nuclear program will not be undermined or hindered by external interference...." "We will offer to place under safeguards only those facilities that can be identified as civilian without damaging our deterrence potential or restricting our R&D effort, or in any way compromising our autonomy of developing our three stage nuclear program. In this process, the

Department of Atomic Energy has been involved at every stage, and the Separation Plan has been drawn up with their inputs."

"Therefore our proposed Separation Plan entails identifying in phases, a number of our thermal nuclear reactors as civilian facilities to be placed under IAEA safeguards, amounting to roughly 65% of the total installed thermal nuclear power capacity, by the end of the Separation Plan."

"There are complex issues involved. Several aspects of the nuclear program lend themselves in the public discussions to differing interpretations, such as the Fast Breeder Program or our fuel-cycle capabilities such as re-processing and enrichment requirements.... Many aspects of the proposed Separation Plan are currently under negotiation. It is true that certain assurances in the July 18 Statement remain to be fulfilled—the supply of imported fuel for Tarapur I and II, for one. Some elements, such as U.S. support for India's participation in the ITER program, have materialized. The issue of the nature of safeguards to be applied to facilities designated civilian also remains pending resolution."

On the completion of second round of talks between Prime Minister Manmohan Singh and U.S. President George W. Bush in New Delhi on March 2, 2006, the Joint Statement stated among other matters and reviewed the progress made in deepening the global partnership between the United States and India since their Joint Statement of July 18, 2005. The President and the Prime Minister reaffirmed their commitment to expand even further the growing ties between their two countries. On the item 'For Energy Security and a Clean Environment' they:

1. Welcomed the successful completion of discussions on India's Separation Plan and looked forward to the full implementation of the commitments in the July 18, 2005 Joint Statement on nuclear cooperation. This historic accomplishment will permit our countries to move forward towards our common objective of full civil nuclear energy cooperation between India and the United States and between India and the international community as a whole.

2. Welcomed the participation of India in the ITER initiative on fusion energy as an important further step towards the common goal of full nuclear energy cooperation.
3. Agreed on India's participation in FutureGen, an international public-private partnership to develop new, commercially viable technology for a clean coal near-zero emission power project. India will contribute funding to the project and participate in the Government Steering Committee of this initiative.

The Prime Minister of India made a statement[7] in Parliament on the 'discussions on civil nuclear energy cooperation with the U.S.' on India's Separation Plan of nuclear reactors of military and civil character, thus:

> Our discussions covered the expansion of our ties in the fields of agriculture, economic and trade cooperation, energy security and clean environment, strengthening innovation and the knowledge economy, issues relating to global safety and security and on deepening democracy. Expanded cooperation in each of these areas will have a significant impact on India's social and economic development.... India will identify and separate its civilian and military nuclear facilities and place its civilian nuclear facilities under IAEA safeguards. In light of the above understandings with the United States, an India-specific safeguards agreement will be negotiated between India and the IAEA. In essence, an India-specific safeguards agreement would provide: on the one hand safeguards against withdrawal of safeguarded nuclear material from civilian use at any time, and on the other permit India to take corrective measures to ensure uninterrupted operation of its civilian nuclear reactors in the event of disruption of foreign fuel supplies. Taking this into account, India will place its civilian nuclear facilities under India-specific safeguards in perpetuity and negotiate an appropriate safeguards agreement to this end with the IAEA. In the terms of the Separation Plan, there is hence assurance of uninterrupted supply of fuel to reactors that

would be placed under safeguards together with India's right to take corrective measures in the event fuel supplies are interrupted.... The House can rest assured that India retains its sovereign right to take all appropriate measures to fully safeguard its interests....

No constraint has been placed on our right to construct new facilities for strategic purposes. The integrity of our Nuclear Doctrine and our ability to sustain a Minimum Credible Nuclear Deterrent is adequately protected. Our nuclear policy will continue to be guided by the principles of restraint and responsibility....

The Fast Breeder Test Reactor and the Prototype Fast Breeder Reactor remain outside safeguards. We have agreed, however, that future civilian thermal power reactors and civilian Fast Breeder Reactors would be placed under safeguards, but the determination of what is civilian is solely an Indian decision.... The accord also ensures India's participation as a full partner in cutting edge multilateral scientific effort in the nuclear field such as ITER and Generation IV Initiative."

Reactions and Fears

Indian scientists have had many of their technical concerns pacified and taken care of. But political opposition in India emphasized repeatedly that India must resist U.S. pressure to link the nuclear deal to any wider strategic realignment. That is, the nuclear civil use future facilities should not come in the way of defence preparedness. It is to be remembered first, that Next Steps in Strategic Partnership (NSSP) initiative was launched in January 2004. Then in April 2005, U.S. and India had signed the 10-year "New Framework for the US-India Defence Relationship" (NFDR) agreement at ministerial level by the Government ruled by political parties that formed the parliamentary 'Opposition' in July 2005. Therefore both the Government and the 'Opposition' had little to differ and President Bush was common factor between the two Governments of India. Secondly, that under the so-called accord, based on Joint Statements, there is no curtailment of Indian defence present or future projects or initiatives. India is to decide on the quality or quantum of 'minimum credible nuclear deterrence' both presently and in future. Thirdly, there is reciprocity of efforts and achievements before the accord might materialize. The U.S. has to obtain constitutional sanction of the Congress and persuade NSG for supplying nuclear fuel to India, while India completes separation of military and civil nuclear facilities. This separation would be worthwhile and affordable even if the accord fails to materialize.

It would be difficult for President Bush to get the approval of Senate. There are some objections for American diehard conservative politicians that President Bush has to tackle. For example:

Will the U.S.-India civil nuclear cooperation deal accelerate the nuclear arms race in South Asia?

Will this initiative effectively recognize India as a nuclear weapons State contrary to NPT?

Will the accord succeed in placing a desired curb on India, on production of nuclear weapons and on existing nuclear arsenal?

Will this initiative create a charge of double standard against U.S. and encourage rogue nations like North Korea and Iran to continue to pursue nuclear weapons programs?

Will this initiative not weaken or demolish by creating exception in the global non-proliferation regime for which U.S. has so ardently worked?

Keeping in view the projected emergence of India as a giant economic power and its self-dependence on nuclear weapons against threat from neighbors, President Bush is offering the nuclear accord to the U.S. Congress as an achievement for the benefit of and in the overall interest of U.S. and Nuclear Suppliers Group.

REFERENCES

1. U.S. Defence Secretary Donald Rumsfeld and Indian Defence Minister Pranab Mukherjee made the agreement in Washington. See, "India, U.S. Ink Defence Pact", Chidanand Rajghatta/ TNN reporting from Washington, *The Times of India*, Lucknow (ed.) 30 April 2005.

2. U.S. Nuclear Non-Proliferation Act (NNPA) of 1978.
3. Report by Kesava Menon & Nirupama Subramanian entitled, 'Nuclear issue: "India is a unique case"', vide, *The Hindu*, Online edition , 28 September 2005.
4. PTI report from Washington "Rice endorses India's Quest to Acquire N-Tech": *The Times of India,* Lucknow (ed.) 7 January 2006. Ms Condoleezza Rice is currently US Secretary of State.
5. PTI report from Vienna of the speech of Chairman of Indian Atomic Energy Commission and leader of Indian Delegation, Anil Kakodkar, on 28 September 2005.
6. *Suo Moto* Statement in Parliament on 27 February 2006 made before the visit of President Bush in India, March 1-3, 2006.
7. Statement was made *suo moto* on 7 March 2006.

2

U.S. Strategic Engagement of India: The Underlying Theme of the Indo-U.S. Nuclear Agreement

—Rahul Bhonsle

> *"The initiative that we are putting before you and asking for legislation to amend the Atomic Energy Act of 1954 will advance international security, enhance energy security, further environmental protection, and increase business opportunities for both our countries."*

United States Secretary of State Condoleezza Rice appearing before the Senate Foreign Relations Committee on 06 April 2006

INTRODUCTION

The Indo-U.S. Nuclear Agreement called as the U.S.-India Civil Nuclear Cooperation Initiative in America (hereafter referred to as the Agreement) was signed by the U.S. President and the Indian Prime Minister on 2 March 2006 at New Delhi as a key marker in the process of strategic engagement of India by the United States. India's strategic significance was recognized by the U.S. in the 1990's much before the present Bush administration came to power. This led to a gradual shift in U.S. as well as Indian foreign policy, adjusting to the realism of a post-Cold War, post-globalized and later a post-9/11 world. The transformation was also due to a shift in global polity from Mackinder's geographical to Adam Smith's economic orientation. Trade, commerce, markets and resources are the key drivers of this new world. China is seen to outpace other economies of the world with double digit growth while India is incrementally emerging as an economic powerhouse determined by the large size of its market, appetite for energy and an information-age aligned youth force. The Indian foreign policy establishment awakened to the new reality of growing U.S. interest in South Asia more gradually. It has always been wary of the hyphenated India-Pakistan approach to the Sub Continent, ignoring the reality of asymmetry between India and Pakistan, seen as a long time protégé of the United States. However, India shed the bind of non-alignment which had prevented equity in relations with the U.S. and watered down its socialism facilitating U.S. engagement.

The visit of President Bill Clinton to India in March 2000 was the first indication of India's enlarged mega pixels in the U.S. eye view. Clinton's warm and charismatic personality was ideally suited to win Indian approval. Thc Next Steps in Strategic Partnership (NSSP) inked in September 2004 under the Bush Administration was a confirmation of permanency of American interest in India. This has now been cemented with the Indo-U.S. Nuclear Agreement. The Agreement is in fact being leveraged by the U.S. as an instrument to draw India closer in the American orbit of interest despite stiff opposition by the non-proliferation lobby at home and anticipated abroad once it is tabled before world bodies such as the Nuclear Suppliers Group (NSG). This paper proposes to explore the underlying theme of the Indo-U.S. Nuclear Agreement pitched as a catalyst for development of strategic relationship between India and the United States in the decades ahead.

The exploration is being developed through a review of conduct of U.S. foreign policy related to the Agreement over the past two years. U.S. Foreign Policy formulation has two distinct features; a small covert and a larger open component conducted in the public domain. The increasing importance attached by the United States to the South Asian Region in general and India in particular is indicated by remarks of U.S. officials and other leaders in their official statements before various committees. The relative transparency of functioning of the United States administration makes these documents available for public viewing virtually in real time. These are then thoroughly dissected by the media, political analysts, contrarians and others interested in the issue. Thus the basic structure of United States policy including prognostications can be successfully gleaned from these discussions.

The direct manner of conduct of diplomacy is another peculiarity atypical to America. There is nothing oblique in the way the United States warns its antagonists. Iran and China are the more recent examples, whom the United States has served notice, the former for suspending nuclear enrichment and the latter for greater transparency in its defense modernization program. The United States Department of Defence is also required to place every year before the Congress its assessment of China's military power and its possible directions. While the merit or otherwise of such a method of conducting diplomacy can be debated separately, it provides a very useful overview of the general intent of the national leadership of the time. Guessing intent is 90 per cent of an analysts task, the remainder being capabilities, which though more laborious is easier to compile and comment upon. Knowing the intent simplifies policy prognostication. The minuscule portion of U.S. foreign policy which is not in the open domain is frequently the subject of speculation. The strategic considerations underlying the Indo-U.S. Civil Nuclear Agreement are thus analyzed based on available documents in the open domain and logical surmises of discussions possibly happening in camera.

Cooperative Security versus Balance of Power

Post-Cold War international policy is torn between the two extremes of balance of power and cooperative security. Nations seem to be progressing through an interlocking grid of cooperative interests in various fields as economy, energy, trade, information and military, while simultaneously engaging each other in a complex miasma of balance of power. This would be evident from the fact that China and the United States are the largest trading partners while both simultaneously pursue a policy of undermining each others interests in conventional and nuclear armament. United States has also been accused of playing the democracy card in the Caucasus, Ukraine and other former Soviet satellites to undermine Russian influence. Americans continue to be wary generally of the Russian Bear and particularly of the Chinese Dragon while engaging them concurrently in trade and energy supplies. The concomitant interplay of foreign policy of nations based on the dyad of cooperative engagement (COE) and balance of power (BOP) is highlighted by means of a graph in Figure 1. Two block of nations have been summated. Block 1 nations are the United States, European Union, Japan, South Korea and India, while Block 2 nations include Russia, China and Pakistan. The conflict-cooperation paradigm between the two blocks is depicted by interaction in the fields of nuclear weapons' proliferation, nuclear energy, energy security, economic security, conventional military capability and terrorism.

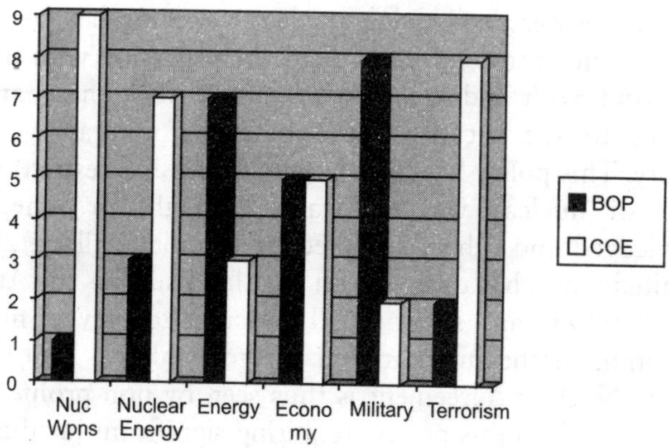

Figure 1

A view at the graph would indicate that the traditional paradigm of balance of power continues to dominate in the fields of energy and conventional military capability, while cooperative engagement is seen primarily in nuclear non-proliferation, including weaponisation and energy and counter terrorism with economy balanced equitably between the two poles. This substantiates the premise that there are many balance of power considerations supplemented by the need for cooperative engagement for the United States in strategic engagement of India through the Agreement.

This is substantiated by statements by U.S. analysts as Robert Galluci who opposed the Agreement in general but was willing to review it based on American relationship with China in the future. If China turns hegemonic, then U.S. would have to balance Chinese dominance with a partnership with India, feels Galluci (2006). The U.S. could thus be developing the strategic alliance with India to undermine possible Chinese influence much as it has been coagulating with other nations in the region such as Japan, Korea, South East Asia and Australia, over the years. The emerging power of the Indian state deems it necessary to include it in the U.S. orbit as a collaborator rather than a competitor.

Basis of U.S. Nuclear Policy

Deterrence is the basis of U.S. nuclear policy. Limiting the number of powers possessing nuclear weapons has been the capstone of nuclear deterrence. Thus the obsession with Iran at present and with India earlier to ensure that there are no accretions to the list of states possessing nuclear weapons capability. This policy has been largely successful, restricting the number of nuclear weapon states to eight or nine, five acknowledged and others accepted by default (Galluci, 2006). The United States has drafted iron clad laws such as the Atomic Energy Act 1954 and supports all measures to prevent nuclear proliferation in the international forum (Galluci, 2006). The Indo U.S. Nuclear Agreement is thus seen by non proliferators as an exception to this policy, requiring significant justification as a concession to India is feared to lead to a cycle of similar allowance being given to future proliferators. The key issues as per Senator Biden were, "India-specific safeguards", or "corrective measures that India may take...in the event of disruption of foreign fuel supplies", U.S. "assurances regarding fuel supply", and "a strategic reserve of nuclear fuel" for India which need to be explained by the U.S. administration (Biden, 2006).

Similar arguments are put forth by Robert Einhorn of the Center for Strategic and International Studies. These include preferential treatment of India, non consultation of the U.S. Congress and the Nuclear Suppliers Group or NSG, allowing India to place only 14 of the 22 existing or planned nuclear power reactors under safeguard, thereby providing it a leeway to expand the scope of its nuclear programs. Abolition of controls is also seen as a signal to other NSG members to supply fuel to India removing the constraints on them. The inability of the deal to stop fissile material production by India has been highlighted as its greatest weakness. The Fissile Material Cut Off Treaty, tabled in the Conference on Disarmament in Vienna by the United States in May 2006, has however obviated this apprehension. Other fears relate to additional reactors which were being built by India with a choice of placing these under international safeguards lying with it, providing a capability to develop greater number of nuclear weapons, up to 50 nuclear missiles per year (Einhorn, 2006). Einhorn feels that an amendment permitting nuclear exports to India except equipment, materials or technologies related to the sensitive fuel cycle should meet the requirement (Einhorn, 2006). The anti-Agreement lobbyists thus seem to be primarily relying on the hazard of proliferation by other states and none have contested the collateral benefits and India's expanded significance in the strategic landscape of the future.

An independent survey conducted by Senator Richard G. Lugar, Chairman of Senate Foreign Relations Committee, has denoted that in the next five years, two nations are likely to join the nuclear weapons club, in the next ten years, four and in the next two decades eight more are likely to produce nuclear weapons. Seventy-nine per cent of the experts polled predicted that a nuclear attack by a terrorist group was more likely than by a state actor (Lugar, 2005). Analysts would not find it difficult to name the states which are likely to be of the two, four or eight most likely to acquire nuclear weapons. The concessions given to India in the current case are not likely to be applicable to any of these countries being signatories of the Nuclear Non-Proliferation Treaty including Iran. Thus the India case is a unique one and the grounds for setting a cycle of similar dispensation to other states into motion appear unjustified.

The Strategic Dimension—Importance of South Asia and India

The first key motivator for greater Indo-U.S. engagement is considered to be the growing importance of South Asia in the U.S. world view. The large population of this region with its challenges as religious extremism, terrorism, weapons of mass destruction lack of democratization, human rights, poverty and illiteracy is a key concern (Boucher, 2006).The United States policy in South Asia seeks to build regional stability by countering terrorism, controlling narcotics and limiting the endemic conflicts in the region. Integration of energy, water, infrastructure, trade and communications in South and Central Asia and building the key foundations of soft power, that is education, economic growth, rule of law, human rights and transparent government are other drivers of policy (Boucher, 2006). The geographic plate of South and Central Asia when linked denotes a paradox of resources and challenges. It is also flanked by two potential adversaries of America—Russia and China. The United States would need a stable, credible and capable regional partner to maintain stability in this region as well as retain it in U.S. orbit of influence.

Pakistan is geographically well suited for this role and is being projected so over the decades. However it is too unstable, lacks India's economic and power potential, international credibility and is also known to balance its relationship with China to advantage. India thus remains the sole option for a strategic fulcrum in South and Central Asia. It has, in the words of Secretary of State, Rice, a large potential for exports, likely to be the world's most populous nation. A rising global power, India is stated to be a, "pillar of stability" in Asia. This makes it a natural partner for the United States and the Nuclear Agreement will consolidate this relationship (Rice, 2006).

India's growing significance to the United States has been summed up by India-born strategic analyst, Ashley Tellis as its economic potential and increased willingness to align itself with the West shedding its long standing policy of non-alignment with a Russian tilt. India's influence will provide the U.S. much needed leverage in controlling what is already the most tumultuous region in the world. India will also benefit with a *quid pro quo* of being acknowledged as a nuclear weapon state, a long cherished national aspiration, frequently prefixed with the word, "responsible", to highlight the country's moral standing on the issue and a largesse of economy, technology, nuclear and military ware.

Economic Motivation

The Economic motivation for United States engagement of India needs to be placed in perspective. Asian share of global economy is estimated to be 43 per cent by 2025. India is likely to have anything from 8 to 10 per cent of this substantial Asian pie. The need for developing economic relations with all Asian states by the United States is thus underlined (Tellis, 2006). India's economic growth of over 8 per cent over the years has been fuelled by trade and investment with the United States as per Boucher. Indo-U.S. Trade has grown by $ 10 billion or 62.5 per cent between 1998 and 2005 (Boucher, 2006). India's vast intellectual capital and the ability to project soft power are also impressive (Boucher, 2006). The emerging Indo-U.S. economic engagement is multifaceted and is supported by agricultural technology sharing, science and technology cooperation and a defense relationship. The broad basis of this association has been highlighted by Rice who emphasized that it went beyond a government to government one to include CEOs of Indian and American companies (Rice, 2006). The U.S. sees broad economic engagement of India contributing to improvement of lives of the people of India (Boucher, 2006).

Multiple economic forums have been formed to foster economic integration. The Trade Policy Forum, the Financial and Economic Forum, the Environment Dialogue and the Commercial Dialogue are viewed as the main vehicles of economic cooperation. Biotechnology and Information Technology forums have also been given special space in the economic partnership (Boucher, 2006). The push given to resolution of the beleaguered Dabhol and other smaller power projects in Tamil Nadu is said to be the first sop provided by the Americans to push-start the cooperative link. The aviation sector has been similarly targeted. Falling margins of American airlines and the tough competition between Boeing and Airbus, the European aircraft consortium could be a motivation for the open skies agreement which saw Boeing winning a $ 15 billion contract in India. U.S. companies are also showing interest in the large number of airport privatization contracts on offer in India in the next few years (Boucher, 2006). The push given to

Intellectual Property Rights by India has acted in its favor (Boucher, 2006). Enhancement of foreign direct investment in telecommunications and retail, the major growth areas has been envisaged in the future (Boucher, 2006). The U.S.-India Agricultural Knowledge Initiative linking universities, technical institutions, and businesses is said to support agriculture innovation. This will set in motion agricultural growth, trade and investment creating rural employment in India (Boucher, 2006).

Analysts like Gary Milhollin are more forthright in highlighting the predominantly commercial motivation of the nuclear deal, to include aircraft orders secured by Boeing, sale of reactors and other equipment by America's nuclear industry, the lucrative, large size of the Indian market and India's defense purchases. India is said to be shopping for billions of dollars worth of military aircraft, including the F-16 and the F-18, letting the assembly lines in America roll on in the years ahead (Milhollin, 2006). Removal of restrictions on arms exports to India thus appears to be a natural corollary to the Agreement.

The Nuclear Dimension

Professor Stephen Cohen appearing before the Senate Foreign Relations Committee made a strong argument in favour of the Indo-U.S. Nuclear Agreement stating that it would pave the way to restrict vertical proliferation through the route of fissile material cut-off, restrictions on testing and limiting deployment of weapons. The nuclear understanding is said to be an instrument to take the relationship of the United States with the people and Government of India to a higher level. Long term civil nuclear cooperation is said to be the principal vehicle of faith for growing cooperation in other fields. As Boucher says, "If we can do nuclear power, we can do anything together" (Boucher, 2006). This would act as a stepping stone for a multilateral agreement between China, Pakistan and India. The Agreement, as per Professor Cohen should be made into a legislation which will allow other states to enter the nuclear club half way. India and Israel were two candidates recommended by Cohen, while Pakistan and North Korea failed to make the grade (Cohen, 2006). This also suggests that the Agreement could eventually lead to legitimatize Israel's nuclearisation. A direct route would have never succeeded given the anti-Israel lobby in the non Western World and sensitivities of Arab states. As a follow up of India, Israel could be benefited in a subsequent time frame.

A best practices center is proposed to be set up by Stephen Cohen to achieve the goal of regional disarmament based on the experience gained in the nuclear arms reduction process between Russia/Soviet Union and the United States (Cohen, 2006). Thus vertical as well lateral proliferation will be restricted. Such a reduction of nuclear warheads in the Sino-India-Pakistan context is however much more complex and appears to be only in the realm of theoretical proposition. It will involve a trilateral agreement between India, China and Pakistan. With reports of continued proliferation in missile testing by North Korea, the issue is further complicated, as it could be seen as a measure undertaken with tacit Chinese support. As of now USA does not have any leverage with China and the least in the nuclear field. Pakistan too will not be amenable to restricting its nuclear rearmament vis-à-vis India for it will lose both the leverages it has against India, terrorism and nuclear weapons. Nevertheless, Cohen's suggestion needs to be pursued.

Space, Science and Technology

The United States and India have proposed a Bi National Science and Technology Endowment Fund with a contribution of $ 15 million each. A Standing Science and Technology Joint Commission is the other initiative in the field of innovation and knowledge economy. Biotechnology, health and infectious diseases, basic space, atmospheric and earth sciences are the key areas identified for growth in this field (Boucher, 2006). India has a large knowledge base in the strategic field of information technology. Its pool of technology manpower is also emerging as one of the largest in the world, with over 250,000 engineers graduating from Indian colleges every year. The United States could benefit considerably from this quasi alliance, as the technological capability matures to that of pure science, research and development in India over the next two to three decades. Cooperation in space technology between India and the United States is also an ongoing process, with two payloads from

NASA planned in India's Chandrayaan Moon Mission. India's successful indigenous space program has now received its due recognition.

Energy

The energy shortfall faced by India has been one of the reasons put forth for greater cooperation (Cohen, 2006). India has set a target of 40,000 MW of nuclear energy by 2030. This envisages a jump of over five to six times from existing capacities. The United States sees this as an opportunity for creating 5,000 new direct jobs and 10,000 to 15,000 indirect jobs in nuclear commerce and trade with India (Rice, 2006). On being queried by Senate Foreign Relations Committee, Chairman Richard G. Lugar, on India's plans for expansion of its nuclear power sector, Secretary Burns indicated that India had opted for a three stage thorium-based cycle with serious proliferation risks. By opening the Indian nuclear market, it was felt that it would be possible to wean away the country from this perilous path (Questions, Lugar, 2005). Energy rationalization is another key area which is directly linked with the nuclear agreement, with a larger share for atomic power envisaged in the overall Indian energy pie. It will provide India an opportunity to develop cleaner sources of energy and also lead to improving environmental security (Boucher, 2006). As Rice testified, nuclear energy is a clean source and will enable India to reduce its carbon emissions which had increased by 61 per cent from 1990 to 2001, second only to China's (Rice, 2006). Indian assurance to assuage apprehensions of the United States have been listed as submission of the civil nuclear program to international inspections and inclination for new non-proliferation commitments in exchange for full civil nuclear cooperation (Boucher, 2006).

Nuclear Non-Proliferation Politics

Despite very convincing reasons for concluding the Agreement, the apprehensions amongst non-proliferators in the United States are essentially three-fold. The first is lack of apriori conveyance of intent by U.S. Administration to the public or the Congress of its nuclear agreement with India.

Milhollin states that the administration is attempting to undermine the Congress by inking the Agreement while shifting the burden of proof on the legislators in seeking an exemption (Milhollin, 2006). The relationship between the Government and the Congress in the United States has always been difficult. U.S. Congressmen are incensed with the point that the Agreement has come about as a *fait accompli* and the administration did not take legislators into confidence. This was the key point stated by Senator Biden, the ranking minority member of the Senate Foreign Relations Committee. The Senator however agreed that time had come to develop a new relationship with India (Biden, 2006). This appears to be an internal turf battle between the U.S. Administration and its legislators and does not have any strategic connotations for India.

The next argument is of India being a non-signatory of the NPT and having carried out nuclear tests is being permitted to legitimatize its nuclearisation. This issue is now a matter of record as the past can hardly be undone. Opinion amongst U.S. analysts, policy makers and legislators on India unlikely to tip off a nuclear war in any part of the world including in South Asia is virtually anonymous. Apprehensions relate to their concern of the Agreement opening the doors for similar proliferators in the years ahead. Pakistan, Israel and North Korea would clearly want to follow this path. South Africa, Brazil, Argentina and others may follow suit (Galluci, 2006).

The key arguments put forth by U.S. Congressmen against the Agreement are that it provides India the benefit of expanding its nuclear power as well as its weapons production program. Congressmen across the board recognized the need for expanding the present scope of Indo-U.S. relations but were not sure if the Nuclear Agreement was the best course to do the same. Thus Senator Biden in his opening remarks indicated his support not because it was necessary but as the ramifications of its failure were much greater. The aim should be to minimize the risks in the whole deal (Biden, 2006). While there appears to be no grouse against the countries need to seek nuclear energy, they have very significant objections to India developing weapons capability (Galluci, 2006).

Making an exception for India is said to affect credibility of the non-proliferation regime thereby allowing other states to seek similar concessions (Galluci, 2006). Milhollin goes even further in naming the states for which export controls will be weakened, to include Iran, Pakistan and possibly even terrorist groups, working through national governments. The United States sponsoring concessions to India may prompt other nuclear weapon states as China and Russia to consider such dispensation to their allies, with weaker non-proliferation laws, they could attain their objectives easily. India thus cannot be considered as an isolated case, argues the analyst (Milhollin, 2006).

Another key poser submitted to Under Secretary Robert Joseph by Richard G. Lugar, Chairman Senate Foreign Relations Committee was on Proliferation Security Initiative (PSI). PSI is the U.S. initiative which seeks to intercept shipments of WMD, delivery systems, and related materials to and from states and non-state actors of proliferation concern. This is to be in consonance with national legal authorities and relevant international law and frameworks, including the UN Security Council (Fact Sheet, 2003). Lugar sought to know why India had not joined the PSI. The administration replied that the United States had encouraged India to join PSI and was keen to have it on board, given its strategic location straddling the key routes of proliferation trafficking and considerable operational capabilities. The Indian response was that an internal review of PSI along with its international and national legal implications was underway before possible participation. The administration was hopeful that India will endorse PSI, and join more than 70 countries around the world in this initiative given that even the United Nations Secretary General Kofi Annan had expressed his support for the same (Questions, Lugar, 2005).

Gary Milhollin has been the most vehement of those who appeared before the Foreign Relations Committee in objecting to the Agreement. The analyst supported his argument by making it out as an issue which will antagonize Muslim opinion in the world with India provided with concessions not granted to Pakistan and Iran, both Islamic countries. It would also put President Musharraf in an awkward position in Pakistan undermining a powerful ally in the counter terror campaign (Milhollin, 2006). Milhollin also debunked the argument that India can be drawn into a future alliance with China and perhaps rightly so (Milhollin, 2006). He highlighted the fact that India has consistently followed a non-aligned policy and would be loathe to annoy a neighbor with which its relations are continuously improving and with which it shares a long physical border. Milhollin has also argued that India may not buy any nuclear reactors from the U.S. at all as France, Russia and even Canada may be able to provide cheaper reactors to India as also it had the ability to construct these indigenously (Milhollin, 2006). While these arguments have an element of logic, the key determinant of any trade-off on nuclear purchases by India are likely t be the political leverages of the seller. The United States through the nuclear Agreement was intending to create just such a relationship of overwhelming advantage over possible competitors.

It would thus be evident that the fear of addition to the nuclear power club is not the real obstacle but that of others seeking a similar route which is of greater concern to the United States' non-proliferation lobby. However, India's detractors tend to forget that India qualifies for being considered as an exception as it is a principled dissenter with an impeccable non-proliferation record. Secretary Rice had also highlighted that in the past non-proliferation policies had not achieved their goals and did not deter India from developing nuclear weapons (Rice, 2006). The country's aspirations and demostrated responsibility in controlling its nuclear capability could thus be acknowledged through the Agreement, argued the Secretary of State.

India's Strategic Culture—Insurance Against Proliferation

Professor Cohen drawing upon his extensive experience through close interaction with the Indian policy establishment of over thirty decades, highlighted the lack of tradition of military or strategic culture in India and supported this argument with the extensive expose on the subject by George Tanham. This would indicate the considerable lead time required in building up strategic consensus before taking any vital decision such as use of nuclear weapons by India. The extensive debates prior to nuclearisation in 1964-65 after the Chinese Lop Nor tests, refusal to sign the NPT in 1967-68, following the peaceful nuclear test in 1973, dubbed by Cohen, as "phony", the Rajiv Gandhi Action Plan of 1988 and the debate over the Indo-U.S. Nuclear Agreement are all as per Professor Cohen, pointers that India's strategic establishment is essentially reactive in nature. India's nuclear policy is said to rest on the rather strong belief of morality of nuclearisation. The country's non-violent, assimilative culture has repeatedly questioned the use of violence as a means of conducting polity in all spheres be it nuclear or terrorism. The need to maintain secrecy to avoid adverse scrutiny by non-proliferation lobby would also have led to keeping a limited number of people in the nuclearisation loop. India's nuclear weaponisation is also believed to be a demonstration of technological capability which had not involved the military; thereby strategic considerations have not been fully factored in the nuclear capability providing cushion for India's ability to proliferate in the future (Cohen, 2006). This assumption may need a review as integration of the service chiefs in the Cabinet Committee on Security seems to have taken place. Indian strategic establishment also follows a feudal hierarchy of a top down approach and thus may not feel the necessity to involve the military establishment as part of the overall strategic decision-making process from the very outset. Such decisions in India are generally made by what can be best described as a, "strategic coterie", dubbed officially as the National Security Council. The National Security Advisor in this loose structure has considerable, if not, overriding influence. Proximity to the Prime Minister appears to be the key qualification for this important assignment. The Brajesh Mishra-Vajpayee and Manmohan Singh-Narayanan relationship will prove this point. As also Indians feel comfortable in creating wheels within wheels of a decision loop with the hope that the ultimate conclusion that will emerge is the most appropriate one. Institutionalization of the process of national security decision-making in India is still in a nascent stage and will take another decade or so to crystallize.

On the other hand involvement of the military could strengthen the deterrent in many ways. Firstly, India's military establishment has always followed in the true British tradition of supremacy of the central government. There are grievances but these are mostly against some of the defence ministers over the years who were perceived to be lacking knowledge of military nuances. George Fernandes and Pranab Mukherjee have considerably redeemed this image. The main grouse is against the Indian bureaucracy which is seen to act as a malign intermediary between the political leadership and the military.

India's strategic culture thus is its greatest safeguard against use of the nuclear option. The decision-making process at present is so obtuse that in case such a situation arises, the nuclear trigger may not be pressed in a great hurry and international influences can play a role in preventing its use.

Summation of Issues

The Indo-U.S. Civil Nuclear Agreement needs to be seen against the larger backdrop of the long term strategic engagement of India by the United States. It places India in the role of a primary power in South as well as Central Asia recognizing its regional primacy. It is designed to provide the impetus to greater U.S. India interaction in the fields of trade, commerce, nuclear energy, agriculture, manufacturing, civil aviation, military hardware, information and biotechnology amongst others. It may induce India into the PSI and also cap the indigenous thorium route of nuclear reactor construction. It may also be a vehicle to induce the international community to grant Israel entry into the nuclear weapons club obtusely following up with India's induction. In the long term it would create a favorable balance of power against an emerging China while limiting the vertical and lateral proliferation regionally.

Conclusion

The Agreement poses a challenge to Indian foreign policy in extracting benefits of cooperation with the United States without compromising on strategic independence. This can be easily achieved by adopting the cooperative engagement route regardless of its likely incursions into the politics of balance of power.

Thus a competitor in one field may not necessarily be an antagonist in general. In a globalised world, nations will alternately cooperate and compete with one another in various fields depending on their national interests. Thus, while China and India can cooperate in the field of oil and natural gas in Africa, there can be competition for the same resource between the two countries in Central Asia. China may pitch Pakistan as a counter to Indian interests in the Arabian Sea but need not be seen as an antagonist state. This is the new nuanced cooperative security order which appears to be emerging, to which India needs to adjust its foreign policy in the future.

The Agreement indicates virtual acceptance of India as a nuclear weapons state (Galluci, 2006). The political benefits of such a status at present are marginal. It is relevant to the extent that it will grant India access to the resources of NSG. The issue of ending India's fissile material production capabilities has lost most of its sting with the introduction of the FMCT. The abrupt introduction of the this Treaty by the U.S. in May 2006, especially when it is not favorably inclined to participate in disarmament talks under the aegis of the United Nations may have possibly been carried out to remove one of the likely objections by the Congress. If this is true, then it adds weight to the argument of the considerable importance that the U.S. attaches to realignment of strategic relationship with India.

Is the nuclear deal an offset for the large aircraft, retail, defense and other markets that India will be providing to the United States corporations in the years ahead? The offset would however not be a dole and since the arms being offered are exorbitantly expensive, we may be able to make do with relatively cheaper armaments in the context of Sub Continental needs. There also seems to be a move to cap India's growing independent nuclear capability. In case India progresses the indigenous route that it has been following over the years, the three stage thorium process it will be beyond the purview of the proliferation regime. By providing alternative sources, this will be obviated and a dependency will be created. India however should not abandon the thorium route and also become a part of the Generation-IV Forum (GIF), the advanced nuclear energy program, considered as a proliferation resistant alternative.

The arguments by U.S. antagonists essentially relate to the politics of non-proliferation. While India technically is on a weak wicket, it has been consistently maintaining that this is due to the discriminatory nature of the international nuclear regime which favors nations who had conducted tests pre 1964. The obvious strength of the country is its consistent non proliferation record. This is being capitalized by policy makers on both sides of the U.S.-India hierarchy. The basic issue which the world community at large has to address is reduction of the currency of power represented by possession of nuclear weapons. Many nations as Iran are aspiring to acquire nuclear weapons to express their sovereignty. Once nuclear weapons do not denote a dominant form of power, the quest for their acquisition will be automatically reduced.

As for India, with the International Atomic Energy Agency already on board, the NSG is the next battlefield. India's supporters there include the Czech Republic, France, Russia, the U.K. and the United States of America, while Argentina, China, Greece, Japan, South Korea, Sweden and Switzerland are likely to raise a number of issues against it. The final answer will be dictated by U.S. ability to influence the antagonists and India's diplomatic initiatives to wean maximum members to its side, poisoned against Indian interests as they would be by India's traditional adversaries.

REFERENCES

1. Joseph R. Biden, Jr. (2006), Opening Statement of Senator Joseph R. Biden, Jr. (D-DE) Senate Foreign Relations Committee Hearing on U.S.-India Atomic Energy Cooperation. April 26, 2006 http://foreign.senate.gov.
2. Richard A. Boucher (2006), The United States and South Asia: An Expanding Agenda. Statement before the United States House International Committee on Asia and Pacific. http://foreign.senate.gov.
3. Stephen P. Cohen (2006), Remarks of Dr. Stephen P. Cohen at the Senate Foreign Relations Committee Panel Discussion on the U.S.-India Nuclear Cooperative Initiative Wednesday, April 26, 2006. http://foreign.senate.gov.

4. Robert J. Einhorn. Statement by Robert J. Einhorn Senior Adviser, Center for Strategic and International Studies before the Senate Foreign Relations Committee, April 26, 2006. http://foreign.senate.gov.
5. Fact Sheet, (2003), Proliferation Security Initiative: Statement of Interdiction Principles. The White House, Office of the Press Secretary, Washington, DC, September 4, 2003. http://state.gov.
6. Robert L. Galluci. Testimony of Robert L. Galluci. Dean of the Edmund A. Walsh School of Foreign Service Georgetown University before the Senate Foreign Relations Committee, 26 April 2006. http://foreign.senate.gov.
7. Senator Richard G. Lugar. Opening Statement for Hearing on the U.S.-India Atomic Energy Cooperation, Wednesday, April 26, 2006. http://foreign.senate.gov.
8. Richard G. Lugar. The Lugar Survey on Proliferation Threats and Responses, June 2005. http://lugar.senate.gov.
9. Richard G. Lugar. Questions for the Record Submitted to Under Secretaries Nicholas Burns and Robert Joseph by Chairman Richard G. Lugar, Senate Foreign Relations Committee, November 2, 2005. http://lugar.senate.gov.
10. Gary Milhollin. Testimony of Gary Milhollin, Director, Wisconsin Project on Nuclear Arms Control and Professor Emeritus, University of Wisconsin, Law School Testimony of Gary Milhollin, April 26, 2006. http://foreign.senate.gov.
11. Condoleezza Rice. The U.S.-India Civilian Nuclear Cooperation Agreement Opening Remarks Before the Senate Foreign Relations Committee Washington, DC, April 5, 2006. http://foreign.senate.gov.
12. Ashley J. Tellis. Senior Associate Carnegie Endowment for International Peace to the Senate Foreign Relations Committee Subject: U.S.-India Atomic Energy Cooperation: Strategic and Non-proliferation Implications, April 26, 2006. http://foreign.senate.gov.

Indo-U.S. Nuclear Deal

—Col. Ved Prakash

3

A LONG, ARDUOUS JOURNEY: VICISSITUDINARY AND UNPREDICTABLE

As is well known, the journey of this Accord started during the time of the Vajpayee Government (1998-2004). The thread, rather, the gauntlet, was picked up by the Congress-led UPA Government, which seemed to have been as determined as its predecessor. The observers were rather keen, even curious, to see how a renowned economist but a green-horn in political arena of the country, would deal with the Americans, as compared to an astute Atal Bihari Vajpayee who after 50 years of practice in the political field, had attained the status of an elder statesman. As the things turned out, the economist Professor, as some like to designate Prime Minister Manmohan Singh, surprised everybody with assiduity, tenacity, and single-minded determination he brought to bear on the subject till he signed the 2 March 2006 Agreement with President Bush at New Delhi, which would be beneficial, according to his lights, for politico-economic and strategic interest of India.

To forestall any possibility of a discordance within the government, when K. Natwar Singh had to resign under the Volcker cloud in the post-18 July 2005 Manmohan Singh-Bush Joint Statement period, he chose not to appoint a new incumbent and ignored the criticism and advice from some cabinet colleagues and senior journalists that the economist must have the services of a professional expert on diplomacy and foreign affairs. This was a statement of not only his self-belief in his own capabilities but also of his faith in the officials who were serving him in the PMO and Ministry of External Affairs (MEA). Maybe, the critics had a point: The Prime Minister was negotiating a sensitive deal with the sole superpower, which would have long-term political and strategic implications for India's future. But as the final results showed, the Prime Minister too had a point in his decision to do without a new External Affairs Minister.

What follows is a resumé of events, assertions, statements, views, and critiques, positive and negative, in the period leading to the agreement signed on 2 March 2006—a procession of thrusts and parries, points and counterpoints, contretemps and ripostes. Taken from the open sources, the headlines from the newspapers have been italicized.

- *Rice takes a hard line, PM drops UNSC Bid:* New Delhi, 16 July 2006. US Secretary of State Condoleezza Rice has told Doordarshan in an interview to coincide with Dr. Singh's first bilateral visit to Washington that her government was supporting only Japan for a permanent seat on the UN Security Council. Dr. Singh virtually dropped the issue from his agenda of discussions with Bush in the forthcoming visit (*AA*, 17.7.05).
- *PM looks to stronger U.S. Ties:* New Delhi, 16 July 2005. Dr. Singh in his departure statement said: "Economy and energy would come in for particular attention during my discussions with Mr. Bush, even as both sides look forward to strengthening their strategic partnership by cooperating in space and civilian nuclear energy." The threats posed by terrorism would also be high on his agenda as his visit takes place in the wake of the London blasts. "As the world's two largest democracies, we have common values and interest" (*AA*, 17.7.05).
- "*Civilian Nuclear Deal will be a breakthrough. It is a way to taking India within Non-Proliferation Frame Work.*" *Rice*: New Delhi, 1 March 06. Talking to reporters en route to India, she said India has to put (some of its) civilian nuclear reactors under permanent safeguards. She said if the civilian nuclear deal comes through, it would be a breakthrough not just for India

and the United States but also for the role of nuclear power in energy development. Asked if India's fast breeder reactors would be kept out of safeguards, she said: "Let us wait and see what the argument says."

Asked if Pakistan would qualify for same kind of special treatment that India might receive, Ms. Rice replies, "Pakistan is not in the same place as India. I think everybody understands that."

At the same briefing, U.S. National Security Adviser Stephen Hadley pointed out that the "basic framework" of the civilian nuclear deal had been agreed to on 18 July 2005 in Washington. "The implementation is going to take a long period of time. The next step in the implementation is this separation (by India of its civilian and military nuclear facilities) agreement, which is what we have been working on. But we have been working on this for four, five, six months; they (Indians) come here, we go there (India); telephone conversations, exchanging documents," Mr. Hadley maintained.

Asked his response to the critics who felt it was an "end run" around the Nuclear Non-Proliferation Treaty (NNPT), Mr. Hadley felt that just the opposite was the case: "This is actually a way to bring India within the non-proliferation framework. It will be adopting the kind of non-proliferation protections we do."

"India has a good record, as a practical matter, in terms of proliferation to third countries. They have been a very responsible party. This is actually the vehicle to bring India on to our page, in terms of proliferation policy," Mr. Hadley added (*The Hindu*, 2.3.06).

- 2 March 06, New Delhi. The Civilian Nuclear Power Agreement between India and the U.S. is signed.
- New Delhi, 3 March 06. "*We are closer than ever before*": President Bush in his address at Purana Qila (Old Fort), New Delhi. He further said: "India and the U.S. are brothers in the cause of human liberty...our partnership has the power to transform the world...India and Pakistan were better off with the US having closer

relations with the two countries. I believe a prosperous, democratic Pakistan would be a steadfast partner for America and a peaceful neighbour for India and a force for freedom and moderation in the Arab world."

A central theme running through his speech was that India, a great democracy, must stand with the U.S. in promoting "democracy" and "freedom" around the world. "India's leadership was needed in the world hungry for democracy. Men and women from North Korea to Burma, to Syria to Zimbabwe, to Cuba, yearn for their liberty. Our nations must not pretend that people of these countries prefer their own enslavement. We must stand with the reformers and dissidents..." Mr. Bush said, defending civilian nuclear cooperation with India. He said this would strengthen the security and economy of both countries while reducing the risk of proliferation.

Freedom was not an American or Indian value—it was a universal value. Appreciating the assistance India provided to a new democracy such as Afghanistan, Mr. Bush asked it to "work directly" with countries where democracy was just beginning to take shape.

Urging India to lift the cap on foreign investment, he felt that the rules governing business in the country needed more transparency. India's leadership was needed to span markets across the world. He hoped that the Doha round of trade talks would be completed by the year end.

Referring to the U.S. food assistance to India in the 1960s, the President said Washington would now help New Delhi achieve a Second Green Revolution. The two nations had agreed on a $ 100-million knowledge initiative in agriculture.

Taking a strong line against terrorism, he said terrorists had misjudged countries such as India and U.S.: "We love our freedom and we would fight to keep it. We both are allies in the war against terrorism."

Thanking Indian Navy for escorting U.S. ships through the straits of Malacca after the 9/11 attacks, he applauded the growing military cooperation between the countries: "We will win this war (against terrorism) together."

Addressing an invited audience at the historic Fort, Mr. Bush had little hesitation attacking Iran with which Prime Minister Manmohan Singh has repeatedly said, India enjoyed "civilisational" ties (*The Hindu*, 4.3.06).

Extensive excerpts from Mr. Bush's speech have advisedly been cited above. It must be clear to the scholars and analysts, barring the cynics and nay-sayers, that bilateral agreements must yield benefits to both sides to succeed. There can be no one-way traffic regime. What either country hopes to achieve from this deal will be clear as we proceed along.

It might be said here and now that Mr. Bush's reference to Iran, a third country, was not in consonance with the international diplomatic etiquettes expected to be followed by the visiting dignitaries, and was expectedly denounced by the Indian Communists. But then the supercilious President of the sole superpower of the world would not care too much about the niceties of such diplomatic correctness—meant more for the lesser mortals!

"China turns to nuclear power to fuel growth."[1]

Even as the U.S. Congress is discussing the ways and means to implement the India-U.S. civilian nuclear energy deal, China is planning for one of the boldest nuclear construction binges since the U.S. expansion in the 1970s. Presently, China has nine operational reactors and two more are under construction, with nuclear energy accounting for about two per cent of its total energy output. Government plans to double it to four per cent by 2020. Even then the percentage of electricity generated from nuclear plants will be far behind today's world average of 16 per cent. Japan, for example, gets about 30 per cent of its electricity from nuclear sources.

Presently, India too gets less than two per cent of its electricity from nuclear reactors, and it has long way to go as the Chinese situation described above shows. Nuclear deal with U.S. is an important step in achieving our targets in the field.

- Singapore, 18 March 06. *U.S. joins Japan, Australia for new strategic dialogue*. At their inaugural meeting, under this new framework, in Sydney, they commended

India for agreeing to place its civilian nuclear energy facilities under relevant international safeguards (*The Hindu*, 19.3.06).

- Washington, 28 March 06. *India's record is good: Burns*. Praising India's record in non-proliferation, Under Secretary of State for Political Affairs Nicholas Burns said, it did not suggest a civilian nuclear energy deal with Pakistan, as the country did not have a record of protecting its nuclear materials.

Asked if the U.S. offered any economic incentive to India for the vote against Iran at the IAEA, Burns said: "Way back in September 2005, and again in February this year, India made its own sovereign decision on the Iranean question" (*The Hindu*, 29.3.06).

- New Delhi, 28 March 06. *Shyam Saran leaves for Washington*. He will hold talks with his counterpart Burns on the civilian nuclear deal and other issues—the first face-to-face contact between the two sides after the early March Bush visit to India. Mr. Saran is also expected to address the conservative Heritage Foundation.

In recent remarks, Mr. Burns has said Washington had presented a draft of a comprehensive civilian nuclear agreement. The Indian plan to separate its civilian and military facilities will, of course, be part of the final agreement.

Presumably, Mr. Saran and Mr. Burns will hold further discussions on the draft agreement even as the Americans try to push the deal through Congress (*The Hindu*, 29.3.6).

- Washington, 12 April 06. *Iran N. enrichment clouds Indo-U.S. Deal*. Iran's crossing of another threshold—its claim of bomb-grade-enrichment—in its nuclear wrangle with the West is certain to complicate the U.S.-India nuclear deal despite expert opinion that Tehran is intentionally overstating its achievement. Citing this exaggerated claim, which is more geo-political in nature rather than any significant technological breakthrough, some U.S. lawmakers and analysts have used the pandora's box argument to object to the Bush administration deal with India—that helping India with its nuclear program will, even in the civilian sphere, trigger a nuclear weapons pursuit by other countries.

Despite repeated assertions by the U.S. officials that India is a unique non-proliferation case and deserves a deal limited to civilian cooperation, the critics refuse to buy the argument, and the Iran claim has given them fresh ammunition. California Democrat Barbara Boxer, who criticized India's relations with Iran at a Senate hearing last week and made sundering these ties a condition for the deal to pass, lost no time in clubbing India and Iran, saying "having nuclear weapons was a matter of personal pride" for both countries.

Even when the U.S. officials stoutly refused to link the Iran development to the Indo-U.S. deal, the flood of commentary generated by Iran's push to N-enrichment often referred to the Indo-U.S. deal while wondering why Washington is being so hard on Iran while giving a pass to India.

The administration's argument that Iran had cheated despite being an NPT signatory while India has stayed clean despite not being an NPT signatory found little resonance among the non-proliferation hawks determined to treat all nuclear latecomers as renegades.

Even when responsible U.S. analysts have seen the Iran claim emanating for geo-political reasons, the chatter here inevitably centers around a possible U.S. attack on Iran. After all, one of the CNN's captions for the story read "War with Iran?"(*TOI*, 13.4.06).

- Mumbai, 16.4.06. *India wanted to end Tarapur pack with U.S. in 80's*: CIA report dated 23 July 1982. The secret CIA document was approved for release in March 2000 but it took six years to get public on 13 April 2006. CIA assessment of July 1982: "India's long term objective is to terminate its bilateral agreement with the U.S., and thereby U.S. control and leverage over the Indian nuclear program...India and U.S. have been deadlocked since the late 1970s over the supply of fuel for the reactors at the Tarapur Atomic Power Station (TAPS). By late 1983, TAPS reactors (which became operational in November 1969) would have used up all available fuel stock, and unless other supply arrangements are made, they would be forced to shut down." The document warned that a long-term shut down would deprive Bombay area of electricity and embarrass (Indira) Gandhi domestically, as well as among countries in the Third World, which respected India's technological progress (*TOI*, 17.4.06).

The rest as they say is history. Just imagine the present contrast to the Indo-U.S. nuke deal, awaiting the approval of the U.S. Congress. An Indian official, admitting that he was aware of the document, refused to comment "because of critical phase of Indo-US ties at the moment".

- New Delhi, 17 April 06. *India 'No' to U.S. clause on Nuclear Testing*. India refused to accept a clause in the new bilateral civilian nuclear cooperation pact, draft of which was handed over to Foreign Secretary Saran during his visit to Washingtom earlier this month, as it included a paragraph stating that the U.S. would cease all cooperation with India in civilian nuclear energy if India decided to detonate a nuclear explosive device (*AA*, 18.4.06).

Saran said: "India is bound only by what is contained in the 18 July Joint Statement, that is, continuing its commitment to a unilateral moratorium on nuclear testing" (*HT*, 18.4.06).

- London, 19 April 06. British Prime Minister Tony Blair has angrily rejected comparisons between nuclear defiant Iran and non-NPT-compliant India, saying he supports Indo-U.S. accord. The comparison was futile since "India is a very very different proposition from Iran" (*TOI*, 20.4.06).
- Washington, 20 April 06. *"N-Sales: No special status for U.S."*. Says Deputy Chairman of Planning Commission Montek Singh Ahluwalia who is also the

co-chair of Indo-U.S. energy dialogue. The U.S. has sought no preferential treatment for its companies in the sale of nuclear equipment and technology as a *quid pro quo* for concluding the nuke deal. The international law permitted no such treatment, he said during a media interaction, hosted by the *Energy Daily* (*HT*, 21.4.06).

- Washington, 21 April 06. *U.S. relents on CMD, insists on no-test commitment.* So delicately poised is the Indo-U.S. deal that a misspoken word here or a misplaced comma there has a potential to cause a chain reaction in the excitable media world. So when the Assistant Secretary for South Asia Richard Boucher, erstwhile long serving spokesman, met the South Asian correspondents on the 20th, he was caution personified as he navigated the verbal minefield around the deal. He clarified two issues. One was his acknowledgement that the idea of a Credible Minimum Deterrent (CMD), the bedrock of India's nuclear stance, is an "evolving concept", rather than a static, fixed one.

This means New Delhi can decide on its nuclear arsenal at any given time depending upon the threat perception, rather than commit to a fixed number of nuclear weapons as Boucher had appeared to suggest in New Delhi during his recent visit there, when he said India defining its CMD was an "absolutely necessary" step towards decreasing tensions in Asia. Separately, in an effort at rationalization, a State Department mandarin put Boucher's remarks in context by suggesting the idea of seeking a definition of CMD was aimed more at nudging India, China, and Pakistan toward an arms control pact on the lines of the one the U.S. and Soviet Union arrived at.

Boucher was even more circumspect on the other controversial issue animating the debate: inclusion of a para in the bilateral treaty, saying the deal is off if India conducts any nuclear tests, a condition the critics see as the U.S. trying to push India into the CTBT through back door. Against India's firm 'No' to the clause, the U.S. officials offered their own take on the issue.: "The U.S. laws still enjoin sanctions against any country that conducts a nuclear test, and India notwithstanding the nuclear deal, is no exception. However, while New Delhi has no problem with the broad U.S. law, the wrinkle is about U.S. including it in the bilateral treaty (*TOI* and *HT*, both 22.4.06).

- Hanover, 22 April 06. Ostensibly here to inagurate the world's largest technology fair, where India figures as a partner country this year, on top of Prime Minister Manmohan Singh's agenda is to try and bring Germany, a vital member of the Nuclear Suppliers Group (NSG), around to see the Indo-US nuclear treaty in a positive light (*The Indian Express,* 23.4.06).
- New Delhi, 23 April 06. Dr Jéan Jacquinot, visiting Scientific Adviser of the French High Commissioner for Atomic Energy, said nations need to deploy nuclear energy because renewable energy or fossil fuel alone would not suffice. He said France was working on building the fourth generation fission reactors after President Jacques Chirac ordered replacing of the present generation of reactors.

He said France meets up to 80 per cent of its energy needs through nuclear energy and claimed that with the incorporation of additional safety elements like secondary containment systems in the "EPR" reactors, the French reactors had become better than the Russian reactors.

Dr. Jacquinot interacted with the AEC Chairman, Dr. Anil Kakodkar, and the Institute of Plasma Research Director, Prof. P.K. Kaw during his visit and held discussions on the status of India's participation in the International Thermonuclear Experimental Reactor (ITER) project.

Joining issue with the skeptics, he claimed nuclear fusion would become the source of energy in 50 years or so, and the projects like the ITER would overcome the problems of storage or reprocessing of radioactive waste and safety. He described nuclear fusion as the model for the fifth generation reactors (*AA*, 24.4.06).

- Hanover, 23 April 06. Here follow some interesting

headlines indicative of German stance towards Indo-U.S. nuclear deal:

One: "Germany cautiously positive on nuclear cooperation" (*The Hindu*, 24.4.06)

Two: "Non-proliferation vow impresses Merkel" (*TOI*, 24.4.06)

Three: "Deutsch drive to power India" German firms pledge staggering FDI (*The Statesman*, 24.4.06)

Four: "Germany lowers reservation on Indo-U.S. N-deal" (*The Tribune*, 24.4.06)

Five: "Merkel mixes hope with caution on N-Deal" (*The Indian Express*, 24.4.06)

The above-noted press observations were made during Dr. Manmohan Singh's visit to Hanover, Germany. Sounding a postitive note, Chancellor Angela Merkel was hopeful on the prospects of the NSG opening the tap of civilian nuclear cooperation for India after the U.S. Congress and IAEA decide on the issue.

Germany on 24 April 2006 once again signaled its willingness to support the Indo-U.S. nuke deal, with its Foreign Minister Frank Walter Steinmeyer telling Dr. Singh that he never opposed the deal, asserting that his earlier statement in Washington was misquoted. He had expressed reservations over the deal because it would not help the cause of non-proliferation at a time when the international community was pressurizing Iran to abandon its nuclear program (*TOI*, 25.4.06).

- Washington, 25.4.06. U.S. Ambassador to India David Mulford said in an address at the American Enterprise Institute, a Washington-based think tank: "The U.S. has not changed its 'goal posts' in the nuclear deal with India and did not see New Delhi's refusal to accept a provision barring further nuclear tests as an issue that could scuttle the deal" (*The Tribune*, 26.4.06).
- Berlin, 25 April 06. The sense in Indian official circles here is that Germany has not only given up its reservations on the nuclear deal, but has also promised

to ask constructive questions on the accord whenever it comes up for discussion at the 45-nation NSG.

- New Delhi, 26 April 06. Robert Blackwell, the former U.S. Ambassador to India and presently, President, Barbour Griffith and Rogers International, said while addressing a CII meet here: "I am optimistic about the Congress approving the Indo-U.S. deal by June, although it appeared to be a very ambitious target.... It is hard to do things rapidly in Congress"(*The Hindu*, 27.4.06).
- Washington, 26 April 06. *Deal draws Flak*. Senate lawmakers criticised the U.S. administration for not being transparent with them on the controversial nuclear deal with India. Legislators were particularly interested in the bilateral agreement being negotiated with New Delhi detailing the landmark deal clinched on 2 March by Mr. Bush and Dr. Singh.

The deal would allow India, a nation not a signatory to the NPT, access to long-denied civilian nuclear technology in return for placing a majority of its atomic reactors under international safeguards.

Speaking at a hearing on the deal, Democratic Senator Joseph Biden alleged that the administration had "reneged" on a promise to share drafts of the bilateral nuclear agreement.

The U.S. had sought a clause in the agreement that nuclear cooperation would terminate if India conducted a nuclear test but New Delhi flatly rejected the suggestion.

Mr. Biden said the administration is yet to share with them the full list of India's civil nuclear facilities, "even in classified form". The IAEA is still negotiating with India on the safeguards.

Republican Senator Dick Lugar, Head of the powerful Senate Foreign Relations Committee, said he himself had submitted to the administration 90 questions, apart from 82 that had already been answered, following an extended 5 April Congressional testimony on the deal by the Secretary of State Condoleezza Rice.

For it to be effective, the nuclear agreement has to be approved by the Congress. Until the administration answered the lawmakers' questions and provided them details on the deal, "we simply should not act on its proposed legislation," said Mr. Biden.

- Bangalore, 29 April 06. Dr. R. Chidambaram, Principal Scientific Adviser to the Union Government, addressing the MS Ramaiah School of Advanced Studies, said India should move towards using more fast breeder reactors and thorium based reactors as it has the world's largest reserves of thorium. "We can become a global leader in this field," he said. India has a lot of potential in the field of nuclear energy and the efficiency of operation of its nuclear power plants are comparable to the best in the world, said Mr. Chidambaram.
- Washington, 3 May 06. *Rice: Be ready for changes in N-deal.* Secretary Rice told a visiting Indian Parliamentary group that as the administration is under pressure from prominent members of U.S. Congress, India must be prepared to accept "amendments" to the nuclear deal not "basic" but some amendments within the framework. Next day, India reminded U.S., through its MEA spokesman, that it would only adhere to the commitments made in the joint statement of 18 July 2005.

This response came after reports that Ms. Rice had told Indian parliamentarians that U.S. Congress wanted to see progress on the safeguards agreement with IAEA and 123 agreements with India before taking the plunge on voting on the deal.

The spokesman also rejected a newspaper report that India had been approached by Britain to send troops to Afghanistan. "There is no such proposal," he said.

- New Delhi, 4 May 06. *Aussies may sell uranium to India.* An Australian delegation headed by Deputy Secretary David Ritchie in the Department of Foreign Affairs and Trade has made a quiet visit here for talks on nuclear issues, and possibly uranium sales, as it also included the Head of Australia's Nuclear Safeguards

Agency, Dr. John Carlson. As Australian Prime Minister John Howard had suggested during his March visit to India, the team was sent to find out more about the Indo-U.S. nuclear agreement.

Australia has some of the largest uranium deposits in the world but its laws permit sales to the signatories to the NPT. So China gets uranium but not India.

- New Delhi, 7 May 06. *Japan may back Indo-U.S. deal at NSG.*[2] Ahead of the NSG meeting in Brazil next month, a key politician from Japan's ruling Liberal Democratic Party (LDP) has indicated that Tokyo would consider supporting the India-U.S. nuclear deal if there is "adequate trust" between New Delhi and international community over its nuclear program. "As far as peaceful uses of nuclear energy are concerned, Japan is not opposed to it," said Mr. Kisaburo Tokai, Director General of the International Bureau of the LDP.
- Washington, 11 May 06. *Lantos twist to N. legislation.* Senior Congressman Tom Lantos said today that he would introduce a "compromise" legislative proposal in a bid to prompt a divided U.S. Congress to support the Indo-U.S. nuclear deal, but promising that he would do so after the Indo-U.S. agreement and India's safeguards pact with the IAEA are submitted to the Congress.
- New Delhi, 11 May 06. The revised nuclear reparation plan tabled by Prime Minister Manmohan Singh in Parliament today has placed 35 facilities across the full spectrum of India's broad-based nuclear program, including 14 nuclear reactors, under IAEA safeguards.
- Washington, 11 May 06. *The Man who heard the "shout from India."* When the world and its media blasted India for its May 1998 nuclear tests, one veteran journalist, perhaps the only one in the West stood up for New Delhi's right to go nuclear. What is more, former *New York Times* editor and Pulitzer Prize

winner columnist blamed the U.S. for India's decision to test: "Americans should understand that it was the West particularly the U.S., that built the policy road leading to the Indian underground explosions. The utter shock in Washington shows more than an intelligence failure. It shows that attitudes towards India are the same Western mush of arrogance, ignorance, and condescension that they have been for the half century since India's independence."[3]

- Washington, 12 May 06. *No headway in securing Congress nod for N-deal.* Extensive briefings to the members of the Congress by senior officials in the Bush administration have so far failed to win bipartisan support for a deal that would permit the U.S. to share civilian nuclear technology with India.[4]
- New Delhi, 12.5.06. *India talks tough.* India today made it clear that it was for the Bush administration to ensure the passage of an appropriate legislation in the U.S. Congress to enable civil nuclear cooperation with India.

The reaction of the MEA came after Congressman Tom Lantos's controversial remarks, saying India first needed to negotiate with the IAEA, and India and the U.S. needed to sign a bilateral agreement before the U.S. Congress takes up the Indo-U.S. deal.

- Paris, 13 May 06. France offers to build six 1000-MW plants. But unlike Russia, which went ahead with Tarapur supplies, it wants to wait till India gets safeguards agreement with IAEA.
- Paris, 16 May 06. *Single phrase stalls the Indo-French N-talks.* Indian negotiators refused to accept nuke-cooperation for "Peaceful, Non-Explosive Purposes". The Franco-Indian nuclear cooperation document, therefore, remains a declaration of intent only.[5]
- Washington, 14 May 06. Despite a lack of adequate support for the U.S.-India deal in the U.S. Congress, India's Ambassador in U.S. Ronen Sen is confident that

the agreement will eventually win over the skeptics. "The deal must not be written off," he told *The Tribune*,[6] "although it is going to be an uphill task."

- Washington, 17 May 06. India and the U.S. will try and revive the fast-withering nuclear-deal in the English summer. Principals from the two sides—Mr. Saran and Mr. Burns—agreed to meet about half way, at least geographically, in London to unravel the boondoggle in a deal that is now enmeshed in domestic politics in both countries.

The main issue now bedevilling the deal is India's voluntary commitment not to conduct further nuclear tests—how to spell it out in the text of the deal in a manner that satisfies Washington's non-proliferation lobby and lawmakers and at the same time does not paint New Delhi into a corner and leaves the impression that it succumbed to U.S. pressure to codify the commitment.[7]

- Paris, 17 May 06. *French N-tech firms eyeing India.* Global energy majors eager to benefit from Indo-U.S. Nuke-Deal.
- Washington, 18 May 06. *No more making yellow cake,* says U.S. The draft Fissile Material Cut off Treaty was introduced today at the Conference on Disarmament in Geneva by U.S. Assistant Secretary of State Stephen Redemeyer.[8] The draft is aimed at freezing making of the bomb grade fuel—'yellow cake' (milled uranium oxide)—across the world.

NUCLEAR DEAL: INDIAN PERSPECTIVE

That the Indo-U.S. deal is a landmark event is widely accepted by now. If an India-born American analyst compares the Bush initiative with the 1971 Nixon visit to China, an Indian journalist thinks the deal is the best India could have got ever. Then there is the section of the media, a very small minority no doubt, which is convinced that India's sovereignty and decision-making independence have been bartered away by New Delhi through this deal.

On the side of military nuclear power, if some Indian scientists and analysts feel India's nuclear policy has been compromised as the deal will cap its nuclear capability, Americans are concerned that the deal will give India unlimited scope to add to its nuclear arsenal.

What follows is a dissection of such arguments and counter arguments, to see what is the truth.

A supporter of the deal, unable to understand its carping criticism from some quarters, is harassed enough to say: yet, despite its pristine simplicity, the India-U.S. nuclear deal is proving uncommonly difficult to understand and accept.

It is a very complex deal and the U.S. exercise of exceptionalising India from a treaty has no precedent. The treaty, NPT, was extended by the international community unconditionally and indefinitely. Non-proliferation has been the major concern of the U.S. for the last three decades and India has been under sanctions ever since its 1974 Pokhran I tests and more so, since the 1998 Pokhran II. That the U.S. ended its over 30 years of nuclear isolation of India imposed by these sanctions in a sudden U-turn is rather inexplicable.

Consider what India is going through presently. In the 1970s India set a target of having 10,000 MW of nuclear power by 2000. In 2006 the number stands at 3,310 MW. The reason? A global US-led embargo on India's nuclear program which is becoming tighter by the year. In 2001 Russia supplied fuel for Tarapur nuclear power plant and agreed to build two reactors in Koodankulam. Come 2004, they regretted their inability to do anything more because of the NSG restrictions.

Consider now what the deal means. In exchange for increasing safeguarded plants from 19 to 65 per cent of the installed power capacity, the embargo is lifted. India retains its nuclear weapons as well as 35 per cent of its reactor capacity to make as many weapons as it wishes to in the coming years.[9]

Yet a section of Indian polity and academia is unable to accept these benefits. On the other hand, across the U.S. sections of the intelligentsia are appalled at the President's decision to give India an exception from its tough non-proliferation policy.

In political terms, it means larger geo-political alignments that will bring India and America closer. Because of its ideological fixation, it will be an anathema to the Indian left and the camp followers.

It is obvious that the sanctions had crippled India's nuclear power industry. Even today, the most mature Indian power reactor design is of mere 220 MW capacity, while the international norm for the past decade has been around 1000 MW. True, India now has 540 MW reactor going, but it is also equally true that it is now running short of natural uranium to fuel even the reactors under construction. Supporters of the deal feel that it will allow India to import fuel and turnkey high capacity reactors, and that should be seen as a 'favor' the U.S. is doing to India.

What are the U.S. motives behind this munificence? There are various interpretations of this motivation—depending upon the author—political or academic, and his persuasion and predilection. Obviously, it can't be altruism, as, like in personal relations, so in international affairs, the commodity does not exist. To put it simply, there are no free lunches in such transactions. Bush's claim that it will ease the pressure on global hydrocarbon resources, and consequent switch-over to nuclear energy will result in the cleaner atmosphere, is only part of the explanation. India, of course, needs all the power it can get today, nuclear power will begin to form a significant part of the energy mix after 2030 only.

Some analysts will place the cause of this U.S. action in geo-politics. For 40 years till the Soviet collapse, India was suspicious of the U.S. Reciprocally, India's non-alignment was immoral for Dulles and his ilk. It forced America, in consequence, into two alliances with Pakistan; first in the mid-1950s and then in the 1980s. Both were aimed at fighting the evil Empire. Pakistan however misused these alliances to fight India, and militarisation of its polity thwarted harmonious relations with India. It also helped Pakistan to nurture delusions of parity with India, buoyed no doubt by the U.S. military and economic aid. For its own geo-political reasons, the U.S. itself followed a hyphenated policy towards the two neighbours. Following the end of the

Cold War, dynamics of the U.S. policy in South Asia began to see a change. The foundation was laid by the Jaswant-Talbot series of talks and the culmination was Indo-U.S. deal of March 2006.

In the globalised world, ruled by the WTO, markets are important, hence the economic and commercial angle. Liberalisation of economy started in mid-1990s. The U.S. had long been the largest trading partner of India but more importantly, by 2001 many U.S. companies also began to see business process outsourcing to India as a means of remaining competitive. Indian software companies began to appear on the American radar. Some economists and influential journals had started seeing India as an emerging power. In early 2005, the National Intelligence Council, a think tank associated with the CIA, noted in a report that China and India would emerge as major global powers by 2020 and their impact will be similar to that of the emergence of the U.S. in early 20th century. The view on China was no surprise but India was a revelation, because the country till the recent years had been seen as an exotic destination, a problem state, and a nuclear flashpoint.

Post 9/11, when the American world was turned upside down by the attack by Islamic radicals, the U.S. started seeing certain congruence with India, which had been facing similar attacks (of terrorist violence) through most of the preceding decade. Though Pakistan was still needed as a partner to fight terrorism, inspite of American disillusionment with it for being a major supporter and sustainer of Taliban, it soon realised that its wider Asian interest demanded much sounder ties with a strong, stable, and democratic India—a proven bulwark against Islamic fundamentalism. Hence, the Indo-U.S. nuclear deal, pointedly excluding Pakistan, is a long-delayed step towards the de-hyphenation of India and Pakistan in the minds of Washington policy makers.

China factor seems to have been played up by some analysts in the U.S. plans. It is undoubtedly there but not as some clichéd thinking would suggest—the U.S. using India to counter China. In the Asian sky, China is a shining star, having started liberalization of its economy full two decades before India's. Its gravitational pull is becoming more powerful by the day. "Whether it wants or not, this force is shifting Asia's tectonic plates." Japan may have economic strength and Russia military power or natural resources, but only India has the combination of population, geographical spread, economic and military potential to exert a similar pull. It also has soft power in abundance. Indian films, music, and media, its cuisine, and parts of its higher education system exert their own power in the world.[10] Its noisy democracy is both resilient and creative. The best proof of its potential lies in the fact that it has achieved high growth rates with a fraction of the FDI China has used and that on an infrastructure that is no one's envy.

The U.S. has no plans, says a senior analyst, to get into an adversarial relationship with China, and is unlikely to encourage countries like India to follow that route. China and U.S. are, after all, each other's major trading partners, and any negative development there would shake the global economy as nothing else could. What the U.S. seeks is the help of a constellation of like-minded powers—Japan, the EU, and possibly Russia—to ensure that the unstoppable rise of China is not too destabilizing.

India cannot be an ally in the mould of Japan, Germany, or even the EU. But India and the U.S. have largely similar views on global issues and common threat perceptions. This is understandable as the two countries share a similar political and economic ethos, the great asymmetry in their situation notwithstanding. There are signs that a more understanding U.S. does not ignore India's advice on Jehadi terrorism, and does not have double standards on the terrorist violence in India's Jammu and Kashmir and the one in the West. The 9/11 event seems to have made the change. The recent past shows the two share convergent views on Nepal and Bangladesh. They also share the strategic goal of preserving stability in the Persian Gulf, even if their approaches on it may differ.

So what is the give and take in the bargain. India needs cutting edge technology to meet its burgeoning energy demand, without in any way constraining its strategic autonomy. In exchange, the U.S. gains friendship of an emerging regional power whose success can ease the global transition to a new world order.

Prime Minister Manmohan Singh tells an American Television Channel in March 2006:

- U.S. agreeing to a civil nuclear deal will be an act of "historic reconciliation".
- India is committed to nuclear separation.
- India and U.S. believe China is important.
- India to diversify sources of weapons purchases.
- Difficulties in Iran, Iraq not to hit ties with the U.S. (*The Hindu*, 1.3.06).

Indian Expectations: Starting Point

The Government of India has created an opening, a favourable enabling environment. It has singed the Joint Statement of 18 July 2005, passed the WMD Export Control legislation in consonance with the NSG and MTCR guidelines, joined the ITER project aimed at development of energy through nuclear fusion and the U.S.-led Generation IV initiative aimed at creating reactor prototypes that are not prone to proliferation.

With the opening up of these favourable circumstances created by the said initiatives and measures taken by New Delhi, it is for our end-users to capitalize the resulting opportunities with vigour and foresight for the benefits of not only their own enterprises but also for overall national good. China, with a much less favourable licensing regime, imports ten times the dual technology that we do from the U.S. For our space and nuclear industries, the completion of NSSP resulted in the removal of many of our organizations from the Entity List, with consequent licensing benefits. Some organisations remain listed and India is continuing to work for their removal too. The 'NSG plus' and 'MTCR plus' restrictions, that were in place, were also done away with. The space industry today is permitted direct cooperation for developing, producing, marketing, and operating U.S. commercial satellites and those of third nations that contain U.S. origin components. It has created the basis that finally led to the eventual conclusion of a bilateral India-U.S. space launch agreement. It has also contributed to a useful dialogue on the subject of missile defence.

India has entered a new phase in its foreign policy. We aspire to be a permanent member of the UNSC. We have extended maximum cooperation to the UN whenever needed and requested. Today, a total of 8,675 Indian Army officers and men are serving with the UN peacekeeping forces world wide.[11] Another contingent of 850 strong Infantry Battalion (2 Rajputana Rifles) left for UN service in Congo on 15 July 2006, bringing the total to 9,525. The Indian Army's participation in the UN peacekeeping operations spanned a period of 50 years, covering 29 UN missions in which over 50,000 Indian soldiers have served in various parts of the world. India is presently the second largest troop contributor to the UN. It has also offered one brigade of troops (about 3,500 soldiers) to the UN Standby Arrangement. India started its contribution with the Korean War. The largest and longest serving contingent (an independent brigade group) was sent to Congo in 1961.[12]

We are demonstrating a growing capability to shoulder regional and global responsibilities. We are focusing increasingly on the transnational issues constituting the priority challenges today: (i) Terrorism, whether of Al Qaeda or Kashmiri jehadis. Serial bomb blasts in Mumbai trains on 11 July 2006 are the latest terror to strike India, leaving 200 dead. (ii) Proliferation. (iii) Pandemic or disaster relief. (iv) Iran nuclear enrichment imbroglio. (v) Israeli attacks in Gaza and Lebanon to have its soldiers released from the Hamas (one) and Hizbullah (three). India can no longer sit out on the debates on the major issues of today. Its vote on Iran in IAEA Governing Council meetings in September 2005 and February 2006 was an unexpected break from the past. Global powers have to make hard decisions. India's interests demand a vigorous and articulate diplomatic effort that explains its positions and advances its national interests. It is worth repeating that non-proliferation is one area where India has a record to be proud of, and it is emphasized that it has and will continue to remain one of India's principal contributions to international security.

India's Support: Even more Important in Future

India, presently, is a rapidly expanding industrial economy with a wide array of technologies that are relevant to proliferation. That in itself makes India a relevant player since its export controls and their effective implementation will matter increasingly for global non-proliferation efforts. Being a Nuclear Weapon State, her support for international norms is critical for their success. But it is not only in its controls and restraint that India can make a difference. The time when NPT was regarded as self-enforcing is long past. The cartelisation alone is not adequate instrument to control the spread of technologies. There are many number of examples to show that political and commercial considerations can defeat that. The challenge that our world presently faces requires more vigorous exertions. This is all the more so since the dangers of non-state actors laying their hands on the nuclear weapons have given the WMD threat an added dimension. UNSC Resolution 1540 is just one example of the global community's response. There are several others, among them a combination of national and multinational efforts. Two such examples are: the Container Security Initiative and Proliferation Security Initiative. Proponents of non-proliferation must seriously analyse whether the support of country like India towards global effort will further their cause. It is obvious that such support will not be easy to muster if India perceives herself as unfairly treated despite its demonstrated commitment to a rule-bound system.

INDIA AND U.S. ARE LOOKING FAR BEYOND THE NUCLEAR ENERGY PARADIGM: A DEEPER AND EXPANSIVE RELATIONSHIP

It was Prime Minister Vajpayee (1998-2004) who first proclaimed India and the U.S. as "natural allies", during his first visit to Washington. After taking over as the UPA External Affairs Minister, Mr. Natwar Singh in an interview, baulked at the phrase "natural allies". A man in the Nehruvian mould, and profoundly conscious of the 'halcyon days' of the NAM mythology, he could not bring himself to go beyond the term "strategic allies" for two nations. Leaving the nuanced implications of the two terms to the scholars and sophists, for an informed individual, the terms are tweedledum and tweedledee.

This could be a truism, knowing how similar are the thinking and practices of the UPA Government and its predecessor, the NDA, on the issue of India's relations with the U.S. Even more interestingly, the U.S. too seems to be continuing with the policies toward the UPA Government that it had initiated with its NDA predecessor. Both the nations seem to be aiming at deepening and broadening their relationship in the recent years.

Multifaceted Relationship

While on way to India for President Bush's 1-3 March 2006 visit, Ms. Rice was asked if the momentum in India-U.S. relations would be lost if there was no civilian nuclear deal during the Bush visit. Her reply was expressly emphatic: "No, not at all. First of all, this trip is not a civil nuclear power trip. This trip is about the relationship between the United States and India." A transcript of her remarks said: "It is business development, it is science and technology development, going back to agriculture. This is a very broad relationship that is deepening, and I think benefitting the world as it did, and cooperation on the tsunami, as it demonstrated in the IAEA board of governors where India joined the consensus on Iran. So, there is a lot that is going to be cemented here."

Strategic Relationship

When asked the same question (What would it mean for his India trip if there was no civilian nuclear deal?) at Kabul where he had halted for a visit en route to India, the President was even more expansive:

> Our relationship with India is broader than our discussions about energy. Ours is a strategic relationship. It is a relationship that's got strong ties because of economics and our military, our desire to help democracies such as Afghanistan.
>
> It is in our interest.... It is in the interests of the countries around the world that India develop a nuclear power industry because that will help alleviate demand for fossil fuels. And by alleviating demand for fossil fuels, it takes the price off gasoline at the pump. And so the faster the Indian economy grows, the more fuel they

demand; the more fuel they demand, it affects our gas prices, and it affects your gas prices.

So what we are trying to do is to have an international consortium that will enable countries to develop nuclear power industries in safe ways, ways that will prevent proliferation, ways that will enable nations to meet their energy needs without excessive consumption of fossil fuels.

After Moon, ISRO may Join NASA into Deep Space

New Delhi, 7 May 06. Tomorrow, NASA Administrator Michael Griffin, after his arrival here, will ink two agreements that will pave the way for two American payloads to be flown to the moon when India undertakes the Chandrayaan mission to the moon in 2008.

Speaking to *The Indian Express*,[13] ISRO Chairman G. Madhavan Nair said his organisation hopes to look at "possibilities of joint inter-planetary exploration" during the visit of Mr. Griffin who arrives tomorrow. "When the U.S. looks around for partners for future inter-planetary exploration missions, India stands a good chance because of our robust, well-developed technologies," Mr. Madhavan said.

Bangalore, 9 May 06. "NASA impressed with Indian space capabilities" (*The Hindu*, 10 May 06). Griffin says he will try to get sanctions on some facilities lifted.

St. Louis, Missouri, 10 May 06."Fully armed: US opens military barn door for India"[14]

In a 30-year arms sale career with Boeing's Integrated Defence Systems (IDS), the lesser-known arms division of the giant airplane firm, Michael Devers seldom had India on his radar—until 2005. Devers travelled far and wide—Korea, Japan, Middle East, Australia—hawking the latest American military wares to U.S. allies and friends. But rarely ever to India, which resolutely bought arms from Moscow, Washington's Cold War rival, and Europe.

One day it began changing. Early 2005, U.S. cleared sale of long held up F-16s (made by Boeing's rival-in-arms Lockhead

Martin) to Pakistan. Then came a stunner from Secretary Rice's office: U.S. was offering to India more advanced F-16s Fighter Falcon and even newer Boeing-made F-A-18 Super Hornets in keeping with the strategic shift in the region. Was Boeing prepared for that?

"We were all stunned," recalled another Boeing executive, "This is a new generation Combat aircraft that we have not sold to our closest allies. Outside the U.S. Navy, no one has it. Yet here was the Secretary asking if we were ready to sell to India, and also ready for joint production." Boeing's reply was swift: Sure thing.

In mid-March 2005, Rice travelled to India for what would only later be revealed as a path-breaking visit of the kind Henry Kissinger made to Beijing in 1970.

Amid a raft of issues that would dramatically redefine U.S. strategic interests in Asia, Rice not only sounded out Prime Minister Manmohan Singh on the nuclear deal, but also suggested India not to be too worried about U.S. supply of F-16 to Pakistan because India could have its pick of U.S. arms from here on. The U.S. was keen on a whole new security architecture in the region, a goal that was written into a 10-year military pact signed by the two defence establishments in June, when Pranab Mukherjee visited Washington.[15]

Suddenly, Washington had thrown open the barn door and Americans could get into the scrimmage, with far greater traction and advantage. Two weeks after the Rice visit, Philip Zelikov, her political adviser in the State Department summed up the historic shift in U.S. policy thus: "The U.S. goal is to help India become a major world power in the 21st century. We understand fully the implications, including military implications, of this statement."

The statement was music to the ears of U.S. arms makers. It was also the round of cash registers ringing. America's notorious "military-industrial" complex was no longer a pariah!

The reason for U.S. relaxation of arms sale to India is clearly as much commercial as strategic. India's defence budget of $ 20 billion a year was an attractive, sizeable cake. And Americans were to partake of it for the first time.

St Louis, 11 May 06. *Defence deals: U.S. may dangle investment bait.* The dog fight among the half a dozen arms makers across the world to bag 126 combat jet that India needs, is getting serious.[16]

U.S.-India Energy Bill Approved

The U.S. Senate Foreign Relations Committee approved the Energy Security Cooperation Act 2005, which is entirely different from U.S.-India Civilian Nuclear Cooperation Deal, on 23 May 2006 and forwarded thereafter for final approval by the full Senate.

This 2005 Act is expected to promote global energy security through increased cooperation between the U.S. and India in diversifying sources of energy, stimulating development of alternative fuels, developing and deploying technologies that promote the clean and efficient use of coal, and improving energy efficiency.

Joint Indo-U.S. S & T Fund Proposed

Prime Minister Singh and President Bush announced at New Delhi on 2 March 2006 the intention to establish a bi-national Science and Technology Endowment Fund and a Joint Science and Technology Commission, aimed at accelerating cooperation in Technical fields of mutual interest. The initiatives build on the S & T cooperation agreement was signed between the two countries on 17 October 2005.

The Endowment Fund could have a corpus of over $ 50 million, and would also be open for contributions from the private industry of the two nations. The income from the Fund would be used to support joint research and development projects in various disciplines selected through a competitive process.

Indo-US Tie-up in Oil, Coal and Nuclear Energy

A fact sheet on the Indo-U.S. Energy Dialogue issued at New Delhi on 2 March 2006 after talks between President Bush and Prime Minister Singh says the two countries have agreed on a host of areas in energy sector including oil, natural gas, coal, and civilian nuclear energy. Some details are mentioned below:

1. In the area of oil and gas, India and the U.S. have decided to hold a national gas conference early May 2006 at New Delhi with a focus on gas infrastructure development and operations, LNG and non-conventional gas, including coal-lead methane, and gas sector regulation.
2. MOUs are ready on offshore drilling for gas hydrates and safety standards. Besides, a dialogue continues on a proposed MOU between the Indian Oil and the U.S. National Renewable Energy Laboratory on hydrogen.
3. In the coal sector, Indo-U.S. Business Advisory Council will be set up by 31 March 2006. Besides, India and the U.S. are finalizing an agreement for setting up an information centre with joint funding by the U.S. Environmental Protection Agency, the U.S. Trade Development Agency, and the Indian Government.
4. The ongoing cooperation between India's Atomic Energy Regulatory Board and the U.S. Nuclear Regulation Commission will continue "in an autonomous manner".
5. Under cooperation on civil nuclear energy, a workshop on best practices for nuclear power plant design, new concepts in construction, commissioning operations, safety, life extension, and regulatory oversight will be held later this year in the U.S. as a follow-up to an earlier one held in New Delhi in January 2006.
6. With India joining the ITER project, both sides have agreed to correspond on establishing a mechanism for cooperation between scientists working on fusion science.[17]

CEOs Forum Moots a $ 5 Billion Fund

Identifying six sectors, including biotech and manufacturing, for deepening Indo-U.S. economic relations, top CEOs from the two countries on 2 March 2006 mooted creation of a $ 5 billion fund to boost infrastructure development. The CEOs Forum headed by Tata Group Chief, Ratan Tata, submitted a report to President Bush and Prime Minister Singh, recommending various measures to strengthen economic and business ties.

The U.S. CEOs wanted further opening up of the economy, especially further liberalization of retail and financial sectors in India.[18]

Indo-U.S. Cooperation in Indian Ocean

Ever since the 18 July 2005 joint statement and 2 March 2006 understanding, the two nations have been looking forward to intensifying the bond of cooperation in the Indian Ocean region. Putting the proposed Indo-U.S. Maritime Cooperation Framework (MCF) on the fast track, the visiting U.S. Pacific Fleet Commander Adam Gary Roughead discussed the final modalities with the Navy and South Block.

INDIA: A SUPERPOWER

It is universally accepted that India is a superpower of the 2050, if not earlier when it will be economic and political equal of China and would have overtaken the economics of the U.S., Japan, and the EU. One must recognise that in India's case, the term will neither be a pejorative, nor indicative of arrogance as some analysts see sole superpower of today. But that experience will not be something new for India because it had cultural and civilisational presence in South and South-East Asia, and commercial links with countries in the West as apart as the Arab lands and Roman empire before the dawn of the Christian era.

Even presently, India is not some distant outback of international political, geo-strategic landscape. It has third largest Army in the world and fourth largest Air Force. It is a regional power in its own right despite persistent endeavors by China and Pakistan with a lot of political and military help from the former to hobble it. That is the reason India has never wavered to act in the region when either its own security interests are threatened or peace and stability of the region are challenged by serious developments be it in an Indian Ocean island nation, Bangladesh, or Sri Lanka.

So it seems and sounds rather strange when, in the context of the Indo-U.S. nuclear deal, some critics have talked of India becoming a client state of the U.S., India surrendering its sovereignty, India losing its independent decision-making in economy and nuclear field, or worst of all, in an obvious rhetoric flourish, dubbing India as the 51st of State of the U.S. If some supporters of the deal have dubbed such assertions, claims or apprehensions as "terrorism of the pen", "obscene exaggerations", "journalism of excess", and "irresponsibly overstating the case", others see some merit in them but no agreement can be without "give and take". If there is no place for "free lunches" in international affairs, neither should a nation be expecting a charity or be seen with a begging bowl. If a nation wants some gains for itself from an agreement, it must be ready to pay certain costs politically, economically but after comprehensive examination of all aspects of the bargain. Once it is convinced of the necessity of a bilateral, trilateral, or multilateral agreement say, Indo-U.S. nuclear deal, Iran-Pakistan-India pipeline projects, or joining other nations in ITER or Gen IV, it should go ahead, ignoring any extraneous considerations.

As for India being a client state, a camp-follower, or a surrender baby, the people who adduce such arguments seem to be unaware of India's innate strengths. Civilizationally, culturally, economically, and even physically, in terms of its size, area-wise or population-wise, we are too proud and too big a nation to be taken for granted, not to speak of being pocketed, by any nation—a sole superpower or any other nation. Of course, it is important to remain united. It is equally important for us to have self-belief, and faith in our future that is beckoning us.

What follows is indicative of our place and position in the comity of nations, even when we have still parts of our nation struggling with poverty.

India Joins Cutting-edge Technology Projects

India joins the billion dollar Future Gen Project, on 2 March, 2006 aimed at creating the world's first zero-emission fossil fuel plant. Invited by the U.S. Government, India will contribute $ 10 million, while the U.S. Government and industry will fund the balance required for the project. The 2 March 2006 joint Bush-Singh statement says India will participate in the governments' steering Committee of this initiative. An international public-private partnership, Future Gen is an initiative to build the world's first integrated sequestration and hydrogen production research power plant. Indian companies are expected to participate in the private sector segment of the project, which will draw upon the best scientific talent to pursue an innovative showcase project focused on design, construction, and operation of a technically cutting-edge power project.

As for India's participation in the multi-billion dollar International Thermonuclear Energy Research (ITER), the joint statement said it is an important step towards the common goal of full nuclear energy cooperation. ITER is an international project that seeks to make use of fusion energy (fusion that occurs in the sun and the stars) for electricity production. The main ITER facility would be in Cadarache, France, and all partners U.S., EU, Russia, Japan, South Korea, and China will participate in its construction, research and development. India was invited to join the initiative as a full partner of ITER at its meeting in Jeju, South Korea on 6 December 2005.

Anil Kakodkar, Chairman, India's Atomic Energy Commission, after initialling the agreement on India's behalf at Brussels on 25 May 2006, said, "This signifies the start of a major international effort in developing an energy source which provides virtually limitless energy." He said, "Even if we are talking about 5000 KWH per capita per year, which is nothing compared to the per capita energy consumption of Europe, that would mean enhancing the electricity consumption in India by a factor of 11 or 12." So India "has joined 6-nation nuclear club."[19]

As part of Indo-U.S. energy dialogue, India has also sought membership of the Integrated Ocean Development Program (IODP), an international drilling program for scientific deep sea research led by Japan and the U.S. It aims to study the unknown deep biosphere by studying core samples and monitoring bore holes, an important first step towards harnessing hydrates as a source of energy. The National Gas Hydrate Program has identified specific areas in Indian deep sea waters for conducting further geo-scientific surveys. It is believed that commercial exploitation of gas hydrates may start some time in the period 2015-20.

What Others Say

"India is a roaring capitalist success story", says the latest issue (June 2006) of *Foreign Affairs*. There is no denying that the 21st will be an Indian Century just as 20th was American. The exuberant self-confidence of Indian economic and strategic thinkers have found their echo in foreign media and foreign policy establishments of various countries. If in July 2005 President Bush decided to assist India's nuclear program, even at the risk of undermining his policy of checking Iran's nuclear ambitions, special reports and covers hailing the rise of India in *Time, Foreign Affairs*, and *The Economist* appeared in June 2006.

It was not too long ago that India appeared in the American press as a poor, backward nation, and saddled with an inefficient bureaucracy. To the same press, it not only seems a "roaring capitalist success story", but also, according to the *Foreign Affairs*, an "emerging strategic partner" of the U.S.

Now comes Dr. Henry Kissinger: "India and the U.S. have no conflicting national interests that could bring them into confrontation and are, therefore, ideally poised to forge a 'Partnership Concord' and emerge poised as natural partners on the global theatre."[20]

Some Indicators about India's Status

1. Prime Minister talks tough, and bluntly, on board Air India One, 9 July 2005. He revealed he had gone to the G-8 Summit at Gleneagle with "no expectations" and he did not expect "they would listen to us". But President Bush and Jacques Chirac endorsed what he said on climate change: "I said the whole world faces a single environment....We all have...to safeguard the essential life support of our planet...certainly the environment cannot be protected by perpetuating the

> poverty of developing nations. That is the balance." He told G-8 leaders: "It is not the negotiating forum... such limited forums cannot be allowed to take upon themselves to arbitrate the fate of the world. The proper framework for the negotiations is the UN Convention on Climate Change or the Kyoto Protocol."

Asked about the agenda of his impending U.S. 17-20 July 2005 visit, he said, "I am not going with any demands. I want to explain to the U.S. Government, to the U.S. Congress what our aspirations are. The bulk of sources for India's development has always been mobilized locally...we are not supplicants."

Asked about Iranian gas pipeline and U.S. opposition to it, Dr. Singh did not mince words: "This is an affair between Iran, India and Pakistan. If the three countries agreed, that should be the end of the matter...we are not a client state!"

2. Sriharikota (India), 1 July 2006. Next to French Guiana, SHAR may emerge as the most favored launch destination. With 11 consecutive successful missions, this spaceport has capacity to launch commercially.
3. Prime Minister attended G-8 Summit's outreach session on 7 July 2005. India (alongwith China, Brazil, South Africa, and Mexico) had been invited to the Gleneagle (Scotland) meet of the G-8, presided over by Prime Minister Blair. Last time India was invited to a G-8 outreach session which was held at Evian in France in 2004.
4. Chennai, 4 July 2006. Bernd Mutzelburg, German Ambassador in India, said: "Science is one field the Europeans can learn quite a bit from the Indians."
5. India was elected on 9 May 2006 to the newly constituted UN Human Rights Council, securing the highest votes in the Asian category, in the largest ever election conducted in the UN history. India secured 173 votes out of the 191 member General Assembly, suggestive of the widespread respect it enjoyed in the UN.

6. India to outpace US, Russia in cell race, thanks to the accelerating growth of the wireless communications network in the country. "Adding five million subscribers per month, India will become the world's second largest mobile phone market by 2008," says an 86-page study report authored by wireless expert Chetan Sharma and conducted for Data Communication Research company. India's regulatory mechanism can serve as a model for both developing and rich nations. India passed Japan in total subscribers in April 2006. In the next few weeks it will break through the 100 million subscriber barrier, says the report released by the St Louis, Missouri-based research firm.[21]

India on World Stage

Prime Minister Manmohan Singh in his second speech from the ramparts of the Red Fort on the Independence Day (15 August) 2005 made a "historic declaration":

> There comes a time in the history of a nation when it can be said that the time has come to make history. We are today at the threshold of such an era.
>
> The world wants us to do well and take our righteous place on the world stage. There are no external constraints on our development. If there are any hurdles they are internal. We must seize this moment and grab this opportunity.
>
> We need to have the resolve to make our country prosperous. We must have the self-confidence to realize that we are second to none, that Indians are as good as the best.
>
> Our political system and leadership must show sagacity, wisdom, and foresight so that we are able to make the best of the moment and make India a truly great nation.

As for no external restraint, Dr. Singh was speaking optimistically after signing the 10 July 2005 Joint Statement with President Bush, and internal hurdles obviously referred to the coalition partners, the Communists in particular.

A leading analyst laments that "When the Prime Minister has delivered such a meaningful speech, most commentaries focused on Pakistan."[22] He claims that no Prime Minister, "in the last 56 years, has made such statement with such optimism". India had been hobbled by various technology denial regimes by the Western countries on the one hand and encirclement and containment strategy of the China-Pakistan combine on the other. "There was, in fact, a tacit alliance among the U.S., Pakistan, and China against India from 1971 to 2000."

It may be a world dominated by a sole superpower, but a new six power-centred balance of power system is already emerging. In this world, the U.S. needs India as much as the latter needs the former, if not more. It is not without any reason that the U.S. is willing to abandon its policy of imposition of multifarious sanctions and denial regimes in force since 1974, and sign a bilateral agreement India-specific on cooperation in civilian nuclear field.

If India was the theme of annual World Economic Forum at Davos a couple of years ago, India (with China) is a regular invitee to the annual G-8 Conference. A globalising world is calling on India to become one of the players in the global balance of power systems which would stabilise peace. Even the Chinese leadership has understood the new developments "and talks of India as a global player in the wake of the U.S. announcement of 25 March 2005 to help in assisting India to become a world power in the 21st century". There need be no unease among the Indians in U.S. wanting to help India to become a world power. China got all the help, initially, from the Soviet Union, and later, from the U.S. to achieve its ambitions to become a world power.

India must be in G-8: World Watch

India and China are positioned to "leapfrog" today's industrial powers and become world leaders in sustainable energy and agriculture within a decade, says the World Watch Institute's State of the World Report 2006. Its main points are:

1. In line with this emerging trend, it wants India and China to be inducted into the G-8 Club, and International Energy Agency.

2. In addition, India should get a permanent seat in the UN Security Council.
3. The two Asian giants can hold the world in balance in the next few years, but much will depend on the choices they make in this period—choices that lead the world to ecological and political instability or to a development path based on efficient technologies and use of resources.
4. People in the U.S. and elsewhere must learn to treat the rise of India and China as a wake-up call and apply their minds on the need to build sustainable economies, says the Washington-based think tank.
5. India and China can develop in a more benign way than other industrialized nations, argues President of World Watch Christopher Flavin. Opinion leaders in both countries are highly commended for increasingly recognizing that resource intensive model for economic growth can't work in the 21st century.
6. Already China's world leading solar industry provides water heating for 35 million buildings, and India's pioneering use of rainwater harvesting brings clean water to tens of thousands of homes says Flavin, one of the leading authors of the report.
7. Some of the positive trends cited include India's commitment to increase renewable energy's share in power from 5 per cent to 20-25 per cent. The country has the world's fourth largest wind power industry. It is also the fourth largest producer of ethanol.
8. Sunita Narain of India's Centre for Science and Environment, says in the foreword to the Report that the South has no choice but to reinvent the development trajectory. "The western model of growth India and China wish most feverishly to emulate is intrinsically toxic," says Narain.
9. Challenges facing India and China include the shortage of fresh water and increased consumption of oil as a result of their burgeoning automobile industries. Since the two have only large coal dominated energy systems

in the world, they are central to future efforts to slow global climate change.

They All Want India to Join Them

Sydney, 18 March 2006. The US, Japan, and Australia create a new strategic forum Trilateral Strategic Dialogue to ostensibly checkmate China. It identified India as the emerging power that must be engaged.[23]

Beijing, 22 March 2006. Russia and China have called for setting up an institutional framework for trilateral cooperation with India. The call made in a joint declaration adapted by President Putin and Chairman Hu Jintao during their summit meeting here on 21-22 March, came two weeks after India dramatically raised the level of strategic interaction with the U.S. It may be noted that the question of trilateral Russia-China-India cooperation has been in the works for last couple of years, but it was seldom paid much attention to by these two countries, China in particular!

A senior analyst[24] put it all in perspective, and aptly too, "Around the world, Mittal's Arcelor bid and the Bush Administration's successful mobilisation of support to their nuclear deal (passed with huge majorities by the House and Senate Committees) are part of the same story: the rise of India."

INDO-US AGREEMENT: WORKING OUT THE DRAFT CONTENTS

The entire edifice of the bilateral Indo-U.S. Civil Nuclear Cooperation Agreement is to be based on the 18 July 2005 Joint Statement signed in Washington by President George W. Bush and Prime Minister Manmohan Singh.

Problem of Indian Nuclear Tests Sorted Out

India has so far been resisting U.S. pressures for formalisation of India's voluntary moratorium on nuclear tests by making it a part of the 123 Agreement. It has now been reported that India has accepted a compromise formula on the issue which was brought to the May 2006 Burns-Saran London meeting by America. Under this formula, legislation by the U.S. Congress to halt all nuclear cooperation with India if it goes in for a nuclear test will be acceptable with the rider that any such decision could be overturned by a Congressional majority. The Bush Administration is keen to get U.S. Congress endorsement for the nuclear deal in some form or other before 4 July recess as further delay could lead to an indefinite postponement.

Such a decision can be overturned by a majority if reasons for Indian tests are accepted by the U.S. Congress, e.g., if the Indian tests follow the Chinese or Pakistani tests.[25]

Another daily[26] of 12.6.06 has a different, contradictory take on the issue detailed above, which is summed up here:

- On the issue of the deal going off in case India were to test a device, the sense is very clear that Washington has this law in place internally but it would not be part of the bilateral agreement. U.S. is inclined to accept a wording that reaffirms India's commitment to voluntary moratorium on testing.
- It was clarified in London that the Congressional waiver will be a one-time affair and not done annually as was being suggested in some quarters.

12-14 June 2006 Talks to Finalise the Draft

India and the U.S. held their talks at New Delhi to prepare grounds for an agreement on civil nuclear cooperation. The two sides will discuss the "123 Agreement on the amendment of the Atomic Energy Act 1954, which stipulates a bilateral cooperation pact before concluding a comprehensive nuclear deal with another country". It also specifies nine criteria that include maintaining the IAEA safeguards, continuing the safeguards in perpetuity, and no enriching or reprocessing without prior approval.

The two sides reportedly exchanged drafts of the agreement when Mr. Saran and Mr. Burns met in London in May 2006. These discussions are a result of the 18 July 2005 political agreement between President Bush and Prime Minister Singh on civilian nuclear cooperation. The Indian team is led by Joint Secretary (America) in the MEA S. Jai Shankar. The U.S. side is led by Director of Nuclear Energy, Safety, and Security in the State Department Richard Stratford.[27]

Another daily[28] has interestingly, different information on these talks as summed up below:

- The draft document of the Agreement will contain significant assurances on fuel supply which would allow India to stockpile fuel for the lifetime of every reactor. The unique fuel supply assurance was agreed upon during negotiations on the separation plan and has not been ever conceded to any country not recognised as a nuclear weapons state. In practical terms there will be no restrictions on how much fuel India can buy. India can import fuel beyond the immediate requirement of its reactors on the ground that it will be part of strategic reserve.
- Other assurances: U.S. help in negotiating an India-specific fuel supply agreement with the IAEA and a back-up arrangement that in case all these assurances fail, U.S. and India will convene a group of supplier friendly countries like Russia, UK, and France to restore supply.
- This is in return for India agreeing to accept permanent safeguards on its civilian facilities unlike other nuclear weapons states.

No Deal-breakers Acceptable: Burns

Under Secretary Burns on 21 June 2006 pledged administration's support to the bipartisan legislation on the deal but said it was against 'deal-breaker' amendments by the U.S. Congress that would force it to "renegotiate" the pact.

Indian Negotiating Skills Need Appreciation

Against America's need to have a viable geostrategic partner, it was India's strong desire to end its nuclear isolation and regain access to the global energy market and cutting edge technologies, that broke the logjam. Driven by these criteria, both nations in a spirit of give and take reached a mutually satisfying compromise. Notwithstanding all this, India made certain that its strategic autonomy, national sovereignty, and economic and political decision-making capability were not violated in any way, now or ever. If still there is criticism about the deal, that is only expected in an open democracy. "As for the critics, they too have their job to do." In any case, any comprehensive bilateral deal of such political implications and economic potentiality cannot satisfy every shade of opinion in either country.

Analysts have showered encomiums on the Indian negotiators of the deal. It was Prime Minister Manmohan Singh who almost single-handedly guided the negotiators and provided the political leadership for such a sensitive deal, impinging on India's security, geo-strategic, and economic interests. Observers of the situation were not surprised when Dr. Singh decided not to appoint a new incumbent, when External Affairs Minister Natwar Singh resigned under the Volcker cloud. In addition, one can imagine the pressure the Prime Minister must be working under when it is well-known that not only was there strong opposition to the deal among his UPA partners like the Communists, Samajwadi Party, etc, to name just two, but even some among his senior Congress ministers were against it, if press reports are to be believed.

Among the officials who assisted him, the foremost was Foreign Secretary Shyam Saran who has to be acknowledged as the public face of the deal. He is always in the public eye and newspaper headlines: holding parleys with the American officials led by Mr. Burns; lobbying for the deal with the U.S. lawmakers, chancelleries the world over, NSG members; addressing U.S. think tanks and public audiences at prestigious institutions like the Institute of Defence Studies and Analysis and India Habitat Centre/India International Centre; interface between the MEA and the PMO; and oversee the work of the negotiating team, consisting of the officials, scientists, and technical experts. Next in line is the Narayanan-led PMO. The public face in America is Indian Ambassador Ronen Sen. As important as Mr. Saran is the scientist Anil Kakodkar, Chairman, Atomic Energy Commission.

Let the final word rest with an analyst who says: "India negotiated the deal with great skill, and self-confidence, a feature rarely seen in the past. In fact, it is the best deal India could have got ever."[29]

Is Ronen Sen on Board?

The Left have been screaming over the 18 July Statement, BJP unhappy, and one daily each from Kolkata and Chennai are convinced that India has been sold down the drain. But things it seem were hardly less discomforting within the core negotiating team, if one daily[30] is to be believed.

When told by the Prime Minister from Washington that it was a done deal, Congress President Sonia Gandhi is said to have asked "if (Ambassador) Ronen Sen was on board!" He, of course, was along with the scientific top brass led by the AEC and ISRO Chiefs.

Ironing Out the 'Difficult' Elements from the Draft

Just before the Indo-U.S. Nuclear Cooperation Bills were to come up for vote on the floor of both chambers of the U.S. Congress, principal interlocutors from both sides Mr. Saran and Mr. Burns met in Paris on 13 July 2006. As the two versions of the Bill are different in some respect, the reconciliations of the two is an important aspect of the entire process. The Administration is in touch with the Congress to ensure that some of the 'difficult' elements are modified or dropped in the final version. India had informed the U.S. that it was not comfortable with some elements in both versions of the Bill which have been passed by a healthy majority of the relevant committees of the House and Senate.[31]

In the Senate version, this relates to not giving India reprocessing technology. India wants it out from the final version.

Then, there is the issue of the Bill stating that the U.S. will stop civil nuclear cooperation in case India violates NSG and MTCR guidelines. While this is unexceptionable, India is worried that minor violations, which can occur when companies do trade, should not lead to termination of all cooperation.

Then there was problem of sequencing, including the signing of a safeguards agreement with the IAEA. For India, this has always been the last step in the process, but Bill in the House has placed it as a precondition. This arbitrary and unilateral change in sequencing has been severely criticized by a section of the Indian media.

Saran conceded to an Indian audience at Delhi's India Habitat Centre on the very next day that New Delhi, "which is waiting for the text of the final legislation after the House and Senate have voted, will have to brace up for some disconcerting 'noises' from Washington as Congress is likely to insist on making certain 'unpalatable' references." A visibly exhausted Saran, delivering a lecture on "Indo-U.S. Joint Statement of July 2005: A year later," within hours of his arrival from Paris, said: "Obviously, the legislation will be the product of an American political process and could well include some references we may find unpalatable."[32]

But he was also quite categorical on the bottomline: India could not undertake any obligations going beyond the 18 July joint statement and separation plan.

Another daily[33] covered the same lecture under the defiant headline, "End of defensive diplomacy." After talking about 'unpalatable' things, he spoke of changing India: "18 July, in retrospect, marks our determination to put behind us an era of defensive diplomacy. If India is to become a credible candidate for permanent membership of the UNSC, then we must adjust our traditional positions. Our foreign policy must reflect our national aspirations and express our confidence as an emerging global player. We cannot duck the difficult issues of the day and display an aversion to risk-taking. July 18 is, in some ways, an effort to usher in a change in mindset."

Seldom has an Indian Foreign Secretary, usually a dyed-in-the-wool bureaucrat, spoken in such a self-assured stance!

Two days earlier, on 12 July, U.S. Ambassador to India David Mulford had made the same points in Washington: "The Bush Administration is aware that some provisions in the legislation...trouble India and would work where it was possible, to address those issues."

St. Petersburg, 17 July 2006.

Prime Minister Manmohan Singh spells out some concerns over the draft U.S. nuclear legislation, saying "it must not go beyond the 18 July 2006 Joint Statement." President Bush assures him: "The U.S. would not shift the goal posts."

BIG PICTURE: GEO-STRATEGIC PARADIGM IN NAVAL FIELD

Maritime cooperation was high on the agenda during the March 2006 Bush visit, with both sides reaffirming their commitment with the existing multilateral efforts aimed at enhancing security in the maritime domain. The proposed Indo-U.S. Maritime Cooperation Framework (MCF) can be deemed as another step in boosting the bilateral engagement through the enhancement of domain and intensity of cooperation. The two have shared interests in securing vital sea lanes of the Indian Ocean in fighting terrorism and finally creating a stable Asia.

Even if Indo-U.S. maritime cooperation increased after the 9/11 attacks, the genesis of this cooperation should be traced back to the end of the Cold War. Before that cataclysmic event, Russian ally's presence in the Indian Ocean was 'comforting' for some Indians against the 'menacing' U.S. navy eyeing for islands and other footholds in that Ocean. It was in some manner 'containment' policy against the U.S. geo-strategic interest here. So in the early 1990s, Soviet Union, being defunct, was not there as an ally, Russia had withdrawn voluntarily from there, and fresh naval competition arising out of a new unipolar power structure compelled India to redirect its military strategy towards great powers. Then on, the existing policy of 'containment' was supplanted by policy of 'cooperation'. The U.S. was no longer seen as a threat as hitherto, but as a partner in naval cooperation.

For the U.S., too, India is a valuable choice as a regional power with the largest navy in the Indian Ocean region. "From the early 1990s, both these navies, as a part of their mutual strategic engagements in the Indian Ocean, began joint exercises and expanded their activities to other sub-regions in the Indian Ocean region."[34] Two major disasters of this decade, the 9/11 attacks and tsunami of December 2004, provided an opportunity to Washington to strengthen its ongoing maritime cooperation with New Delhi.

Post 9/11, the new convergence of interests with Washington on the war against terror persuaded India to give up its traditional policy of resistance and go for military cooperation with the U.S. The visit of the U.S. aircraft carrier Carl Vinson to Mumbai port in December 2001, a surprise move by the U.S. brought the first cue for the new dawn of Indo-U.S. friendship. This visit washed away the bitter memories of the infamous hostile entry of the legendry U.S. Enterprise into the Bay of Bengal during the 1971 war.

Post 9/11, Washington's request to India for escorting its naval vessels in the Malacca Straits marked the beginning of a new chapter in Indo-U.S. strategic engagement, and it was also America's endorsement of India's strategic imprint stretching beyond South Asia to neighbouring South-East Asia. So the Indian Navy can be seen as a stabilizing force through its partnership with the U.S. and other navies to secure this region. The U.S. decision to craft a four nation coalition group with India, Australia, and Japan for relief operations in the tsunami affected nations was another high for Indo-U.S. Naval cooperation in the Indian Ocean. Such a cooperation was unthinkable in the Cold War days when India deemed Soviets as allies and the U.S. a devil incarnate! Chinese growing naval presence in the region is also a factor that fuels Indo-U.S. naval cooperation.

Nations Supporting the Nuclear Deal

Even before the Indo-U.S. deal is passed by the U.S. Congress, nay, before it was approved by the House and Senate Committees, which they did on 27 and 29 June 2006 respectively, India was getting signals of support from various countries. Here is a sample:

1. Hanover, 23 April 06. Germany cautiously positive on nuclear cooperation. Will watch progress in U.S. Congress and in IAEA and then decide.
2. New Delhi, 7 May 06. Ahead of NSG meeting in Brazil in June, a key politician from the ruling Liberal

Democratic Party (Mr. Kisaburo Tokai, its Director General of International Bureau) indicated that Tokyo would consider supporting the Indo-U.S. deal if there is "adequate trust" between New Delhi and international community over its nuclear program.

3. Paris, 16 May 06. The Indo-French nuclear cooperation document would have been signed but for differences over a single phase. Indian negotiators refused to accept nuke cooperation for "peaceful, non-explosive purposes". It is obvious that Paris will move with India only after the deal with the U.S. is singed, sealed, and delivered.
4. New Delhi, 3 July 06. India signed three pacts with Spain and Prime Minister Manmohan Singh held discussions on Indo-U.S. deal with his counterpart, Jose Luis Rodriguez Zapatero, and sought Spain's support at the 45-member NSG.

Nuclear Deal a Step Forward: ElBaradei

In June 2006, the deal got important support from IAEA Director-General Mohammed ElBaradei, who wrote in the *Washington Post*: "The deal allows India access to sensitive technology in exchange for bringing its nuclear reactors under safeguards. With this creative break from the past...India will get technology to help lift its 500 million people from poverty...and combat nuclear terrorism and rid our world of nuclear weapons."[35]

India and Nuclear Tests Conundrum

After the flurry of activity induced by the visits of French President Jacques Chirac and U.S. President George W. Bush, the momentum seems to have slowed down considerably between India and its international interlocuters on nuclear cooperation. The sticking point, ironically, seems to be India's voluntary moratorium on nuclear tests.

Indo-French nuclear cooperation negotiations in Paris stumbled on a single phrase. French document, sent to India even before the February 2006 Chirac visit, said the proposed nuclear cooperation would be for "peaceful, non-explosive purposes." Indian negotiators refused to include this in the final document which stalled talks. India had also refused to include phrases in the document that referred to NSG guidelines at the time for understandable reasons, because this was just before the Bush visit. Consequently, the Franco-Indian nuclear cooperation document remained only a declaration of intent. It seemed obvious that France would move with India only after the deal with India was signed, sealed, and delivered.

Paris has also shown a great deal of interest in the content of 123 Agreement that India will be signing with the U.S. The U.S. draft presented to India also had the contentious clause that nuclear cooperation between the U.S. and India would be off if India conducted nuclear tests again. There was crossing of swords on this provision, as was only to be expected.

The French and American caveats in both agreements are remarkably similar, and the analysts say this is the clause likely to appear again and again in India's nuclear dealings with other countries, particularly the members of the NSG. France, Germany, Spain, Japan *et al.* are more likely to keep the lines of negotiation open till the issue is settled the way it is spelt out or left out in the 123 Agreement between India and the U.S.

It is clear by now (10 July 2006) that the Indo-U.S. bilateral agreement will not have this particularly contentious demand in its text, as was the case when this deal sailed through with huge majorities in the committees of the House (37-5) and Senate (16-2) without this clause. But sources say they expect the "testing clause" to be part of the U.S. Congress resolution, in 'one form or other,' if and when it happens. A lot of hard bargaining is expected at that stage—even the mutual acrimony is not ruled out.

To the U.S., India has been insistently telling that its commitment would be totally confined to the letter and spirit of the 18 July 2005 agreement. With other members of the NSG, India has been working the diplomatic wheels overtime, assuring them that any nuclear cooperation would only be for civilian use and in reactors that would be under international safeguards.

According to the opponents of the deal and serious analysts, scepticism about the India agreement emanates from two issues: (i) the diversion of imported equipment, materials, and technology from India's civil to (military) nuclear programs; (ii) the apparent failure of the nuclear deal to curb the production of fissile material. These two could, as well, be the concern of some of the NSG members. That obviously is the reason that but for Russia, no other members of the NSG—like France, Germany, Japan, etc. have come forward to supply nuclear fuel for Indian reactors. They prefer to politely wait in the wings till the final 123 Agreement is signed between India and the U.S.

The concern for the production of fissile material is a bit of a smokescreen, even among non-proliferation oriented countries. But it is a strong demand from, rather an article of faith with, non-proliferation Ayatollahs, who have been particularly vocal on India committing itself to the FMCT.

China recently reaffirmed its commitment to an "early negotiations" of FMCT, "even though it is well known among the nuclear policy circles that Beijing is not really interested in the FMCT."[36] Its active and long standing help in proliferation of nuclear and missile technologies to Pakistan and North Korea is a matter of common knowledge.

As far the U.S., a subterranean debate has been underway in that country where the diplomats are ready to begin talks on FMCT, even if the Pentagon remained reluctant, even skeptical, participant. Now that the U.S. has introduced the draft FMCT at the CD in Geneva on 18 May 2006, it should be of some interest to us how the US strategy on the on-coming negotiations on the issue evolves—particularly the dynamics of inter departmental policy predilections. One way America may want to achieve quicker results is to launch an earnest effort to get the world's nuclear nations together on the subject in Geneva.

As for India, it is pushing the NSG and IAEA hard to work out an "assured fuel supplies" agreement. This was a major concern weighing on India's policy makers when it was debating whether to put its civilian nuclear reactors under perpetual safeguards. India has already held parleys with leading members of NSG like France, Germany, Japan, and Spain. The U.S. has agreed to guarantee fuel for India's reactors. "French officials at Paris said they were working with the IAEA to structure a three-tier fuel supply system, in case political conditions prompt one of India's international suppliers to cut off fuel supplies." One happy augury has been the hearty welcome of the Indo-U.S. nuclear agreements by IAEA Secretary General ElBaradei soon after its announcement.

Then came the news that a via media has been found on the subject: If India conduct tests, cooperation will be off, but the decision can be reversed by a majority vote in the Congress.

But of late, there has been some criticism on another aspect of this subject. From day one, the Indian side has insisted that the 18 July 2005 agreement is about energy and not arms control. The U.S. too sees the deal primarily about fashioning India's energy choices. "But there is also a non-proliferation impulse as reflected in the reference to India's unilateral moratorium on nuclear weapon testing in the joint statement issued that day." Now comes the finger-pointing. Accepting reference to India's voluntary moratorium without extracting reciprocal reference to the United States' own moratorium was a serious error of tactics and principle. Today it is this commitment that is proving the most difficult to work around as India resists U.S. efforts to convert its voluntary no-testing pledge into something more legally binding. Specifically, the U.S. is trying to link the assurance of perpetual nuclear fuel supply as envisaged by the Indian nuclear separation plan into a "no nuclear testing" condition. As per the normal practice in such situations, these clauses form part of the "bracketed" portion of the Nuclear Cooperation Agreement (the so-called '123 Agreement') currently under negotiations between the two sides.

Is India Surrendering to America on Agni-III?

This is a pet charge of the Indian Communists, a Kolkata daily, and some Indian critics, particularly two among them (let us call them KB and CB), being bandied about freely in the domestic debate in the country.

Apprehension about American pressure or, at least the perception of such pressure, occasionally surface in India with reports that New Delhi has deferred testing the long range Agni-III missile because of Washington's strong disapproval. It is a fact that the scientists[37] working on Agni-III had told the press that the missile was ready for test firing since January 2006, implying political go-ahead was holding it up.

A senior U.S. official scoffed at the reports, saying the issue "has not even come up for discussion here (Washington).... There is not any U.S. pressure here that I am aware of". He was also frank enough to say that any missile test at this junction may not exactly be helpful in the context of the nuclear deal but it would be wrong to say the deal rested on the issue.

One should indeed appreciate the honest expression of views about present being inappropriate time to test launch Agni-III as it would give a handle to anti-deal critics to go at India. Defence Minister Pranab Mukherjee had, in similar vein, cited, "a self-imposed restraint" to justify the Agni-III test hold up in May 2006. There is something known as political prudence which is useful in conducting relations between two nations, the same may as prudence is useful for inter-personal relations between two individuals.

Finally, when India did conduct Agni-III test launch on 9 July 2006 to prove rubbish the theory of U.S. pressure on India, the Kolkata daily had the story ready for this eventuality too: "India went ahead with the flight test held up for more than half a year after it was cleared by the U.S. The Chairman of the U.S. Joint Chief of Staff, Gen. Peter Pace, gave the 'public' go-ahead to test the Agni-III during a visit to India last month" (*AA*, 10.7.06). It is obvious that a country or its government can never win against a free-wheeling, determined journalist and his/her newspaper!

US Defends Agni-III Test

"For U.S., India can do no wrong," screams a news headline in a daily.[38] It was nice to see the U.S. offering an unprecedented defence of India's missile test and nuclear program, attesting to the growing close ties between the two democracies.

White House said Agni-III test was transparent, non-threatening, unlike that of Korea's missile firing. It disclosed that India had notified the U.S. and Pakistan about the test.

How and What of Indian Gains

Once the U.S. Congress clears the deal and once it passes muster in the IAEA, where the chief Indian interlocuter Anil Kakodkar has already visited Vienna for the initial powwow and the IAEA team visited India early July 2006 for discussions on the safeguards, and the NSG, for which India has already started meeting up its leading members, the agreement would come into force. Admittedly, all three are yet some distance away. But once India and the U.S. reach these three destinations with some mutual pushing and pulling, the denial regimes would cease to exist.

The boost this could provide to IBM, Intel, Microsoft, General Electric, not to mention our own high-tech enterprises, is bound to go a long way to help sustain and even augment our growth rates. The way is already being cleared for import of cutting edge technologies, dual-use material, and finally nuclear reactors.

Moribund ideological qualms and frozen mindset resulting from the ephemeral political calculations should not be allowed to result in our missing out on an unprecedented opportunity to place the entire gamut of our relationship with the U.S. on a sound footing. "Mindsets in both our countries have been changing for the better, thanks to the efforts of Presidents Clinton and Bush and Prime Ministers Vajpayee and Manmohan Singh." The deal will allow the two countries to build on them.

Genuine differences over some issues must not be allowed to cloud the big picture. The big picture suggests that a robust relation with America will help enhance our security and economic interests for decades to come.

Nuclear Energy: Major Gain

Here is Chairman, Indian Atomic Energy Commission Anil Kakodker speaking at the IAEA 49th General Conference at Vienna on 28 September 2005:

> India, constituting one-sixth of the global population, is

> on the rapid economic growth path. A recent study has revealed that we will need to augment our electricity generation nearly ten-fold in next four to five decades. A large fraction of this energy coming from nuclear power would be of immense benefit in the context of environment and sustainability concerns.
>
> India would like to see a rapid increase in nuclear power capacity well above planned 20,000 MWe by 2020.

It is to be noted that India had a mere 2,000 MWe nuclear energy in 2000 against planned 10,000 MWe.

The nuclear cooperation deal with the U.S. encourages India to revise its nuclear power generation target to 40,000 MWe by 2030 from 20,000 MWe by 2020.[39]

Are American Fears Indian Gains?

It will be good for "surrender theorists" to know what the U.S. critics say on the deal. The *New York Times* was so furious at the pro-Indian tilt of the nuclear deal that it thundered editorially: "Kill the deal."

An exasperated *Guardian*, the left-leaning British daily, has noted in March 2006 that "the U.S. is now treating India like its uniquely special ally Israel, also outside the NPT...believed to have 200 warheads."[40]

Under the heading, "Did Bush Blink"? in the *Washington Post,* Dan Froomkin said: "It appears that to close the deal during his visit, Bush directed his negotiators to give in to India's demands that it be allowed to produce unlimited quantities of fissile material and amass as many nuclear weapons as it wants." Another article expressed the same fear. During their joint news conference, Mr. Bush and Dr. Singh praised the deal but did not say that "it would allow India to produce vast quantities of fissile material," something which all the P-5 nuclear powers have voluntarily halted.[41]

Robert J Einhorn, a U.S. expert, is more direct: "It is not meaningful to talk about 14 of the 22 reactors being placed under safeguards. What is meaningful is what the Indians would do at the unsafeguarded reactors, which is, vastly increasing their production of fissile material for nuclear weapons." Questions will also be asked about the future when, as Under Secretary Burns hints, the percentage of safeguarded reactors would rise from the present to a higher figure as most of the new reactors come under the IAEA supervision.

It is indeed interesting, perhaps intriguing, that there are fears also from the safeguarded reactors. The above has been briefly repeated here for the Indian critics of the Indo-U.S. deal, the likes of a daily from Kolkata and another from Chennai and the two inveterate if incurable critics (CB and KB) who feel India has bartered away its nuclear sovereignty with this deal. Here are the U.S. and Western analysts who feel India through this deal can build as many warheads as it wants. They accuse Bush of wilting under the Indian pressure. This should be music to the Indian ears who daily hear of India surrendering to the USA.

Indian critics should note the dramatic changes. From the earlier threats to India to freeze, cap, and roll back its nuclear program, America is now helping India's transformation into a major nuclear power. Will those die hard critics accept the change in the American position in favour of India as genuine?

As it seems today, "the pros would seem to outweigh the cons so far as the 300-million middle class Indians (minus Arundhati Roy) are concerned."[42] They would agree with the views of Leonard Weiss, one of the architects of the NPT, that India has gained de facto recognition as a nuclear power and can make as many nukes as it can even as it obtains nuclear fuel, equipment, and technology for its civilian program apart from recurring international cooperation in space technology.

Another gain of the deal that should please Indians beyond the middle class is the end of the delusional parity between India and Pakistan artificially built up and maintained by the earlier U.S. administrations for their own geo-strategic reasons. That it was fizzling out anyway was evident when Clinton, after spending five days of hype and bonhomie in India, deigned to spend just five hours in Pakistan, a kind of refueling break and that too to deliver a stern lecture to an unruly junior! "But now Bush's Pakistan has friends."

The U.S. finally ending its hyphenated stance towards India and Pakistan has infuriated the 'mighty' *New York Times,* as it wants Washington to treat India on equal footing as hitherto fore, and it has its reasons. After dubbing the Bush trip as "spectacularly misconceived," the *Times* failed to understand why the U.S. made a distinction between India and Pakistan although they are longstanding military rivals and have pursued the same nuclear path outside the NPT. It says editorially: "It is just baffling why Mr. Bush travelled half way around the world to stand next to one of his most important allies against terrorists—and embarrass him" by his refusal to provide the same "privileged treatment"to Pakistan.

The fact that India's stature is no longer what it was in the sixties and seventies has gone home the world over, and presently it is seen as an emerging world power on its own, not only by the international community but also by the leading lights of its press. It is a pity that the 'mighty' *Times* refuses to realise the change while the 'uncomplicated' man has! Reference to India being "different" (much like F. Scott Fitzgerald's famous quotation about the rich) has put all doubts at rest."[43]

SEPARATION PLAN

The separation of its civilian and weapon facilities was an important commitment made by India in the 18 July joint statement. Even when the President and Prime Minister arrived at their joint press conference venue in New Delhi on 2 March 2006 during the visit of the former, the final touches were being given to this plan by their officials. It was undoubtedly a very intricate complex, and involved process.

When India was building its nuclear facilities a number of common use facilities must obviously have been planned as would be expected and so natural in a developing nation. If all facilities primarily meant for civilian use are handed over for safeguards, how does the country ensure its strategic weapons independence for years to come? How does the government ensure that firstly it calculates the amount of fissile material needed in stock to ensure independence, and secondly build up that much stock? The important question for India is, how much is enough? How big is the fissile material 'hedge' to be?[44]

It was necessary for Mr. Bush to have the final Indian Separation Plan that would enable him to approach the Congress to amend certain parts of the Nuclear Non-Proliferation Act, 1978 that strengthened the U.S. Atomic Energy Act, 1954. Clearly India needed to achieve a substantial fissile material to reserve ratio to ensure that it can go through with a workable plan on separating its civilian and weapon facilities while safeguarding the independence of its deterrent. But this is all in the air for common Indians barring the select few who are in the know. No government will provide any information on the subject.

What are the criteria or yardsticks for separating two types. For the American interlocuters the 'plan' must be reasonable and not outrageous. Beyond this macro stipulation the deails of the plan were left to the Indians. Secretary Saran says some non-proliferation advocates contend that since it for India to determine what is civilian and what is military, this would open the door for flouting non-proliferation norms. This betrays a lack of understanding of the 18 July joint statement. The Indo-U.S. Agreement is not about India's nuclear weapon program. It is about civil nuclear energy cooperation. The Agreement aims at advancing India's energy security through full civilian nuclear energy cooperation. It is legitimate for our partners to expect that such cooperation will not provide any advantage to our strategic program, and hence the need to separate it from our civilian nuclear sector. But it makes no sense for India to deliberately keep some of its civilian facilities out of its declaration for safeguards purposes, if it is really interested in obtaining international cooperation on as wide a scale as possible. This would be quite illogical.

Prime Minister tabled the updated version of the Indian Separation Plan for its civilian and military nuclear facilities in Parliament on 11 May 2006. Under this plan, 14 reactors are offered for safeguards and 8 will remain unsafeguarded. All the fast breeder reactors, currently operational and under construction, will remain outside the purview of inspections by the IAEA.

Reactors Not under Safeguards

S. No.	Name/Location of Facility	Capacity MWe	Date/Target Date of Completion
1	MAPS-1 Kalpakkam	220	1984
2	MAPS-2 Kalpakkam	220	1986
3	TAPS-3 (Tarapur)	540	2007
4	TAPS-4 (Tarapur)	540	2006
5 & 6	Kaiga 1 and 2	220 Each	2000
7 & 8	Kaiga 3 and 4	220 Each	2007

Reactors under Safeguards

S. No.	Name/Location of Facility	Capacity MWe	Date/Target Date of Completion	Safeguarded by
1 & 2	TAPS-1 and 2	150 Each	1969	2006
3	RAPS-1 Rajasthan Kota (Rawatbhata)	90	1973	2006
4	RAPS-2 Rajasthan Kota (Rawatbhata)	187	1981	2006
5	Kudankulam-1	917	2007	2006
6	Kudankulam-2	917	2008	2006
7	RAPS-5 (RAPP-5)	202	2007	2007
8	RAPS-6 (RAPP-6)	202	2008	2008
9 & 10	RAPS-3 and 4 (RAPP-3 and 4)	202 Each	2000	2010
11	Kakrapar 1 KAPS-1-(KAPS-1)	202	1993	2012
12	Kakrapar-2 (KAPS-2)	202	1995	2012
13	NAPS-1 Narora	202	1991	2014
14	NAPS-2 Narora	202	1992	2014

Note: Sl. 1 to 6 are already safeguarded or committed to safeguards.

Nuclear Separation Plan: Almost Elusive till the End

It was a touch and go till the very end, as the story pieced together from various sources confirms.

Prime Minister Singh and President Bush held most of their one-on-one meeting on 2 March 2006 without knowing whether their negotiators had actually managed to strike the deal. It was only when Ms. Rice entered the meeting room at Hyderabad House that the two principals learnt that it had been done.

In the meanwhile, a snippet did manage to escape the four walls of secrecy to say that in the freewheeling discussion between the two, Dr. Singh gently advised Mr. Bush not to be too zealous in his crusade for "democracy" worldwide. "As an older man to a younger one, let me say that one should not expect all societies to be transformed overnight mechanically," Dr. Singh cautioned his guest.

Describing Mr. Bush "an uncomplicated man," the sources disclosed it was only because he had sent a clear signal to his negotiating team that the deal was clinched. "Quite honestly, we never believed the U.S. would agree to us keeping 35 per cent of our capacity out of safeguards."

Two days before Mr. Bush's arrival in India, Ms. Rice rang up Dr. Singh to say his negotiators were making "impossible demands". She insisted that the fast breeders must come under safeguards and India must agree to include larger number of its reactors in the civilian list. Having just made the statement in Parliament on India's nuclear Separation Plan, Dr. Singh told her he could not go beyond that paradigm.

To this, Ms. Rice raised two further issues. She said, "India cannot have conditional safeguards, and that if it did not agree to permanent safeguards there would be no deal."

She demanded that India must place all its future civilian reactors under safeguards, to which Dr. Singh agreed provided the U.S. recognized that the decision to classify future reactors as military or civilian was India's alone.

Even so, the safeguards conundrum persisted. When Mr. Bush and Ms. Rice alighted from the Air Force One at the

Delhi airport, she returned to the issue of permanent safeguards. The Prime Minister turned to the President, saying since India wanted permanent fuel supply for its safeguarded reactors "there was a difference only of language". At this point President turned to India's National Security Adviser M.K. Narayanan with, "I want the deal" (*The Hindu*, 5.3.06).

Thorium Route

India's experience so far is that light water reactors imported from outside have performed outstandingly better. It is also true that the world's experience with nuclear power generation has finally settled upon the light water reactors as the safest and easiest to run, especially for larger outputs such as 1000 MWe. The trouble of course is that these reactors are the "once through' variety where enriched U 235 is used once and thereafter sent to the waste disposal storage facility.

The Indian science is looking at distant but certain thorium route, "In fact, the Indian scientists have a noble vision." It is necessary to understand what exactly they are trying to achieve. Thorium is more abundant in the world than uranium. Thorium can be used as a nuclear fuel if it can be bred into U 233 which is an isotope of uranium. If thorium is used in a full fuel cycle, far fewer transuranic toxic waste products are produced. Of about one million tonnes of uranium reserves in the world, almost 300,000 tonnes are in India which has the second highest reserves, next only to Australia. Due to these factors, Indian scientists earlier had decided to develop a fuel cycle which would make the country independent of imported uranium—a view in which they have been proved correct by the restrictions in force for years on the supply side, in case of India since 1974. The thorium fuel route may be a distant vision, but it is a vision deserving a vigorous and sincere pursuit.

During the course of debate on the Indo-U.S. deal, its critics were positing against India bartering its nuclear independence by planning its nuclear energy needs to be met by the imported uranium under the deal. They wanted India to pursue the thorium research more vigorously. Anyway, the issue has been settled for now after the 2 March 2006 Indo-U.S. agreement on the Separation Plan. It was in this context that a brief para above has been added in this text, explaining the thorium route.

Fast Breeder Reactors

There was contentious debate between India and the U.S. on placing these reactors under the safeguards. American insistence on the issue was so vigorous that a senior journalist,[45] known for his accurate analysis on such topics because of his knowledge of the ongoings behind the curtains, had publicly given up any hope of India winning its argument for keeping the fast breeders unsafeguarded. At the end of the day, Indian negotiators had the last laugh. These reactors remained in unsafeguarded list.

Number of Operational Reactors Worldwide

Country	No. of Reactors	Total installed capacity Gwe (Percentage of total production)
India	15	3.04 (2.8)
USA	104	99.21 (19.9)
France	59	63.36 (78.1)
UK	23	11.85 (19.4)
Russia	31	21.74 (15.6)
China	9	6.602 (2.2)

Source: Nuclear Energy Institute, Washington.

Apsara and CIRUS under Separation Plan

India agreed to shut down CIRUS and shift Apsara out of the Bhabha Atomic Research Centre.

Canada supplied the CIRUS reactor at the BARC in Trombay, Maharashtra. India decided to permanently shut down the CIRUS in 2010, rather than allow intrusive inspections in a facility (BARC) of high national security value. Significantly, the size of the nuclear force is determined primarily by the supply of reprocessed plutonium from CIRUS and Dhruva heavy water research reactors at the BARC.

The entire Apsara reactor at the BARC will not be shifted but only its fuel core which was purchased from France. The core would be shifted from its present location at the BARC and put under safeguards in 2010. The step was necessary to keep BARC out of the intrusive inspections.

The Apsara is a swimming-pool reactor with its fuel core hanging in a large pool of water, explained Dr. S. Banerjee, Director, BARC. The Apsara would continue to be located at the BARC but would operate with the indigenous fuel of enriched uranium, and would not come under safeguards, he said on 12 June 2006 at the Indira Gandhi Centre for Atomic Research at Kalpakkam, near Chennai.

The Apsara was the first research reactor to be built in India indigenously, although its fuel was imported from France. It became critical on 4 August 1956 and was named Apsara by Pt. Nehru.

Far too many Facilities under Safeguards

There has been criticism that far too many facilities like the Nuclear Fuel Complex (NFC) are under safeguards apart from 14 reactors. It is, however, learnt that what has been undertaken is a firewalling within the NFC so that separate processing can be feasible for civilian and military facilities.

Sources clarified that entire NFC will not be under safeguards, just units that will be needed for processing fuel obtained from abroad have been separated from the rest which can be used for strategic purposes. This is a logical step in separating civilian and military fuel cycles.

The Separation Plan tabled in Parliament lists nine research facilities as civilian. But these will be "safeguards irrelevant," which means they will not be part of any safeguards arrangements—as was largely interpreted—but have been declared civilian so that they can enter into international cooperation.

Besides this, India has nuanced its position on the FMCT by welcoming the U.S. draft in the Conference on Disarmament in Geneva but has not given up its stand for a verification mechanism.

U.S. dropped this in its draft. This is in line with Indian commitment in the July 18 agreement while at the same time not divorced from its original position.[46]

Critique in Snippets

- "The India-America nuclear dialogue." While nothing substantive is likely to result from the Indo-U.S. nuclear dialogue, the climate is opportune to resolve the contentious issue of spent Tarapur fuel.

  (R. Ramachandran, *The Hindu*, 16.7.05)
- "Friends yes, but not allies, please." (Editorial, *The Hindu*, 16.7.05)
- "Swallowing some pride to win the nuclear game." In bartering away the country's independence in nuclear policy-making, the trade-off Dr. (Manmohan) Singh has attempted to secure the prospect of a dramatic scaling up of nuclear power capacity. Belying his sedate and conservative visage, Prime Minister Manmohan Singh has cut a deal with the U.S. on the nuclear issue that none of his predecessors dared, or perhaps wished to do.

  (K. Venugopal, a senior scientist, *The Hindu*, 22.7.05)
- "Musharraf's discloser on A.Q. Khan raises questions." Gen. Musharraf disclosed for the first time that Dr. A.Q. Khan, the Pak metallurgist who confessed to having proliferated to Iran and Libya, also provided centrifuge technology to enrich uranium to North Korea. The General has not explained what was the quid pro quo Dr. Khan received from the North Koreans.

  (K. Subrahmanyam, *The Tribune*, 26.8.05)
- "Learning and doing." Whether it is the nuclear deal or capital account convertibility, national interests are paramount, many of us, particularly "responsible leaders," cannot resist the attraction of grandslanding. (Yoginder K. Alagh, former Union Minister and an economist, *The Tribune*, 25.4.06)
- "One nuclear deal, two narratives." The Western media have savaged the Bush visit and the nuclear deal shows India acted in its national interest. Yet looked at

another way, India is befriending a world leader seen to pursue an agenda against Muslim countries.

(Vidya Subrahmaniam, *The Hindu,* 15.3.06)

- China: Nuke deal a bad example.

  (Chinese media comments, 3.3.06)

- In opening up the door to nuclear commerce with India, Washington has confirmed how much an alliance with New Delhi is worth to it. But is anybody on the Indian side doing the maths?

  (Siddarth Varadarajan, *The Hindu*, 29.7.06)

- "An agreement and a problem with romantics." India would seem to be caught in the semantics of the agreements that equates it with the non-nuclear weapon states. It would rather like to see the language used for nuclear weapons states in the Indo-U.S. deal, though operationally it matters little.

  (R. Ramachandran, *The Hindu*, 19.4.06)

  Here it is worth quoting another analyst (C. Raja Mohan) who chided Indians for spending too much time worrying about the issues of sequencing rather than getting on with the job of expediting talks with the IAEA and NSG to help some skeptics in the House and Senate to overcome their nibbling doubts about India wanting this nuclear deal as much as do the U.S.

- "A case of sour grapes." Pakistan is in no position to ask for nuclear deal. Pakistan lost little time in mounting a campaign against the Indo-U.S. nuclear deal, arguing that any such arrangement should be a common passage for both. The element of terror and blackmail in its campaign is hard to overlook. When Gen. Musharraf made this plea to President Bush when the latter visited Islamabad on 3 March 2006, Bush replied: "This was not possible because India and Pakistan were two different countries, with different needs and different histories."

After this rebuttal, Pakistani officials and diplomats launched a worldwide campaign, of not so subtle blackmail, that the deal would unleash an arms race in Asia.

IAEA has documented nuclear proliferation from Pakistan to Iran, going back to 1987. If Pakistan wants to be a part of civil nuclear energy package, it should repair damaged confidence about its past nuclear proliferation transactions. Given the vast confidence deficit between the U.S./international community and Pakistan, the latter must launch various CBMs, starting with giving international access to Dr. Khan. Holding out veiled threat to the international community about initiating a nuclear arms race in South Asia can only prove counterproductive.

(K. Subramanyam, *TOI*, 3.5.06)

- "The nuclear deal and 'minimum deterrance.'" The Indo-U.S. nuclear agreement will raise the financial and political costs of the Indian nuclear weapons program but it does not impose a legal bear on production of fissile material or the testing of nuclear explosive devices by India.

  (Siddarth Varadarajan, *The Hindu*, 10.7.06)
- "Assessing the nuclear balance sheet." The U.S. wants a decisive say in the scripting of India's safeguards and additional protocol agreements with the IAEA but is withholding "full" civil nuclear cooperation.

  (Siddarth Varadarajan, *The Hindu*, 7.7.06)
- "For durable ties with U.S., India must define its core security interests."
- A strong, economically viable India provides a stable balance to the strategic architecture of Asia and the politically volatile Middle-East.

  (G. Parthasarathi, diplomat and former Ambassador to Pakistan, *The Tribune*, 13.07.06)

CRITICISM AND OPPOSITION IN INDIA

There has been strong opposition to the Indo-U.S. nuclear deal from some public figures, senior analysts, and ranking lawmakers. Their objections can roughly be grouped under different groupings. It is interesting to note that while in U.S.A. some analysts have argued that "India took too much for too little." In India, on the other hand, there are scholars and analysts who feel the U.S. has trapped Indians into surrendering their sovereign decision-making after promising—mind you, not giving—a pittance. This section would examine the two sides of this argument at some length.

NAM Supports Iran: May 2006

Issued in *PutraJaya,* Malaysia on 30 May 2006 after a ministerial meeting, the NAM resolution refused to back action against Iran, as recommended by the IAEA 4 February meet. India and Egypt both had voted for referral of Iran to the UNSC. NAM had supported the rights of state to develop research, production and use of atomic energy for peaceful purposes without any discrimination.

Press reported the U.S. officials "chiding India for the NAM statement."

Western Media's Strong Opposition

President Bush has been called a man with an uncomplicated mind who has black-and-white view of the world that makes him rush in where angels fear to tread as he did in Iraq. Yet again, later he turned America's nuclear policy upside down with the sole objective of befriending India. Besides the political opposition, there is also academia ranged against his policies. On Indo-U.S. deal, the press has been particularly strident. The *New York Times* thundered editorially: "Kill the deal."

It is not only some U.S. politicians and influencial dailies and journalists who are perturbed over the deal, even the left leaning *Guardian* of Britain has noted: "The U.S. is now treating India like its uniquely special ally, Israel, also out of the NPT, which maintains a policy of deliberate ambiguity about its nuclear capacity and is believed to have about 200 warheads."

Surprisingly, opposed to some Indians thinking and accusations ad nauseam that India was becoming a client State of the U.S., at least one influential daily, *Washington Post*, feels Mr. Bush wilted under U.S. pressure! Under the heading, "Did Bush blink?" Dan Froomkin wrote in the *Post:* "It appears that to close the deal during his visit, Bush directed his negotiators to give in to India's demands that it be allowed to produce unlimited quantities of fissile material and amass as many nuclear weapons as it wants."

Another article expressed the same fear: "Bush and (Manmohan) Singh praised the deal at a joint news conference but they did not mention that it would allow India to produce vast quantities of fissile material, something which the U.S. and four other major nuclear powers—China, Russia, France, and Britain—have voluntarily halted." Robert J. Einhorn, a senior adviser at the Centre for Strategic and International Studies in Washington said: "It is not meaningful to talk about 14 of the 22 reactors being placed under safeguards. What is meaningful is what the Indians can do at the unsafeguarded reactors, which is, vastly increasing their production of fissile material for nuclear weapons."

The change in U.S. stance towards India is dramatic. From the earlier posture of asking India to freeze, cap, and roll back its nuclear program, America is now helping India's transformation into a major nuclear power. Will it set off a new arms race in Asia? Question will also be asked about the future when, as Burns hints, the percentage of safeguarded reactions would rise from the present "to a higher figure as most of the new reactors come under IAEA supervision".

Hans Blix Contradicts BJP Objections

On a visit to Delhi on 21 June 2006, former IAEA chief opposed the deal: "No one can argue with the energy aspect, it has certainly raised the proliferation concerns....India will have greater freedom to directly import uranium for the enrichment of the nuclear plants, one does not know what resources this will free up."[47]

"Nuclear Deal Cynics, take note:" A Daily

While former Indian foreign ministers (Natwar Singh and Jaswant Singh) are busy giving the Indo-U.S. deal a political twist, China has accepted sweeping new conditions to gain access to natural uranium from Australia, its second largest exporters. As a nuclear weapons state under the NPT, China is under no obligation to separate its military and civilian nuclear program, yet Beijing has agreed to set up a "Delineated Chinese Nuclear Fuel Cycle Program," that would be eligible for Australian uranium under international safeguards. When under NPT, China has no need to do so, it has yet accepted separation and permanent safeguards to ensure that it has access to natural uranium beyond its borders to make success of its plan to increase nuclear power generation four-fold in the coming decade. As a result, it was eager to satisfy all Australian political demands on separation and safeguards under the agreement signed in June 2006.

Then the analyst[48] makes a stinging remark on Indians: "While China is focused like a lazer beam on the 'outcomes'—in this case a permanent lock on the lucrative Australian uranium—a section of the political establishment and bureaucracy in India is paralysed by quibbling over language and sequence."

Beijing and Canberra have also agreed that the bilateral safeguards agreements would have to kick in the event of IAEA safeguards being suspended for some reason or the other. Then comes the exhortation: "If China were to be India's benchmark for nuclear diplomacy, New Delhi should be getting off its haunches to quicken the pace of its safeguards negotiations with the IAEA and make sure that the U.S. Congress quickly approves the nuclear deal."

China Understands Balance of Power Game

The China-Australia agreement also shows that China does not allow minor sensitivities or perceived slight to its leaders come in the way of its long-time national interests. It signed the agreement on uranium supply in April 2006 after the Indo-U.S. joint statement of 2 March 2006. So, the Chinese should have been aware of India contesting the perpetuity clause and getting satisfactory assurances on fuel supply. They also knew about India's Separation Plan determined solely by India. Yet China, one of the "legitimate" five nuclear weapon powers, yielded more ground on both issues than India. "Their Separation Plan is to be finalised jointly between China and Australia."[49] Their perpetuity clause will not be offset by collateral and multilateral guarantees on fuel supply. Why did China yield to such stiffer conditions, even after knowing that India had got away with less stringent conditionalities?

America put pressure in stopping the EU countries from selling arms to China. But it had no problem in Australia selling uranium to China. This only shows Americans are sincere in their campaign to spread civilian nuclear energy around the world, and especially to large energy demanders like China and India. Does it also mean the U.S. and Australia have relatively more trust in India than in China, the proliferator?

This also shows that the Chinese are more pragmatic than the Indians. They do not waste time on rhetoric but concentrate on their goal—in this case, getting assured long-term uranium supply for the large-scale expansion of their civilian nuclear energy program.

The Chinese yield when they have to and wait for an opportunity to retrieve the situation. China had fought a bitter war with U.S. early 1950s in which 200,000 Chinese lives were lost. Still Mao and Zhou had no hesitation in closing the 1971 Sino-U.S. deal with Kissinger when he made a path-breaking visit to Peking, says K. Subrahmanyam. In Kissinger's view, China is a closed society with an open mind while India is an open society with a closed mind.

Burning two billion tonnes of coal, it is the second biggest polluter in the world, next only to the U.S. In a hurry to change the situation, it accepted harsher conditionalities to achieve its aim—stooping to conquer.

China does not see the U.S. as an adversary bent upon containing it. Having overtaken Japan as the largest holder of foreign exchange balance, it has invested most of it in the U.S. It is economic pragmatism. They discarded their Marxist dogma against multinationals and made full use of the U.S. interest to advance their economy. Politically shrewd, they would not mind being on the U.S. side, if not embracing it, to play the balance of power game with Japan, Russia and the EU. If emerging India needs some help from the U.S., it should be seen as pragmatism to play an effective role in this multi-polar world, dominated by six power centers. Being close to the U.S. does not prevent India being friendly to other major powers.

It is time Indians learn some lessons from the pragmatic Chinese, and not be distracted by traders of trivia, railing against Indo-U.S. deal under one pretext or others. As the Foreign Secretary said, it is time we change our mindset.

Criticism and India's Response

As the 27 June 2006 Congressional voting in the influential relevant committees of the House and Senate was close, New Delhi took the unusual step of rebutting some mischievous comments on the Indo-U.S. deal, in particular by former Additional Secretary of RAW, J.K. Sinha who said in the *Indian Defence Review* that India would have the capacity to produce 50 nuclear warheads annually. Such reports are usually ignored but this one could not be as it was deemed important enough by the second ranking Democrat on the House International Relations Committee, Howard Berman to cite the figure in a discussion in Washington to fortify his argument that the Bill needed conditions to limit India's fissile material production (*The Statesman*, 24.6.06).

MEA Spokesman Navtej Sarna's statement said there had been "considerable amount of misinformed speculation" about the nuclear program. Contradicting critics in India as also in the U.S., he said, "The argument that the nuclear deal with the U.S. would enhance our strategic capacity is as misplaced as its opposite extreme—that it would cripple our program." He also referred to the Rice testimony in the Congress where she noted that the nuclear deal will have no impact on India's strategic program.

But Mr. Sarna added that India remains "committed to a credible minimum deterrent." Earlier this year, U.S. officials demanded publicly that India should define the "credible minimum deterrent". Rjecting it outright, India contended that it was up to it to define it and it had no responsibility to declare such a definition. He said the nuclear deal was about civilian nuclear energy cooperation and not about the nuclear weapons program. This and other issues mentioned in such reports have all been covered by the 11 March 2006 Separation Plan, already tabled in the Parliament. "It is clear and unambiguous, just as the 18 July Joint Statement is. There is no room for misinterpretation," he said.[50]

Communists Criticise Indo-US Deal

The Indian Communists of all hues have made strident proforma criticism of the Indo-U.S. deal. This has not surprised the observers of the Indian scene. But what did raise the eyebrows among the cognoscente was the "unholy and unusual" company they were travelling in! But before coming to that, a word on their views, or rather contrary views, on the nation, and other issues.

For them, India was never a nation, it was a grouping of nationalities. They hardly participated in India's freedom movement. They have abused, one time or other, the leading Indian figures, not excluding Gandhi, Nehru, and Bose. It is different matter that in the recent years, they have changed their mind on this, as on so many other issues. After all West Bengal Chief Minister Buddhadev Bhattacharya is openly defending capitalism. For them, World War II turned "patriotic"only when Hitler attacked Stalin's empire. To them, China was not the aggressor in 1962. They welcomed Chinese—as also Soviet-nuclear tests, but for India, it was 'No, No'. Again, it was "false" independence in 1947. Considering this all, some would not deem it worthwhile to give any weight to their "ideological" criticism of the Indo-U.S. deal. But a brief look is worthwhile because of the type of the company they have on the issue and also because the UPA is in power with their 'outside' support.

The comrades have been, thus at odds with the Indian scene but their present doubts on the deal may push them further into a corner. The reason: "They are lining up with some of the queerest characters in opposing the deal—Muslim fundamentalists in India and Cold War dinosaurs in America."[51] Obviously, something strange is happening if the Communists find them on the same side as Muslim bigots and the *New York Times,* which thundered editorially "kill the deal" before the March 2006 Bush visit. There is a stong opposition in the West, and particularly within the U.S. itself because President Bush is seen to be turning America's nuclear policy upside down with single-minded aim of befriending India. In this scenario, the Communists cannot even accuse India of walking into the U.S. trap. This has queered the pitch for them. Then the huge Muslim rally in Delhi's Ram Lila grounds was not so much to protest against Indian government than with the "uncomplicated Bush's blunders in West Asia. Will the Communists ever learn a lesson?

BJP-NDA Criticise Nuclear Deal

In a memorandum submitted to the President on 21 June 2006 by Messrs Vajpayee, Advani, Fernandes, and Jaswant Singh, important points were: "The Government must be restrained from dismantling India's nuclear program.... The deal will bind India in future, and it was worse than CTBT."[52]

Earlier, speaking to the press on 21 April 2006, senior BJP leader Jaswant Singh asked the UPA government to explain if it accepted CTBT in disguise, agreeing to forsake all nuclear testing.

A daily aptly replies to the BJP criticism: "Perceptions change with the change of role, and of course time." Mr. Singh may not remember but it was the then Prime Minister Vajpayee who said at the General Assembly on 24 September 1998: "After concluding this limited testing program (Pokhran II) India announced voluntary moratorium...we conveyed our willingness to move towards a de jure formalisation of this obligation.... In announcing moratorium, India has already accepted the basic obligation of the CTBT."

As for Jaswant Singh himself, U.S. Under Secretary Strob Talbot, who had held eight sessions of strategic talks with him, says in his book, *Engaging India,* that "fully expecting Jaswant to tell us to forget about Indian signature on CTBT... to my surprise, he told me that Vajpayee was still prepared to...sign the treaty...."

The current MOS for External Affairs, Anand Sharma, has said all this publicly: "BJP was ready to go far beyond what we have conceded to the U.S. It is all on record."

Overdoing the Criticism: A Sophistry

A critic, who has never seen anything right in the Indo-U.S. deal, in an article headed "India capped," in a daily,[53] gives ten reasons for Pakistan to celebrate India's nuclear deal. An analyst, who sees this deal as beneficial for India, gives a short shrift to the article with a simple question: "Pray, tell me if the deal is such a shackle for India, why does Pakistan wants it for herself?" Then came the rapier thrust: "Surely, Musharraf does not enjoy being humiliated repeatedly, from President Bush downwards, requesting for a similar deal for Pakistan—if it was that worthless!"

Sam Nunn: A Sceptic

Critics including former Senator Nunn are skeptical of the recent agreement signed by Mr. Bush during his 1-3 March 2006 India visit. It requires Congress to exempt India from U.S. laws that restrict trade with countries that have not submitted to full nuclear inspection.

His concerns are that the deal would promote a regional arms race with China and Pakistan and make it more difficult for the U.S. to win support for sanctions against Iran and North Korea.

Critics in the U.S.

What is reckoned to be the first ever clash of perceptions over the Indo-U.S. nuclear deal came on 23 June 2006 on the floor of the Senate, virtually on the eve of the 27th meetings of the powerful committees of the House and Senate. Democrat Byron Dorgan lashed out at the Bush administration for signing an agreement that "legitimises India's nuclear weapons". Republican John Cornyn came up with a swift rebuttal citing India's non-proliferation record and willingness to work with peace-loving partners like the U.S. to reduce the dangers of proliferation.

Criticism from Unexpected Quarters

The Indo-U.S. nuclear deal has another critic. Al Qaida number two and Osama bin Laden protégé, Ayman al Zawahiri criticized on 29 April 06 American President Bush for giving a "strong impetus" to India's nuclear program while doling out orders to Pakistan (video released on a fundamentalist Islamic website).

Is Civil Nuclear Energy Risky?

Some scientists and academics issued a statement, asserting that excessive dependence on the civil nuclear reactors to meet nation's energy requirements may not be best option for the decision makers. They said it may not be all that "clean" as claimed by its proponents, and it also involves certain element of risk from the reactors producing it. Moreover, excessive dependence on the imported reactors and technology could result in loss of our autonomy in the important field.

Here is the searing comment from an analyst, a little disappointed with such "nit-pickers,"to use his term for them: "Those who fell extremely short of meeting even 30 per cent of energy from our indigenous reactors have no right to be heard by our nation. Likewise, people who cannot supply more than 5 to 10 hours of electricity to our countrymen from fossil fuels might as well remain silent. Their talking about India losing its autonomy is ridiculous!

Nuclear Autonomy, Strategic Independence, Minimum Credible Nuclear Deterrent, and Capping India's Nuclear Arsenal

Asserting that India's ability to sustain a minimum credible nuclear deterrent remains adequately protected, Prime Minister on 7 March 2006 assured (both houses of) Parliament that India-U.S. nuclear deal and the Separation Plan of civil and military nuclear facilities will not adversely affect the country's strategic program.[54]

He said no constraint has been placed to construct new facilities for strategic purposes. The integrity of our Nuclear Doctrine remains adequately protected.

Hidden Costs

By now, "the fact that the U.S. offer of civil nuclear cooperation carries hidden political costs is well accepted."[55] But if the political costs are tangible and have already begun to accumulate, what of the charge made by a section of the Indian strategic community, and echoed by the BJP, that the nuclear deal will compromise the credibility of India's "minimum nuclear deterrent?"

The U.S. Congress may make noises,"[56] or try to bring it in some form or other such "unpalatable phrases"[57] in the bills—123 Act—to be passed by it, there is nothing in any agreement India has signed that commits it to cap or reduce its weapons-grade fissile material stockpiles. Of course, Washington is already citing its domestic legal obligations as a reason to pressure India on this point but New Delhi itself will be under no compulsion to obey. Truth to tell, much will depend on the way FMCT negotiations are conducted at the Conference on Disarmament (CD) in Geneva. If the U.S. is rapidly able to establish a consensus around its draft FMCT, India will be hard pressed not to go along with others to put an end to fissile material production. But India has already announced a day before the U.S. draft was introduced in the CD that it will readily join other nations if the FMCT is a non-discriminatory legislation. Yet again, such multinational acts can't be passed in a hurry. But if the U.S. ploy of blackmailing the CD into accepting an FMCT by the end of this year (2006) fails—which it is likely to, for the simple reason that most nations demand parallel progress on the proposed treaty preventing an arms race in outer space—then India would be home and dry.

Now the issue that touches Indian sensitivities: will this agreement lead to a cap or constraint on India's nuclear weapons arsenal in either quantitative or qualitative terms? In the 'statement of the U.S. policy' section, the House of Representatives Bill on nuclear cooperation says the U.S. should seek to achieve a moratorium on fissile material production by India, Pakistan, and China and promote the "reduction and eventual elimination" of nuclear weapons in South Asia. In the Senate version, the President is expected to report annually to Congress about U.S. efforts to get India and Pakistan to secure, cap and reduce their fissile material stockpiles. While this may be U.S. policy, there is nothing in any agreement India has signed that commits it to cap or reduce its weapons-grade fissile material stockpiles.

Thus it follows there is no constraint on the quantitative enhancement of India's nuclear weapons, but what about qualitative improvements"? The Senate Bill authorising nuclear commerce with India is explicit that the waiver of existing prohibitions for India will "cease to be effective" if India "detonate[s] a nuclear explosive device" after the Act comes into force. It is reasonable to assume that the NSG rule change for India will also become null and void if India conducts an explosive test.

While India has its reasons for its voluntary renunciation, do these clauses amount to the decision being pushed down its throat, that too by a state that refuses to be bound by any legal no-test covenant? Here are three relevant factors: One, India has already "bilateralised" its unilateral moratorium in a joint statement with Pakistan during Prime Minister Vajpayee's 1999 Lahore visit. Any India test will violate that agreement. Two, sub-critical tests and computer simulations of the type the U.S. conducts in order to validate weapon designs would not attract any penalty. Three, there would in any case, still be no legal obligation on India not to conduct an explosive test.

But it must be clearly understood that if and when, compelled by national security interests, India conducts nuclear test, it will have to bear economic and political costs.

NSG MILESTONE AND IAEA

Amidst the din created by the debate in the U.S. Congress (May-July 2006) on the nuclear deal, it is often forgotton that there are two more equally important, if not more, milestones before this deal is home and dry: the safeguards agreement with the IAEA and approval by the 45-member NSG.

But some analysts aver that getting an Indian exemption from the NSG is the most important act in the unfolding drama of ending three decades of technology denial and discrimination against India. "The NPT may have outlined the principles of nuclear apartheid, but it is the NSG that converts theory into practice. This is where the beef is."[58]

While the NSG has a stand alone significance for the Indo-U.S. bilateral relations, the 123 legislation currently under hammer in the U.S. Congress would not have been of crucial importance to India's future nuclear stakes if the NSG had opened its door to India. Nuclear fuel and technology would then be available from any number of its members.

But unfortunately, the beginnings have been anything but auspicious. This became obvious during the May 2006 NSG Plenary in Brazil.

It is worth emphasizing that the NSG is the beating heart of the non-proliferation regime—the main link in the chain that has kept India in the atomic doghouse since 1974.

This is how the mighty failed against the midgets. The U.S., backed by the likes of France and Britain, tried to get the NSG members to insert a paragraph in the press release "taking note" of the Indo-U.S. nuclear deal. Imagine who are India's "curious foes" in the early 21st century! It is Dublin-Wellington axis that frustrated the U.S.-U.K.-France-India axis. Ireland and New Zealand backed by the likes of Austria and Norway insisted that the relevant paragraph mention the NSG had "concerns about the deal". "The moral mites stood their ground." The plenary failed to give the Indo-U.S. deal a hope for and much-needed boost. How helpless the sole superpower was!

France Push at NSG: Indo-U.S. Deal

Dismissing suggestions that its nuclear dealing with India was "predicated upon successful passage of the Indo-U.S. nuclear deal, France (through its New Delhi Ambassador Dominique Girad) said on 13 June 2006, "It will continue to press for waiver of restrictions on India at the NSG and IAEA. He said: "Indo-French Feb 2006 Nuclear Cooperation declaration is independent of the Indo-U.S. deal."

India Lobbies Japan

Foreign Secretary Saran, visiting Tokyo in June 2006 to ostensibly look into mundane issues like property matters for the Indian Embassy, utilized the visit to push for Japanese support for the nuclear deal. This would be crucial in the NSG of which Japan is an influential member.[59]

India-IAEA Talks on Safeguards

Dr. Anil Kokodkar travelled to Vienna to hold preliminary discussions at the IAEA headquarters in March 2006 for concluding a nuclear safeguards agreement as a follow-up to the Indo-U.S. nuclear deal.

The discussions continued when on IAEA delegation visited New Delhi later on for the purpose. The officials and scientists from the Department of Atomic Energy and India's Atomic Energy Commission were the Indian interlocuters.

A Dangerous Precedent: Fears of Proliferation

Several experts have warned that forgiving a civilian nuclear agreement with non-NPT member India would not only make it harder to enforce rules against nuclear renegades like Iran and North Korea but also set a dangerous precedent to other countries with nuclear ambitions.

"If we do this deal, ask how we will avoid offering a similar one to Brazil or Argentina if they decide on nuclear weapons acquisition, or our treaty ally South Korea", Robert Gallucci of Georgetown University told the Senate Foreign Relations Committee hearing on 26 April 2006. This flows from lack of understanding of India's commitment to non-proliferation and its having been a responsible nuclear weapons state.

Commitment to Non-proliferation

India's commitment to nuclear non-proliferation is not new. In this field, it can claim to be among the founding fathers! Pt. Nehru's call in 1954 for a 'stand still' to nuclear weapons tests and then for a test ban began a process that eventually led to the 1963 Partial Test Ban Treaty. En route this debate was also introduced the 1959 Antarctica Treaty that created a nuclear free zone on that continent.

In 1956, India proposed the international control of military reactors and then co-sponsored the non-proliferation proposal in the UN. Nehru prophetically warned the world as far back as 1957 not only of nuclear proliferation but also of connected dangers of terrorism. But from being an early and enthusiastic supporter of this concept, India was dismayed to watch the evolution of an international treaty that was blatantly discriminatory, lacking a mutuality of obligations between the weapons states and non-weapons states. On a matter of principle, India chose not to be a party to the NPT, precisely because it was inherently discriminatory in nature.

The above is to emphasise that India had sensitivities about nuclear weapons from the very inception of that technology and these were reflected in its approach to international security. Today, when it is fashionable among the nations to speak about the non-proliferation, they must remember that India's activism in this regard well pre-dates the NPT. The developments since 1968 only further underline India's non-proliferation credentials. Unlike some other states who eventually joined the NPT, India did not undermine the NPT—even when it differed with many of its premises, and was not its member. "At no stage did we support irresponsible theories that projected nuclear proliferation as a new version of balance of power".[60] India scrupulously followed all the basic obligations of an NPT member even of the weapon state category, some of whom encouraged and abetted proliferation for political or commercial reasons. Our export control performance during this same period also contrasts favourably with those of many developed nations who could not stop their companies from supporting clandestine WMD programs. At a policy level, this was an important component of a larger commitment to disarmament enunciated most recently, by Prime Minister Rajiv Gandhi in India's 1988 Action Plan. As is well known, the indefinite extension of the NPT and the enactment of the CTBT forced India to exercise its weapon option in 1998.

Responsible Nuclear Power: India

India has been extremely conscious of its responsibilities about the control of WMD technologies and their delivery systems. What follow are very important components of India's approach to global non-proliferation and international security, particularly as it has evolved since India's emergence as a nuclear weapons state in May 1998:

- Even as a nuclear weapons state (NWS), India remains committed to the goal of complete elimination of the nuclear weapons on a non-discriminatory basis.
- A new global consensus on non-proliferation is called for because some NPT members both NWS and non-NWS have not only not complied with the provisions of this treaty but have also violated them flagrantly. Obviously, there is a need to go beyond the NPT. For instance, India has agreed in the Indo-U.S. joint statement of 18 July 2005 that it would not transfer reprocessing and enrichment technologies and would support international efforts to limit their spread. India has also adopted a very comprehensive WMD Export Control Act and harmonized our export control lists with those incorporated in the NSG and Missile Technology Control Regime (MTCR) guidelines. This has enabled India to fulfill the obligations prescribed in the UNSC resolution 1540.
- The States must adhere to the commitments they made under international treaties because our own security interests have suffered due to clandestine nuclear weapons program in our neighbourhood aided and abetted by some of the NPT signatory countries themselves.

As of today (July 2006), India believes it has the responsibility and the capability to participate fully and actively in global R&D efforts to evolve proliferation-resistant nuclear technologies, which will enable us to derive the full benefits of nuclear energy, minimizing the risk of diversion to military uses. It is a matter of satisfaction for it that India has been accepted as member or dialogue partner in several regional groupings, is a serious contender for UNSC seat, hence its decision to form G-4, has put up a candidate for the post of UN Secretary General, and more importantly, it has signed a joint statement with the U.S. on 18 July 2005 to enable it to get international cooperation for its civilian nuclear reactors operations. For that purpose, India and U.S. have agreed on 2 March 2006 Separation Plan to offer certain Indian civilian power reactors for IAEA safeguards.

Since 1998, a major challenge to India's foreign policy, and consequently, its strategic and security analysts, has been to seek global recognition and understanding of its impeccable record on non-proliferation, its decision to acquire nuclear weapons notwithstanding. This recognition was important even if some may not see it that way. It is of course, no surprise that the world is, gradually but surely, coming to see India as an emerging superpower, with its burgeoning economy and increasing political stature. To achieve its full potential, sooner rather than later, India will need access to cutting edge technologies in virtually all fields. In today's increasingly globalised world, it is imperative that Indian economy shifts toward greater technological sophistication. It was with this technological imperative in mind that India signed the 18 July 2005 Joint Statement with the U.S. More importantly, it is a matter of gratification that the so-called sole superpower has seen the futility of denying India access to sophisticated cutting-edge technologies through the instrumentality of the archaic denial regime imposed by the political opponents of India to satisfy the non-proliferation enthusiasts in that country, since 1974, and even more harshly since the 1998 tests. It is with the very same aim —the hunger for these cutting-edge technologies— that India has joined the ITER and Generation IV, Glonars and Galileo Satellite Navigation Systems, the Indo-U.S. Space Launch Agreement, and several others.

If America has seen the light, so have others as can be seen in Russia and China inviting India to join them in a trilateral set-up for world peace and regional stability in the east. It may not be out of place here to mention that there have been talk of the

Russian-China-India axis over the last couple of years among the geo-strategic community, but Chinese attitude has been rather lukewarm, if not cold. But after the U.S.-India 2 March 2006 Nuclear Separation Agreement, things seem to have changed for the better for India. The recognition also came from British Prime Minister Tony Blair when the press reported on 13 July 2006 that "Tony Blair will call this weekend for five leading developing countries (other four being China, Brazil, South Africa and Mexico) to be allowed to join the G-8 in order to secure multilateral deals on climate change, trade, and Iran" (G-8 summit holds its meeting in St. Petersburg, Russia from 15 to 17 July 2006). It is not only in the world chancelleries that India has been accorded such recognition, but the same has been the case with the international press. Some instances of the later have already been cited. The latest being 15 July 2006[61]. "Mukesh Ambani on *Newsweek* Cover" reads in a self-obvious manner: India's Mister Big, Mukesh Ambani, could Spark Asia's Next Boom.

To further add to the world community's faith in its responsible conduct till date and its capability to absorb the gains of latest technologies that would come its way, India has already taken certain important policy decisions: (i) Adopting a very comprehensive WMD export control legislation and harmonizing its export control lists with the ones incorporated in the NSG and MTCR guidelines. It has fulfilled India's obligations laid down in the UNSC Resolution 1540. (ii) The separation of India's civilian and military nuclear facilities. (iii) Negotiations of an additional protocol with the IAEA. The cumulative results of these steps is to increase the confidence of the international community in the robustness and effectiveness of our export control systems making us a more viable destination of advanced dual-use technologies. With the U.S., India already has a more liberal and predictable licensing of dual-use technology for Indian industry.

The above-mentioned, brief narrative shows that India has never breached, or wavered from, its commitment to non-proliferation even when it has not been a member of the NPT. It also shows that India has also been a responsible nuclear weapons state. So in concluding a bilateral civilian nuclear deal with India, the U.S. will neither be setting a dangerous precedent, nor will this single exception unravel the NPT, which in any case, as we have seen, has failed to check illegal (and unauthorised) proliferation by certain countries.

Necessity for Making One Single Exception

The following should not only clear some apprehension and negative perception about India's nuclear policy but also address criticism at home:

- There is a continuity and consistency in India's approach, even if it might have sometimes been marked by the particularities of a specific decision.
- What might have appeared to some critics an inordinate external influence over India's decision-making in sensitive areas is, in fact, "rooted in our own well-considered and independent judgement" of where its national interests lie. This is in keeping with its tradition of non-alignment.[62]
- It is only natural that India must adjust to change, change inherent in its emergence as a Nuclear Weapon State, change inherent in the sustained dynamism and technological sophistication of its economy, and consequently, change in global expectation of India as an increasingly influential player on the international stage.

Now, coming to the exception part, what does the international community gain making an exception to the current regulations for India? How does it answer and mollify the concerns of the apostles of non-proliferation who fear making an exception for India might unravel the three decade old NPT regime.

One, the very enviable record on non-proliferation even when it was not a party to the NPT demands, deserves and justifies the exception for India. Significantly in the preface to the 18 July 2005 agreement, President Bush conveys his appreciation for India's strong commitment to preventing WMD proliferation, and acknowledges India as a responsible state with advanced nuclear technology. Today, there is no other state which has this record of responsibility and is still denied non-discriminatory access to civilian nuclear technology. Two, our export controls are today at global standards and our policy of non-transfer of re-processing and enrichment technologies, in fact, put us in an "NPT plus" category. Three, in considering to approach towards the resumption of full civil nuclear energy cooperation with India, the world must ask itself whether India is a partner or a target for the global non-proliferation regime. It simply cannot be both at the same time. India emphatically believes it is a partner and technology denial regimes in force since 1974, and then more harshly since 1998, must be dismantled. Four, the world needs to ask whether the global non-proliferation cause is better served with India inside the tent or outside. Would not the civil nuclear cooperation with India strengthen that regime? Of course, India is convinced of its case.

INDO-U.S. DEAL: U.S. PERSPECTIVE

U.S. Endeavors to See the Deal Through

By May 2006, all the important officials of the U.S. administration, including Secretary Rice, had testified before the Congress. In addition, necessary steps to muster support with international institutions and bilateral visits to foreign governments were also utilised to advance efforts to see the deal through.

In March 2006, two Assistant Secretaries of State, Richard Boucher and Stephen Redeymeyer were dispatched to Vienna to promote the plan with the NSG, an assembly of 45 nations that export nuclear technology.

Is it Geo-Strategic Motives Only?

To start with, the U.S. sceptiks criticised the nuclear deal on many counts. Perhaps, they fail to comprehend larger political objectives—the "big picture", as the phrase goes. Yet as the significance of the deal began to sink, the quibbling seen before too began to subside.

The realisation that India's nuclear program is there to stay was an obvious reason for the U.S. to bring India into nuclear mainstream. Having discovered China with that Nixon visit, it was time the U.S. started looking for a geo-strategic partner as China was growing too fast and too big for its comfort. And India fitted the bill.

The geo-strategic and security may be the prime reasons for the Indo-U.S. deal, the economics of it all can't be ignored. Trade and economy, after all, are of cardinal importance in any inter-state relationship. India's growing economy, its political and geo-strategic influence, and stability of its democratic institutions were simply too attractive an option that had to be grabbed.

Pro-Deal Views: U.S.

In a report released on 7 June 2006, the U.S. think tank, Council on Foreign Relations recommended that the Congress should formally endorse the deal's basic framework, while delaying the final approval until it is assured that critical non-proliferation needs repeatedly cited by critics of the deal, are met. The deal will strengthen the strategic partnership. The administration wants the Congress to pass amendment to the 1954 Atomic Energy Act that would give India-specific waivers and allow the civilian nuclear cooperation to proceed.

The report's authors Michael Levy and Charles Ferguson say: "The Bush administration has stirred deep passions and put the Congress in the seemingly impossible bind of choosing between approving the deal and damaging nuclear non-proliferation, or rejecting the deal and thereby setting back an important strategic relationship."[63] Indian nuclear testing and fundamental changes blocking growth in the number of Indian nuclear weapons are important.

U.S. Supporters

President Bush and Under Secretary Burns urged the Congress to approve the landmark plan to share nuclear technology with India, as it would be in the U.S. interest. They were speaking in West Virginia on 23 March 2006. The further points made were:

- India can be trusted as it has proved itself a non-proliferator over 30 years.

- It is in our interest that India use nuclear power to power its economic growth...since there is a good connection between demand for fossil fuels elsewhere and price here.
- U.S. would be far better off having India submit to supervision under the agreement than having it isolated.
- "India is accepting international verification and who can argue with that."
- Legislation to implement the plan was introduced in the Congress on 14 March 2006. "We are going to make a convincing case."
- The agreement reflects the emergence of a new global partnership between India and the U.S.

Individual American Supporters:

- "Kissinger hails pact". Welcoming the agreement as "an unprecedented level of cooperation and interdependence between the two powers", he said on 22 March 2006: "In a period preoccupied with concerns over terrorism and the potential clash of civilizations, the emerging cooperation between the two great democracies introduces a positive and hopeful perspective" (Former Secretary of State, Henry Kissinger).
- "Experts urge U.S. Congress to support deal". Debunking criticism of the agreement by the non-proliferation lobby, some foreign policy experts in Washington urged the Congress to support the pact and warned that failure to implement it would be a "body blow" to development of strong ties with India. The signatories included:

  Frank Wisner : Former American Ambassador to India.

  Selig Harrison : Convenor and senior scholar at Wilson Centre.

  Walter Anderson : Formerly a senior official at state department, and now at the school of Advanced International Studies of the Johns Hopkins University, Washington, DC.

Karl Inderfurth : Former Assistant Secretary of State.

Harol Gould : Scholar at the South Asian Studies, University of Virginia.

- "Nixon to China, Bush to India": Farid Zakaria, File 2006.

  Strategists in India and the U.S. will both have to prevail over ideologues at home. The Bush administration has been far-sighted on this issue. With China rising and Europe and Japan declining, it sees India as a natural partner. It also recognised that 30 years of lectures on non-proliferation and sanctions have done nothing to stop, slow down, or make safer India's nuclear program. Most important, it recognised that India was a rising and responsible global power that could not be treated like a rogue state.

  India has many ideologues who are fighting against its forward looking Prime Minister.

  (*The Indian Express*, 22.02.06)

Is the U.S. Changing Goalposts?

It all started on 3 May 2006 when Ms. Rice told visiting Indian parliamentarians that the administration was under pressure from some ranking Congressmen to add some amendments to the Indo-U.S. nuclear deal. India reminded the U.S. on the 4th of May that it woud only adhere to the commitments made in the joint statement of 18 July 2005.

It seemed the U.S. Congress wanted to see progress on the safeguards agreement (with the IAEA) and 123 Agreement (with India) before taking the plunge on voting on the deal. This was the key demand of the Senators and Congressmen during their marathon hearings with Rice some weeks back. Washington sources said U.S. lawmakers were not insisting on scrutinizing the text of the agreement but record 'progress'. The sources insisted that the U.S. Congress' position on the nuclear deal is more or less the same as it was when the U.S. was negotiating with the former Soviet Union on strategic arms reduction.

Here comes the crunch, because India is yet to move in a substantive manner to get safeguards agreement discussions off the ground with the IAEA. Sources said this is part of the "simultaneity", agreed between India and U.S.—that the U.S. would move with their Congress and the NSG, while India would move with the IAEA on a safeguards agreement.

While Department of Atomic Energy Chief Anil Kakodkar made one trip to Vienna to start the discussions, it is reported the talks are still stuck on the mechanics of working out on India-specific template. "The real problem seems to be that New Delhi is yet to focus on working out this agreement which needs more than draughtsmen—it needs political and strategic direction."[64]

When the American Congress moves from the hearing stage to the mark-up, that is, from the committee to the floor, India will need to show that it is making progress with the IAEA on the safeguards—which is a quiescent front at the moment.

Indian officials have stepped up work with the U.S. on the 123 Agreement—so called after the clause 123 of the U.S. Atomic Energy Act, 1956 that requires to be amended to permit civilian nuclear cooperation with India,. The Congress members wanted to add "exit" clause to the nuclear deal, laying down that all nuclear cooperation with India will stop if India tested another nuclear device. Though India has been observing voluntary moratorium on the nuclear tests since 1998, still it stoutly rejected the U.S. attempt to formalise the same by its inclusion in the bilateral nuclear agreement. Still India is aware that such a provision does exist in the U.S. domestic laws. Then what is the way out? An acceptable language that maintains the veracity of U.S. laws without forcing India into CTBT through the side door!

It is for note that nature of criticism is similar in both the countries. What Congress is saying about the deal—lack of transparency, negotiations details not being shared with it, too much being given to India under the treaty, *et al.*—is also the theme song of the BJP and Communist critics, who feel India will come under the U.S. tutelage.

Production of Bomb-grade Fuel by India

U.S. critic of the Indo-U.S. deal felt that India could have a free run on production of bomb-grade fissile material under the terms of this Bush-Singh agreement. They obviously do not trust India's voluntary commitment against any more nuclear tests, presently given by the Manmohan Singh Government, and initially by its predecessor, the Vajpayee dispensation immediately after the 1998 tests. There is a whole lot of debate going on in U.S., in administration, Congress, and the think-tanks and analysts.

Mr. Burns said he spoke to Mr. Saran on 16 May 2006 and they both agreed to "meet in London next week (24 May) to try and unravel the boondoggle in a deal that is new enmeshed in domestic politics in both countries." The analysts felt it was time that the two addressed the issues that threaten to undo the hard work that has gone into bringing the deal close to fruition. The main issue now bedevilling the deal is the one surrounding India's commitment not to conduct further nuclear tests, as mentioned in the preceding paragraph.

The intractable problem about this commitment is how to spell it out in the text of the bilateral agreement, presently being worked out between New Delhi and Washington, in a manner that satisfies U.S. non-proliferation lobby—some Indians dub them as non-proliferation Ayatollahs—and some lawmakers seriously opposed to the deal and at the same time does not paint New Delhi into a corner and conveys the impression that it is succumbing to U.S. pressure to codify the commitment. It is worth noting that a Kolkata daily has been declaring in one article after another that India is taking dictates from the U.S. and if this deal goes through, it would have surrendered its independent decision-making authority and even sovereignty as a nation to Washington. An equally thoughtless, may be irresponsible, comment came from another scribe, dubbing India as having already become the 51st State of the U.S. One is tempted to see such journalistic flourish as avoidable "excess", or even "terrorism of the pen". More on it later.

It is natural for Washington to insist that no-test proviso be part of the bilateral agreement between the two sides. The 18 July 2005 Joint Statement has a reference to India's moratorium on nuclear testing. Making this point at a Carnegie endowment meeting on the nuclear deal on 16 May 2006, Mr. Burns had said emphatically: "That was a very important commitment made to our government by the Indian government and it provided some of the backdrop to the negotiations that subsequently took place towards the Separation Plan that India engaged in. This is very important commitment this moratorium on nuclear testing."

But New Delhi believes it is a general commitment and it is not necessary to codify it in a bilateral agreement and make the deal hostage to such codification. But U.S. has its own take on the issue. Privately, the U.S. officials say their insistence on codification is based on their experience in 1974 and 1998 when the Indian tests caught them completely unaware.

The U.S. is not depending upon this codification route only to thwart any possibility of India producing bomb-grade fuel from the nuclear reactors placed under the IAEA safeguards to ensure civilian nuclear cooperation with the U.S. Another route the U.S. decided up on was through the Fissile Material Cut-off Treaty (FMCT). U.S. Assistant Secretary of State, Stephen Redemeyer introduced a draft of FMCT on 18 May 06 at the Conference on Disarmament (CD) in Geneva aimed at freezing the making of the bomb-grade fuel—'yellow cake' (milled uranium oxide)—across the world, including in India. The immediate aim of this move is to reassure critics of the U.S.-India deal who feel India can add unlimited quantities of bomb-grade fuel for its nuclear arsenal under this deal. Addressing this concern through FMCT, the administration hopes to galvanise domestic and international support for "the floundering Indo-U.S. deal", as some critics see it.

One hopes the Indian hawks on the Indo-U.S. deal will concede that India did one-up on the U.S. at least in this case. In a well-thought move, India pre-empted the U.S. by making the statement at the CD a day before the U.S. introduced its draft there and calling for "structured negotiation" on the proposed cut-off treaty. Indian ambassador Jayant Prasad said India had historically supported such a treaty. Unlike the U.S., India called for "non-discriminatory" treaty that is verifiable. It was an intelligent demarche by India to endorse new talks on FMCT as the India-U.S. deal was entering home stretch in the U.S. Congress as also the NSG. Indian statement came not only a day before the U.S. introduced its draft FMCT, but also days before a crucial plenary meeting of the NSG in Rio de Janeiro, which was discussing the Indian deal for the first time.

So, as the non-proliferation Jehadis in Washington[65] and other NSG capitals were drumming up the chorus against fissile material cut-off before the forthcoming NSG Plenary, New Delhi took up the FMCT gauntlet at Geneva. "Any treaty banning the production of fissile material must be non-discriminatory: it must stipulate the same obligations and responsibilities for all States. Full compliance by all States with their obligations under international instruments to which they are party is crtical to the achievement of the goals envisaged."

It is obvious that there is a long way to go before such a multilateral treaty can come into force after contentious, protracted negotiations and India and other countries cease production of the so-called 'yellow cake.' Again, the critics point out that the draft treaty reportedly does not contain any verification provisions, and consequently take years to negotiate, considering it has been on ice for so long. The critics are already shouting themselves hoarse about the revival of the treaty being a ploy to push through the Indo-U.S. deal. Here is a trenchant critic of the nuclear deal, Michael Krapon of the Stimson Centre: "Tabling a draft treaty now is a smart idea politically to improve chances that the Congress will approve the Bush Administration's proposed nuclear deal with India."

In a critique of the draft FMCT, Krapon said, "a treaty could also be wise and substantive move, depending upon its provisions. The administration's draft text is weak in a number of areas, notably in its dismissal of President Ronald Reagan's dictum of 'trust but verify'."

May be notionally, the draft treaty at least meets a major complaint of the non-proliferation lobby that India is being allowed to continue cranking out fissile material while other recognised nuclear countries have stopped production, or at least claim to have done so.

New Delhi has agreed to sign on the FMCT if all countries agree to it, though it has genuine concerns and has rather learnt about how much fissile material China and Pakistan have stacked up. It has always espoused non-discriminatory treatment for all nations on all such geo-strategic issues, and followed this principled tenet since the dawn of its independence. It was no surprise, therefore, that at the Congressional hearing on 17 May 2006 a senior U.S. official indicated that it was just one of the measures the Bush administration was considering to convince lawmakers and the global community that India can be dealt with in good faith.

"Civil nuclear cooperation with India will elevate Indo-U.S. ties to heights we have never achieved. The significance of the initiative should not be underestimated," Assistant Secretary of State Richard Boucher told a Congressional sub-committee as part of the administration's hardsell of the deal. He further told the panel: "India has pledge for the first time to submit its entire civil nuclear program to international inspection and take on significant, new non-proliferation commitments in exchange for full civil nuclear cooperation with the international community. With this initiative, the world expects India to be full partner in non-proliferation and India expects the world to help it meet its growing energy needs."

THE BATTLES IN THE CONGRESS

The U.S. Congress is co-equal partner in governing the nation, along with the administration (the Executive) and the judiciary. The President must work in close cooperation with it if he wants his bills to be approved.

There are examples where the Senate refused to ratify the international agreements signed by the administration. The Comprehensive Test Ban Treaty (CTBT) is one such example.

As for the Indo-U.S. deal, it has been passed by the relevant committees of the House of Representatives and the Senate. The last battles of this war will be fought as the Bill goes to the floor of the two houses before the end of July 2006, as expected. India has already raised objections to certain "bracketed" parts of the Bill in the Senate.

Washington, 16 March 2006. Showing some speed and sincere intent, the U.S. administration introduced legislation in Congress, 13 days after the finalisation of the Separation Plan at New Delhi, setting in motion the process of implementing the Indo-U.S. nuclear deal.

"India Took Too Much for Too Little"

There were interesting arguments by the supporters and opponents, all experts and prominent defence analysts of the nuclear deal at the second hearing of the Senate Foreign Relations Committee on 26 April 2006.

The Bush administration has given too much to India in return for too little in the nuclear deal and this imbalance should be corrected by getting New Delhi to commit to American geo-strategic objectives, including on Iran and proliferation issues, said the former administration officials William Perry and Ashton Carter, a former top Pentagon aide.

"We have given them a nuclear quid, we should expect a geo-political quo," Perry, former Defence Secretary and currently with the Hoover Institution, told the panel whose chair, Richard Lugar, seemed progressively inclined to support the agreement. Carter said Washington should expect greater purchases of American military hardware and civilian nuclear technology, besides enlisting India's help to achieve non-proliferation objectives.

Three of the four experts who testified in the first panel—Perry, Carter, and Dr. Ashley Tellis—spoke in favour of the deal while former top non-proliferation official at the State

Department, Robert Gallucci vehemently opposed it, using familiar non-proliferation arguments that the other experts see as flawed. As senators probed the experts to see if they could tighten any aspects of the deal, formally or informally, Gallucci said he would prefer Congress vote down the agreement. Tellis, a Mumbai-born analyst and one of the architects of the deal, argued that it is important for the deal to go through to realise that remained unrealised during the Cold War. Failure of the deal to go through would be a major setback to ties, he warned. Gallucci agreed it would be so in the short-term but the effect would not be catastrophic.

Referring to the commitments other experts expected from India, Tellis suggested that this could be achieved by speaking quietly to New Delhi on the sidelines rather than making demands which would stir issues of national pride.

In a second panel, the Clinton administration's non-proliferation guru, Robert Einhorn, of Centre for Strategic and International Studies, picked up Gallucci's argument to oppose the deal, asserting that it would be a windfall for India's nuclear weapons program and would destabilise the region.

Ironically, Einhorn raised the bogey of Pakistan and China expanding their nuclear arsenals and cooperation if the Indo-U.S. deal went through. How one wishes someone from the Senate Committee had politely reminded Einhorn that it was under his watch that China proliferated to North Korea and Pakistan; and the latter opened a nuclear Wal-Mart and operated it not-so-clandestinely for years till its CEO A.Q. Khan was consigned to the infamy of life under house-arrest two years back, mainly because of the exertions of the western intelligence agencies.

The only way Einhorn would countenance the deal was if U.S. get India to commit to a fissile material cut-off unilaterally, pursuant to a multilateral arrangement. A critic of the deal in its current form, he said a multilateral cap on the accumulation of the fissile material would make a major contribution to fighting nuclear proliferation and preventing nuclear terrorism. "Making U.S.-India civil nuclear deal a catalyst for achieving such an outcome would transform the deal from a substantial loss to a substantial gain," he said.

Dr. Tellis, at the Carnegie Endowment for International Peace, told the Panel that renewed civilian nuclear cooperation "becomes the vehicle by which Indian people are reassured that the U.S. is a true friend and ally responsive to their deepest aspirations." He further added: "By altering the existing web of legal constraints on civilian nuclear cooperation with India, Congress would also expand simultaneously India's access to a wide range of controlled technologies that are useful for numerous peaceful economic endeavours going beyond merely the production of electricity. This session was marked by the blunt talk delivered by top Democratic Senator on the Senate Foreign Relation Committee, Joseph Biden, and also its Co-Chair. Biden, who had earlier indicated that he would support the deal, hinted that his backing would be conditional. He said: "I and many others are considering amendments that might deal with what I believe to be the shortcomings in this negotiated agreement." This, in view of the clear stand by New Delhi and Washington that any conditions attached to this finely balanced agreement would be a deal breaker! Critical points made by the Senator are: (i) Bush administration did not consult with the members of the Congress before signing the deal on 18 July 2005, paying little attention to our concerns as it negotiated with India its plan for separating civilian nuclear facilities from the military ones. (ii) "Legislative proposal" submitted to the lawmakers and a "decision proposal" to the NSG "were so poorly drafted as to cast doubt on the administration's seriousness of purpose". (iii) The Senate and its Committee should not be taken for granted, just because some analysts feel the deal will sail through the Senate Committee but will face a tougher time in the House International Affairs Committee. (iv) The administration has yet to share with members of Congress the full list of India's civil nuclear facilities—even in classified form. (v) The White House has reneged on an earlier promise to share drafts of the peaceful nuclear cooperation agreement that it is negotiating with India. (vi) The administration is yet to share its negotiating record or explain just what it agreed to when it accepted the idea of "India-specific safeguard" or "corrective measures that India may take...in the event of disruption of foreign fuel supplies" or U.S. "assurances regarding fuel supply", or "a strategic reserve of nuclear fuel" for India.

Mr. Biden warned the deal is not a "slam dunk", as they say. But to avoid sounding too hawkish, he noted despite his reservations regarding the deal, he had indicated in the past that he would probably support it "because I agree that the time has come to develop a new relationship between India and the parties to the Nuclear Non-proliferation Treaty". He also believed that undoing the deal could do more damage to the U.S. relationship with India, "than approving it, with carefully drafted conditions. This deal brings risks, and I believe the administration and Congress must minimise these risks."

Now a tongue-in-check remark, perhaps, aimed at his repulician friends: "The administration has done a lot more to lobby us than than to work with us."

Mr. Perry, despite demanding a geo-strategic support from India as reported above, espoused the deal fervently. Having played an active role in earlier administration on issue of non-proliferation, he said U.S. should back India in the development of nuclear power. He also cautioned the Senate against trying to modify what has now been agreed upon.

Eight specialists from the non-government sector, including Stephen Cohen of the Brooking Institution, came before the committee during this hearing. While a majority supported the deal, Carter and Gallucci were the two to oppose it. But one overriding theme was that the agreement should not be tinkered with at this stage.

Mr. Cohen, who has earlier argued that the civil nuclear deal if properly implemented will advance and not retard American non-proliferation objectives, said it was his judgement that this agreement need not trigger an arms race with Pakistan and neither did it give a green light to India to build a thousand or more nuclear weapons.

He remarked, "it does provide the U.S. with an opportunity to work with India to prevent a broader nuclear arms race that is not in the interest of India, Pakistan, China, or America". To this effect he proposed three steps:

1. The agreement with India should eventually be folded into legislation that will develop criteria that would allow other states to enter such a nuclear "half way house" which would provide civilian nuclear assistance to those nations with an impressive horizontal proliferation record.
2. The administration should take an initiative that comes to terms with vertical proliferation through a nuclear restraint regime in Asia that would include India, Pakistan, and China.
3. With the civilian nuclear agreement in place, India should feel "less paranoid" about talking of its own nuclear capabilities.

He further told the lawmakers: "This agreement does much to repair the torn U.S.-Indian strategic tie, it is important in reshaping and revitalising India's massive energy shortfall and it has already been helpful in our attempt to constrain an Iranian program, but this administration and its successor with Congress assistance should regard it as a beginning, not as an end as far as our non-proliferation and strategic interests are concerned."

Here comes the counterpoint, a quaint mix of rhetoric and fact: "It is impossible to weaken export controls for India without weakening the same for other nations such as Iran and Pakistan and even for terrorist groups and that the 'great flow' in the administration's civilian nuclear energy proposal is that it considers India as an isolated case."[66]

Rice Testimony before the Congress Analysed

Secretary of State Ms. Rice made an effective rebuttal of criticism of many aspects of the deal, but when strategic reasoning has to contend with irrational belief it is not always the former that wins. She failed to convert the proliferation Ayatollahs, who persist in repeating their dogmatic assertions just as religious extremists elsewhere in the world do. Ironically, many liberals considered friends of India turned out to be dogmatists on non-proliferation theology and so are against the deal while many conservatives proved to be pragmatists who accepted the merits of the agreement.

It appears the liberal attitude was often more in terms of partronization than true respect for India's rising to potential. The cold warriors of U.S. were used to either client-patron or adversary relationships with the rest of the world and they had only contempt for the non-aligned. They find it difficult to adjust to Secretary Rice's perspective of "a more lasting and durable form of global security—a balance of power that favours freedom" in which India is counted as a balancer.

She tells the lawmakers that history is irreversible and India is a nuclear weapons state and that can't be changed. India, a democratic country and an open society, shares values with U.S. A proven non-proliferator, it can't be compared to other proliferators who, having signed the NPT, are trying to circumvent it. India will not stop weapon or fissile material production at this stage, and that can be regulated by regional dynamics.

She then explained the benefits of the deal for U.S. India, growing at 8 per cent annually and relying on fossil fuels only, would become yet another emitter of greenhouse gases like China. Reactors to India will create additional jobs in U.S. India is offering additional civil reactors for safeguards, thereby enhancing the effectiveness of non-proliferation regime and the IAEA.

The spirit of the proceedings was summed up by Senate Democratic Party leader Joe Biden and former Democratic Presidential candidate Senator John Kerry, saying they may disagree with some parts of the Bill. The consequences of allowing the agreement to fail are so enormous that they would vote for it (From "Rice sets the menu for a swing in N-deal support" by K. Subrahmanyam, *The Tribune,* 8.4.06).

Principle of Simultaneity and Reciprocity

At the Congress hearing during the second week of May 2006, Democratic lawmaker Tom Lantos proposed a calibrated approach to the nuclear deal, seeking to move legislation that would allow the deal to proceed lock-step with the signing of a U.S.-India bilateral nuclear treaty and New Delhi agreeing on a system of inspections of its civil nuclear facilities by the IAEA. Simply put, Mr. Lantos is laying down sequencing process: that the U.S. legislation will become operational only after the 123 Agreement with India is in place. And funnily enough, the 123 Agreement also comes into effect when the legislation comes into effect. Therefore, for the legislation to succeed, details of the negotiation on the 123 Agreement will need to be made available to Congress leaders. Here comes the Indian demand for simultaneity and reciprocity: the two processes must proceed side by side.

The safeguards agreement is similarly bedevilled: India will not conclude a safeguards agreement with the IAEA unless it receives conclusive signals from the NSG that an exemption is at hand. Conversely, the NSG wants to see "progress" on the safeguards agreement as it debates the exemption. This puts India in a unique but awkward situation of being unusually transparent in concluding this deal with the international community.

At the NSG, the U.S. is expected to make a strong pitch for an Indian exemption, backed by U.K., France, and Russia.

Situation before the Committees Passed the Bills

Inspite of the initial apprehensions, a week before the House Committee was due to take up the Indo-U.S. bill on 27 June 2006, it was clear that the House and Senate Committees would endorse the key proposals of the Bush administration to allow the transfer of the nuclear materials and technology to India. But according to some sources, the 'mark up' bills could well include in the preamble and elsewhere the language that is bound to grate on Indian sensitivities. So the lawmakers are widely expected to offer a sugar pill with a bitter coating.

For example, after reiterating the sacrosanct nature of the NPT as a rampart against nuclear proliferation, they may attach a laundry list of what should and should not be done to extend cooperation to countries which are not signatories to the NPT. In addition, the lawmakers will seek to oblige India to fall in line with the American designs to curb the nuclear ambitions of Iran, endorse its stand on FMCT, and seek India's participation in the Proliferation Security Initiative. This is just a sample, there could be more.

Finally, it could urge the President to present an annual report to the Congress on whether India has adhered in letter and spirit to the terms and conditions of the deal.

All this is bound to further enrage the opponents of the deal and even embarrass its vociferous supporters as they will certainly compromise on India's pride as a sovereign nation. The UPA government will therefore need to summon all its persuasive skills to convince the sceptiks that the deal does serve the larger national interest without eroding India's sovereign prerogative to address its security concerns. Indians must learn to draw a line between substantive and operational aspects of the deal and what are not more than rhetorical flourishes.

It is good to remember that the Bill has three main parts concerning the operational, the processes, and the non-binding. India should be ready to accept some 'noises', some unpalatable phraseology in the latter two parts.

U.S. Suggests 2-Stage-Plan for Nuclear Deal

In their May 2006 meeting in London, Burns suggested a 2-part approach to the Nuclear Deal to his counterpart Saran.

1. Stage one. U.S. Congress would pass a "Sense of the Congress" resolution expressing support for the deal and laying out conditions for India to meet, without taking up the Waiver Authority Bill.
2. Stage two. U.S. Congress will take up the Waiver Bill, but only after India has negotiated a safeguards agreement with IAEA, and has met the conditions imposed on it by the U.S. legislature.[67]

Indian reaction to the approach was not known immediately.

Another daily[68] in its report datelined 11 June 2006. New Delhi has given dramatically opposite report on the issue of two-stage plan detailed above. The contrasting reports on the same subjects and motives behind them are intriguing but cannot be the subject of detailed comments for this essay.[69] The contrasting observations are summed up here:

- On the India-specific legislation pending with the Congress, it has been agreed that even the agreement will be put on vote.
- In the Saran-Burns London discussions, Washington conveyed that it had come up with a compromise that Congress takes up the legislation and puts it on vote but will also get a chance to vote up on the bilateral agreement once it is negotiated.
- This puts to rest speculations over the Tom Lantos proposal—it has not been withdrawn—that the Congress will first pass a "Sense of the Congress" resolution and vote on the bill only after other conditions like the bilateral agreement and the safeguards agreement are negotiated.

Cheney Battles for Nuclear Deal

Vice President Dick Cheney stressed the "strategic importance" of the deal and urged the legislators to vote for it as "our strategic partnership with India gives rise to a broad and ambitious agenda, and that is the way it should be for two great nations in a time of challenge". He also spoke of employment opportunities the deal would open for the Americans. Indian Ambassador Ronen Sen was of the view that the accord would "lead to the betterment of the lives of the people of India."[70]

Both were addressing the U.S.-India Business Council on 22 June 2006.

Interestingly, an influential Democrat Ed Markey, Co-Chair of the Bipartisan Task Force on Non-Proliferation, called the deal "a dangerous proposal and a great threat to the NPT". He was launching a campaign with the Friends Committee on National Legislation to defeat the deal. The Federation of American Scientists is also lobbying hard against this nuclear deal.

Both Congressional Committees Approve the Bill

House International Relations Committee passed the Indo-U.S. Nuclear Cooperation bill on 27 June 2006 with huge bipartisan support. The voting was 37 to 5.

Senate Foreign Relations Committee followed suit on 29 June with 16–2 voting. While the House Committee mentioned Iran in its resolution, the Senate avoided the mention.

Rice Urges Congress to Vote before August 2006

Secretary Rice on 10 July urged both Houses of Congress to vote on the Indo-U.S. agreement before the month-long summer recess in August.

She emphasised that the U.S. does not support India joining the NPT as a nuclear weapons state. The goal of the U.S. initiative is to include it, for the first time ever, in the global non-proliferation regime.

U.S. Congress on N-deal, Enormous Disapproval to Positive Mood: Walter Anderson Gives Reasons

"Several weeks ago (Mar-Apr 2006), the chances of the nuclear deal with India any time soon seemed unlikely." Yet when the draft bills came before the relevant committees of the House and Senate in the last week of June, the mood was much more positive.

- 'Trust' was the word by many Senators to feel that the deal will not undermine U.S. nuclear non-proliferation goals.
- Likely strategic gains of close association with a rising India far outweighs the risk to non-proliferation.
- On the eve of the 29 June Senate Foreign Relations Committee meeting, Republican Party majority leader described the nuclear deal as the most important strategic diplomatic initiative by President Bush—a sentiment echoed by both Democratic and Republican Senators as they voted 15 to 2 in favor of the bill.
- Members of the House Committee two days earlier, with almost identical sentiments, had voted 37 to 5 for a similar bill.
- Three reasons for this turnaround are: (i) Judicious White House decision to accept modification of the draft bill to give the Congress a role in the implementation of the deal that was missing in its

original version. (ii) Supporters were quite effective in convincing Congressmen that gains outweighed the risks. (iii) Most importantly, vigorous lobbying, especially by the increasingly influential Indo-American Community.

Win-Win Situation for Both

If there is any common ground between the critics and supporters of the Indo-U.S. deal, it is that the document signed on 18 July 2005 by the two nations was "historic" in every sense of the term. If America turned its back on decades of non-proliferation policy and did so in order to cement a strategic relationship with India, India on its part was seen by the strategic analysts as taking hard foreign policy decisions and saying goodbye to the fudgy, mushy days of non-alignment. If India was planning its future keeping in mind its status as a world power of the future and its strategic interests to be served thereof, the U.S. saw this deal doing for itself what its alliance with Japan and Germany did after World War II. "By any yardstick, this precisely is the stuff world orders are made of."[71]

One analyst feels this deal serves India's enlightened national interest as the Indian and American strategic interests in Asia and the wider world overlap. His arguments: (i) India does not want another nuclear weapons state (Iran) in its neighbourhood. (ii) "Bush invasion had less to do with weapons of mass destruction...than the ideological motivation to promote democracy in the Middle East." (iii) There is a good fit between the 'unilateralism' of the U.S. and the 'revisionism' of India as far as the world order is concerned. (iv) India and the U.S. have common interest in balancing the rise of China—not its containment.[72]

Any bilateral pact to be acceptable must be a win-win for both sides, and so seems the case with the Indo-U.S. deal. Because of the present asymmetry in political and economic powers of the two sides, it is natural for some Indian analysts and political figures to feel uneasy about the U.S. motives for befriending the India of Cold War days perceived to have staunchly been in the anti-U.S. camp!

A leading strategic analyst[73] believes the Americans have a strategy to ensure that they remain the foremost power in military, economic, technological, and cultural terms in a group of six major powers—U.S., China, EU, Japan, Russia, and India. Now to implement this strategy, they want to enlist India as a partner as they have already ensured mutually beneficial relationship with the other four powers in this group.

If this association, partnership helps, India to become a prosperous nation economically and powerful one politically and strategically, Indians should have no problem with that.

It needs to be emphasised that all four countries now partnering with the U.S. were its enemies not too far in the post: (i) China lost 200,000 men in early 1950s in war with the U.S. The latter blocked its entry into the UN for long years till the Nixon policy U-turn of 1971. (ii) In the 1950s, instead of facing the Soviet Union militarily, they decided upon its containment and to borrow from President Reagan, the "Evil Empire" collapsed in 1989 as a consequence. (iii) Japan was the only country to be atom-bombed and who perpetrated this atrocity? America, of course. (iv) Germany was destroyed as much by the U.S. munitions as by those of the rest of allies during World War II. How come that all these four countries are merrily partnering with the U.S., forgetting the bitter past! It stems from the mature analysis of their geo-strategic security and national interests by all the five nations. Here is a brief picture of their current level of engagement.

China has an over $ 200 billion annual trade deficit with U.S., has invested $ 250 billion in U.S. bonds and banks, and is a partner with U.S. in a number of international economic and technological arrangements. So the U.S. policy towards China is engagement, not containment. "So China is as capitalist as the U.S.", a fact Indian Communist will not acknowledge and Karl Marx rues! Russia too is a partner in G-8, having just (July 2006) presided over its St Petersburg Session. Russia will soon emerge as largest supplier of oil. The depth and expanse of relationship of America with Japan and Germany/EU hardly need to be detailed.

In contrast with these four powers, India had no enmity with the U.S., except the contempt some culturally and spiritually "superior" Indians poured on this merely 200-year-old upstart of a country. Of course we looked down upon the U.S. from the Nehruvian heights, and it also was the butt of the Krishna Menon jibes. So we seem to be 'natural allies', nay 'natural partners', as the former phrase is not palatable to some non-alignment days Indians. In brief, India expects energy security through nuclear power and clean coal energy, and some help to become a strategic power which counts in the comity of nations, a la China. Of course, we have people in India who want us to follow China in all other spheres but this one!

There is fear that the U.S. is entrapping India through this deal not to carry out nuclear tests, thus compromising its strategic autonomy. It is said India is being pushed into the CTBT in a devious manner.

It has already been mentioned that India was ready, post-1998 tests, to convert its voluntary renunciation, a de facto act on nuclear tests into a de jure one under certain condition. This was Prime Minister Vajpayee telling the UN in 1998. Strobe Talbot says so in his book: *Jaswant was Ready to Sign CTBT.*

But what is the status of the CTBT as on date. Of the five recognised nuclear powers, three—U.K., France and Russia—have signed and ratified it. The U.S. Senate has denied ratification to the Treaty, and China, matching the U.S., has also not ratified it. But there are no indications that any nation is in a great hurry to carry out nuclear testing. Here is Ms. Rice in the *Washington Post* of December 2005: "For the first time since the Peace of Westphalia Treaty in 1648, the prospect of violent conflict between great powers is becoming even more unthinkable. Major powers are increasingly competing in pace, not preparing for war. To advance this remarkable trend, the U.S. is transforming our partnership with nations such as Japan and Russia, with the EU and especially with China and India.

Together we are building a more lasting and durable form of global stability, a balance of power that favours freedom.[74]

Analysts agree that reasonable assessment of the international political scene reveals that resumption of nuclear testing is of extremely low probability.

In March 2006, President Bush explained the new U.S. policy towards India simply with: "things change, times change." India's own attitude towards nuclear testing would illustrate the above axiom, says K. Subrahmanyam, who traces our stance on the tests:

1. Nehru proposed a complete test ban treaty as far back as 1954.
2. India was the first non-nuclear nation to enthusiastically sign the Partial Test Ban Treaty (PTBT) in 1963. Because of this, India dubbed the Pokhran I test as a peaceful nuclear explosion.
3. Indira Gandhi attempted to test in 1983, even as she exposed the 'six nations, five continents initiative', which urged comprehensive test ban.
4. Rajiv Gandhi followed up this initiative and held a conference of six nations in Delhi in 1986.
5. Comprehensive test ban figured in his disarmament plan 1988.
6. In 1990 the bulk of non-aligned nations used the relevant clause of the PTBT to convene a conference to urge comprehensive test ban. This was vetoed by nuclear weapons powers.
7. In 1994 CTBT found a mention in the joint statement of Narasimha Rao and Bill Clinton.
8. Even as India had been urging a complete test ban, Rao attempted to carry out a nuclear test in December 1995, but was thwarted by the Americans.
9. All through this period, successive PMs denied any intention to acquire nuclear weapons.
10. For the first time in June 1996 when Inder Kumar Gujral was Foreign Minister, India declared in the

Conference on Disarmament (CD) that nuclear testing was a matter of national security concern for the country.

11. When the CTBT was to be adopted by the CD, India blocked it and compelled it to be taken to the UN General Assembly. There it was passed with near unanimity, with India opposing it.

This narrative shows that India could adopt a publicly declared policy on nuclear testing from 1954 to 1996 and when compelled by national security considerations could make a complete U-turn.

Seen in this light perhaps, vociferous outpourings in the issue of nuclear test are really not of much relevance or practical importance—if not a mere triviality in the context of the Indo-U.S. deal.

PAKISTAN AND INDO-U.S. NUCLEAR AGREEMENT

Pakistan has always seen itself as co-equal of India and often behaves accordingly. Indian analysts often felt India has suffered because of this hyphenated treatment of two countries by the Western countries, particularly the U.S. Things changed a little after 9/11, and with the U.S. initiating a nuclear pact with India in July 2005, Pakistan got a message clearly and unambiguously. Statements and actions of the Pakistani leaders in relation to the 123 Agreement are briefly given below, without any comments:

- Islamabad, 20 July 2005, Prime Minister Shaukat Aziz's visit to Washington was cancelled because the Bush administration was unwilling to accord him more than a business-like welcome. Pakistani suggestions that he be hosted a White House dinner, a la Indian Prime Minister Manmohan Singh, or be invited to address a joint session of Congress, were turned down politely but firmly (*AA*).
- Washington, 27 August 2005. The U.S. State Department has said that President Pervez Musharraf's confirmation of Dr. A.Q. Khan's involvement in supplying nuclear

technology to North Korea does not alter Washington's trust in the Pakistani leader (*AA*).

- Islamabad, 2 March 2006. Pakistan would seek a deal similar to the one the U.S. has made with India on civil nuclear cooperation, said its Information and Broadcasting Minister Sheikh Rashid Ahmed (*The Hindu*).
- Islamabad, 3 March 2006. Mr. B. Muralidhar Reddy writes: "With most of its expectations dashed during the run-up to the U.S. President's visit, Islamabad is hoping at least for a few trade concessions" (*The Hindu*).
- Islamabad, 3 March 2006. "We have China and U.S.", says Musharraf. His Information Minister said Washington had succeeded in "pocketing" New Delhi (*The Hindu*).
- Islamabad, 4 March 2006. "No nuclear deal with Pakistan", says President Bush: "Islamabad needs to do a lot more to defeat the Al-Qaeda".
- Islamabad, 18 March 2006. Musharraf says: "India-U.S. deal disturbing to Pakistan. It will upset the balance of power in the region" (*The Hindu*).
- 1 May 2006, Issue of *TOI:* "Nuclear cloud over South Asia. U.S. deal may hit Indo-Pak diplomatic engagement." The lead article by Maleeha Lodhi, Pak High Commissioner in U.K.
- Washington, 13 May 2006. "Khan supplied N-Tech to Syria", says a U.S. intelligence report to Congress, adding a new dimension to A.Q. Khan's 'Wal-mart' saga (*HT*).
- Islamabad, 22 May 2006. Less than a month after Pakistan said it has closed the chapter of investigation into its disgraced nuclear scientist A.Q. Khan, House of Representatives Committee on International Relations will hold a public hearing of its sub-committee on international terrorism and non-proliferation in Pakistan

on the subject "The A.Q. Khan Network: Case Closed?" (*The Indian Express,* 23.5.06)

- Islamabad, 23 May 2006. "Pak nuclear chief involved in smuggling". Anwar Ali, new chief of Pakistan Atomic Energy Commission was involved in at least one 1980 nuclear-related smuggling operation in Canada, a U.S. defence think tank has alleged (*AA*).
- Islamabad, 28 June 2006. A day after a key committee in the Congress endorsed a bill to implement the Indo-U.S. civilian nuclear deal, a bitter Pakistan today said it would not accept any "discriminatory treatment" and that a "package deal" for two neighbouring countries would have better served the strategic stability in South Asia.
- Washington, 12 July 2006. Claiming that Pakistan's nuclear weapons program was driven by the threat perception of India, Pak Foreign Minister Khurshid Mahmud Kasuri has said that Islamabad would "say yes" to a bilateral fissile material moratorium. Addressing the Washington-based think tank Carnegie Endowment for International Peace, Kasuri also said that the U.S. would eventually "begin to see the logic" of giving a "package civilian nuclear deal to Pakistan similar to the one it has reached with India.

IRAN VS IAEA AND INDIA

Iran-Pakistan-India pipeline project has been a contentious issue for long years. Also held up in controversy is $22 billion gas deal with India. The two issues further got complicated when India voted at the 24 September 2005 IAEA meeting at Vienna for referring Iran to the Security Council for its nuclear proliferation being a member of the NPT.

Undoubtedly, this vote stunned many analysts of the Indian foreign policy, most of all Iran itself. At a time when even they had been more mature in their responses, they were taken aback by the support they had suddenly received in the Indian political system. CPM General Secretary Prakash Karat had threatened the UPA Government that he "will not countenance its vote against Iran's nuclear proliferation at the IAEA meeting in September 2005". Karat had conveniently ignored the most important fact that Iran had been caught cheating in its secret pursuit of an undeclared nuclear enrichment program, which would have given it the capacity to produce atomic weapons. Some scholars would advise India not to take the Communists too seriously. But that is suicidal advice as the Government runs with their support, and they have the power to pull it down any time. If they have not done so till date, it is because they are prepared to tolerate any "misdemeanors" of the UPA Government than their pet hate, the BJP, bouncing back into power. Still it is worth recording that, according to many seasoned politicians and serious analysts, the Indian Communists had welcomed Chinese nuclear weapons, but vehemently opposed their own nation's nuclear tests of 1975 and 1998.

Coming to the commercial deals with Iran, an analyst wrote that driving hard bargains is a centuries-old Persian skill. A former oil minister of India told his interlocutor in mid-2005, in his more candid moments, "how exasperating it has been dealing with the Iranians over the past months of negotiations". They have "generally ravaged on one commitment after another, squeezing India for the last possible dollar".[75]

Iranians reportedly became even cockier after knowing that India's compulsions on the pipeline are not merely commercial but also political. The UPA needs the pipeline disparately, they think, to keep its leftist allies in good humour. So why should not they exploit the compulsions of India's domestic polities for their own commercial benefits. They also must be calculating India's declining oil production. Then India depends on imported energy[76]—about 76 per cent of oil, 20 per cent of gas, and 4 per cent of coal consumption. So Iran refused to sell gas to India at $ 2.2/MMBtu, as decided/accepted in 2004. It later (late 2005) reportedly upped the price by a factor of 5.

Latest on Gas

July 2006, Iran has finally and firmly rejected India's demand for a price equivalent to international long-term gas supply contracts for the Iran-Pakistan-India pipeline gas, saying, rather curtly, that New Delhi should forget about buying Iranian gas at a low price.

Tehran is seeking at least 7.2 dollars per mBtu price for gas it wants to sell to India and Pakistan through the over 7 billion dollar pipeline while New Delhi is willing to pay no more than 4.2 dollars per mBtu for gas delivered at its border.[77]

There is other side of the picture also. Iran needs a credible customer for its LNG. This is India's strength. Despite the brave rhetoric, Pakistan alone cannot simply fill the bill. The hysteria on the IAEA vote is a side show. The stakes are so high that the global oil industry is completely divorced from human rights and political considerations. Iran will no doubt continue selling oil to those which voted against it at the IAEA—Singapore being one of them. "The mature missives from the Iranian authorities suggest they will not scrap the LNG deal with India for this one vote (and, perhaps, others to come). Analysts feel the Iranians are not about to cancel anything in a fit or emotion or anger. They need the dollar much more than we need their gas. We can buy it elsewhere, but who else can they sell so much gas to, given their imbroglio with the G-8 on their nuclear enrichment? For the present, situation is too fluid for any definitive assessment of the issue.

As for the Indian vote against Iran on 24 September 2005 and 4 February 2006, it has been widely accepted as a strategic decision in the national interest. There were domestic pressures on the UPA Government due to the Left's ideological problems, and to an extent, BJP's opportunistic policies. Independent of domestic politics compulsions, New Delhi weighed its options. India's interests in Iran are easily summarised: (i) India's need for its territory for geographic access to Afghanistan and Central Asia in view of Pakistan's obdurate attitude. (ii) Source of energy. (iii) Muslim politics of India: Here are our interests in voting with the U.S.: (i) Developing a long-term strategic partnership with the sole superpower. (ii) Help in implementing our nuclear deal with the U.S., which will not only end our nuclear isolation, it will also make us a player in the global nuclear field. (iii) Credibility of India's claim as a responsible nuclear weapons power.

Prime Minister Manmohan Singh has emphatically given the answer to the contentious issue: "India does not want another nuclear power in its neighbourhood."[78] When asked about U.S. opposition to the pipeline project, he said India was not a client state, and he was categorical that it was the issue between Iran, Pakistan, and India and when the three agree, the work will start.

"Iran Vote: Matter of National Shame"

Thus wrote a daily from Chennai. In view of such strong reactions from certain quarters, it is worth having a look at Iran's record vis-à-vis India.

Iran has Seldom Supported India

Iran and Turkey provided Pakistan with military materials during its 1965 war with India. After the war, Iran purchased ninety F-86 Sabres from Germany and passed them on to Pakistan. In the 1971 war, Tehran provided Pakistan with a squadron of F-5 fighters. On the other hand, when Saddam Hussein attacked Iran to unleash a bloody and ruinous 8-year war, India terminated its long-standing military training program in Iraq. In summit after summit of the organisation of Islamic Conference, Tehran has been party to the Pakistan-backed anti-Indian resolutions on Jammu and Kashmir. But when the national interests of two countries converged, they acted in concert—India and Iran jointly backed the forces opposed to the Taliban in Afghanistan.[79]

But it is amazing how the press can spread disinformation in the name of non-aligned solidarity or ideological affinity!

Now the last word on the Iran's stand-off on its nuclear enrichment issue. The EU had sent in June 2006 a package of incentives for Iran to end its nuclear program. Iran said it would send its response by 22 August. The EU set 12 July as the deadline for the purpose.

Dr. Ali Larijani, Iran's top nuclear negotiator, was to meet EU Foreign Policy Chief Javier Solana at Brussels on 5 July to discuss the issue. At the last moment, Iran postponed the crucial talks by a day, without offering any explanation. Later, it never took place.

> Paris, 12 July 2006. World powers said today they would refer Iran back to the UN Security Council after Tehran failed to respond to the package of incentives aimed at defusing a nuclear stand-off by the EU deadline.[80]

The decision taken by the foreign ministers of P-5 nations and Germany, could clear the way for eventual economic sanctions against Iran but does not open the door for possible military action threatened by the U.S.

REFERENCES

1. Lead article by Pallavi Aiyar, *The Hindu*, 18.3.06.
2. *The Statesman*, New Delhi, 8.5.06.
3. Chidanand Rajghatta, *TOI*, 12.5.06.
4. Ashish Kumar Sen, *The Tribune*, Chandigarh, 13.5.06.
5. *The Times of India,* New Delhi, 17.5.06.
6. *The Tribune*, Chandigarh, 14.5.06.
7. *The Times of India,* New Delhi, 18.5.06.
8. *The Times of India,* New Delhi, 19.5.06.
9. Manoj Joshi, *Hindustan Times,* New Delhi, 10.3.06.
10. Superstar Amitabh Bachchan is a case in point. He has been awarded an honorary degree by a British University on 18 July 2006; subject of EDM (early day mention) in British Parliament; and was received by three senior cabinet ministers/politicians, back to back on 19 July—all three rare honors.
11. The breakdown of the total of 8,675: Congo (3,756), Sudan (2,420), Ethiopia/Eritrea (1,625), Lebanon (672), and Golden Heights (187). In addition, 15 officers are serving in Ivory Coast (7), Burundi (6), and Department of Peacekeeping at the UNHQ, New York (2).
12. *The Asian Age,* New Delhi, 15.7.06.
13. *The Indian Express*, New Delhi, 8.5.06.
14. *The Times of India,* New Delhi, 11.5.06.
15. Chidanand Rajghatta, *ibid.*
16. *The Times of India*, New Delhi, 13.5.06.
17. *The Hindu*, New Delhi, 3.3.06.
18. *Ibid*.
19. *The Hindu,* New Delhi, 25.5.06.
20. *The Statesman*, New Delhi, 11.5.06.

21. *The Asian Age,* New Delhi, 11.5.06.
22. K. Subrahmanyam, *The Tribune*, Chandigarh, 19.8.05.
23. *The Hindu*, New Delhi, 24.3.06.
24. C. Raja Mohan, *The Indian Express*, New Delhi, 29.6.06.
25. Seema Mustafa, *The Asian Age,* New Delhi, 9.6.06.
26. Pranab Dhal Samanta, *The Indian Express,* New Delhi.
27. *The Hindu*, *New Delhi,* 12.6.06.
28. *The Indian Express*, *New Delhi,* 12.6.06.
29. Air Marshal (Retd.) R.S. Bedi, *The Tribune*, Chandigarh, 18.4.06.
30. *The Indian Express*, New Delhi, 25.7.06.
31. *The Indian Express*, New Delhi, 14.7.06.
32. *The Asian Age,* New Delhi, 15.7.06.
33. *The Statesman*, New Delhi, 15.7.06.
34. Amit Kumar, *The Tribune*, Chandigarh, 14.6.06.
35. *The Hindu*, New Delhi, 15.6.06.
36. Indrani Bagchi, *The Times of India,* New Delhi, 17.5.06.
37. The Head of the Defence Research and Development Organisation, Dr. M. Natarajan is on record saying so; *The Asian Age,* New Delhi, 10.7.06.
38. Chidanand Rajghatta, *The Times of India,* New Delhi, 14.7.06.
39. *Frontline*, 16.6.06.
40. Cited in *The Asian Age,* New Delhi, 10.3.06.
41. *Ibid.*
42. Amulya Ganguli, *The Asian Age,* New Delhi, 10.3.06.
43. *Ibid.*
44. Rear Adm (Retd.) Raja Menon, *Strategic Analysis*, Oct-Dec. 2005.
45. C. Raja Mohan.
46. Pranab Dhal Samanta, *The Indian Express*, 12.6.06.
47. *The Asian Age,* New Delhi, 22.6.06.
48. C. Raja Mohan, *The Indian Express*, New Delhi, 5.5.06.
49. K. Subrahmanyam, *The Tribune*, Chandigarh, 8.5.06.
50. *The Statesman*, New Delhi, 24.6.06.
51. Amulya Ganguli, *The Asian Age,* New Delhi, 10.3.06.
52. *The Tribune* and *The Asian Age,* New Delhi, both 22.6.06.
53. *The Asian Age,* New Delhi, 20.5.06.
54. *The Hindu*, New Delhi, 8.3.06.
55. Siddarth Varadarajan, *The Hindu*, New Delhi, 10.7.06.

56. Foreign Secretary Shyam Saran's words when speaking in Delhi on 14.7.06.
57. *Ibid.*
58. Pramit Pal Chaudhuri, *Hindustan Times,* New Delhi, 26.6.06.
59. *The Times of India,* New Delhi, 21.6.06.
60. India's Foreign Secretary Shyam Saran, speaking at New Delhi on 24 October 2005.
61. *The Times of India,* New Delhi, 16.7.06.
62. See n 60.
63. *The Tribune*, Chandigarh, 9.6.06.
64. Indrani Bagchi, *The Times of India,* New Delhi, 5.5.06.
65. To be fair, they have their counterparts in India, but due to certain reasons they will not be recognised in this essay.
66. With inputs from *The Asian Age,* New Delhi and *The Tribune*, Chandigarh, both 28.4.06.
67. *The Asian Age,* New Delhi, 8.6.06.
68. *The Indian Express,* New Delhi.
69. That will need a separate study at a later date.
70. *The Asian Age,* New Delhi, 24.4.06.
71. Siddarth Varadarajan, *The Hindu*, New Delhi, 16.5.06
72. C. Raja Mohan, *Impossible Allies: Nuclear India, United States, and the Global Order.*
73. K. Subrahmanyam, *The Times of India,* New Delhi, 3.7.06.
74. K. Subrahmanyam, *The Indian Express*, New Delhi, 19.4.06.
75. Shekhar Gupta, *The Indian Express*, New Delhi, 1.10.05.
76. Himraj Dang, *The Indian Express*, New Delhi, 5.10.06.
77. *Hindustan Times,* New Delhi, 17.7.06.
78. He repeated this assertion on 18 April 2006 at New Delhi when a Muslim delegation of representatives of Muslim organisations was led by Delhi Jama Masjid's Imam Syed Ahmad Bukhari (*Hindustan Times,* New Delhi, 19.4.06).
79. Manoj Joshi, *Hindustan Times,* New Delhi, 3.10.05.
80. *The Indian Express* and *The Statesman*, New Delhi, both of 13.7.06.

Indo-U.S. Civil Nuclear Cooperation

4

—K.R. Gupta

The Indian Prime Minister, Dr. Manmohan Singh's visit to the U.S. in July 2005 was hailed "as a historic step forward" in their bilateral relations. A senior American official stated that the mutual interests of India and the United States were coinciding more than ever before. It was the time that the U.S. began to see India as one of its most important partners worldwide, given the fact that India is a rising economic power and an established democracy. The PM's visit led to the Indo-U.S. Joint Statement on July 18, 2005, announcing a series of bilateral measures on areas such as information technology, business, commerce, energy, space, disaster response, agriculture, science and technology and other economic issues.

One of the most important developments was to initiate the measure to strengthen energy security and promote the development of stable and efficient energy markets in India with a view to ensuring adequate and affordable energy supplies. Stage was set to start a U.S.-India Energy Dialogue which led to the Civil Nuclear Cooperation Agreement between the two countries in March, 2006 following the U.S. President George W. Bush's visit to India.

The development of close Indo-U.S. relationship is said to be "one of the most important undertakings the U.S. has embarked on in its foreign policy," and is considered to be the beginning of a new relationship. These relations, however, have not catapulted into closeness suddenly. Certain developments that took place in the international geo-politics have shaped these relations over a period of time. It is necessary to understand the finer points of these developments as a background to the Indo-U.S. partnership.

Background

For nearly forty years, i.e. till the disintegration of the Union of Soviet Socialist Republics (USSR) in 1991, India's relations with the U.S. were viewed through the narrow prism of Cold War. For geo-political reasons America considered Pakistan as its closer ally and had two alliances with it, first in the mid-fifties and second in the eighties, aimed at containing and fighting the erstwhile USSR. However, militarisation of polity in Pakistan and nuclearisation of that country brought non-proliferation concerns in the American attitude.

The 9/11 attack by Islamic radicals on twin towers of World Trade Centre and the Pentagon made America see some congruence with India which had been facing such attacks through most of the preceding decade. In the months following 9/11 attack when India survived a body blow of terrorists to its Parliament, America began to realise India's security concerns and the rationale behind its nuclear tests. It started finding merit in India's arguments to refuse to sign Comprehensive Test Ban Treaty (CTBT)*. India's changing profile was written into the U.S. National Security Strategy in 2002. For the first time, the U.S. administration began to take cognizance of India's geo-political virtues, economic strength as well as genuineness of its security concerns. Experts feel that it was during that period that India began to emerge as a strategic partner to the U.S.

The Indian Prime Minister had meeting with President Bush on the sidelines of United Nations General Assembly in New York in September 2004. The Joint Statement called "U.S.-India Partnership Cooperation Trust" was issued after the meeting laid out the directions for future relationship and noted that "bilateral relations had never been as close as they were in the present." The meeting served to underline the strategic areas including commitment to combat proliferation of Weapons of Mass Destruction (WMDs), terrorism and enhance global security. The leaders on both sides noted that the implementation of the first of the Next Steps in Strategic Partnership (NSSP)

---

* In fact, CTBT could not come into existence because the U.S. failed to ratify it.

marked the beginning of a new era of cooperation and trust. Emphasis was also laid on advancing economic cooperation in multilateral institutions including Doha Development Agenda (DDA) of the World Trade Organisation (WTO) and also through other bilateral mechanisms, such as India-U.S. Economic Dialogue, and the High Technology Cooperation Group.

At the political level, the high-level engagement continued throughout the year. India's External Affairs Minister visited Washington in June 2004. He also had meetings subsequently with the then U.S. Secretary of State, Colin Powell on the sidelines of ASEAN Regional Forum in July 2004 and January 2005 in the aftermath of Tsunami, both held in Jakarta. Those meetings served to consolidate political contacts between the two countries after the formation of new Government in India under the prime ministership of Dr. Manmohan Singh. The response from the U.S. came in the shape of visit of then Deputy Secretary of State, Richard Armitage and U.S. Defence Secretary, Donald Rumsfeld to India on July 13-14 and December 8-9, 2004 respectively.

The U.S. Secretary of State, Condoleezza Rice visited India in March 2005 as the first stop on her 6-nation Asian tour. She had meetings with the Prime Minister, the External Affairs Minister and the Chairperson of the United Progressive Alliance (UPA) and discussed the entire range of issues of bilateral, regional and global importance. Most importantly, there was a forward movement on starting an energy dialogue which cleared the pathway for the historic nuclear deal.

Global Nuclear Energy Partnership

The Bush Government launched a Global Nuclear Energy Partnership with an allocation of $250 million during the year 2005-06. Under this initiative, the technologically advanced countries would supply small-scale nuclear reactors to the developing countries to help them meet their energy requirements and reduce their dependence on oil and other fossil fuels. The U.S. disclosed plans to work with France, Russia and Japan and to co-opt India in due course.

In line with the above and in the context of India emerging as a global power, President Bush reached the historic July 18, 2005 agreement with Dr. Manmohan Singh. Dr. Singh agreed to a separation plan of India's civil and weapons reactors, while Bush committed to provide New Delhi access to nuclear know-how, fuel and technology. The agreement is aimed to strengthen U.S.-India relations, American security and the global non-proliferation order.

After weeks of intense diplomatic activity, India and the U.S. reached the historic Indo-U.S. Civilian Nuclear Cooperation Agreement during President Bush's visit to India in the first week of March 2006. The Indian Plan to separate civilian and weapons reactors facilities met the United States' benchmarks of being creditable, verifiable and defensible from the non-proliferation standpoint. The main points of the deal are:

- Fourteen of India's 22 reactors are to be separated as civilian and placed under safeguards. The U.S. concedes that Breeder Reactor be kept outside until India decides otherwise.
- The reactors once safeguarded will remain so permanently. India secures the right to take corrective action if the reactors' fuel supply is cut off.
- India will decide whether it wishes to safeguard future reactors.
- Enrichment and reprocessing plants can switch back and forth from safeguards, depending upon whether they handled safeguarded material or not.
- The nuclear separation plan will be done in phases but will be concluded by 2014.

If approved by the U.S. Congress, India would be provided with access to nuclear know-how, fuel and technology. It would integrate India into the global non-proliferation regime after having remained outside of it ever since the nuclear Non-proliferation Treaty (NPT) was signed in 1968.

Key Factors

The following five key factors explain why the U.S. has pursued the agreement despite stiff opposition from some quarters including the Nuclear Suppliers Group:

(i) It does not provide any assistance to India's nuclear weapons programme.

(ii) The supply of civilian grade fuel or building new power reactors does not free up fissile material for India's military programme.

(iii) It places nearly three-fourths of India's hitherto unsafeguarded fissile material and facilities under International Atomic Energy Agency (IAEA) safeguards.

(iv) India is non-signatory to the NPT but has maintained its impeccable non-proliferation credentials throughout and was committed not to divert any nuclear material designated for civilian use or to export to other countries. Each time some foreign state such as Libya and Iran approached New Delhi for assistance in developing nuclear capabilities, they were firmly refused.

(v) China and India represent the two biggest nuclear energy markets for the next two decades, estimated at $ 40 billion and $ 25-30 billion respectively. The provision of alternate energy options reduces New Delhi's dependence on regimes whose policies might undermine regional or global security.

Benefits for India

For Indian negotiators the deal ensures the following benefits:

(i) It gives India the benefits of peaceful nuclear cooperation while transforming the unilateral Indian commitment to non-proliferation into a veritable international obligation. It creates the only viable international framework that can resolve India's nuclear 'outlier' status.

(ii) Despite creditable progress made by India on the basis of indigenous technology in the face of decades of technology embargoes, the Department of Atomic

Energy's three-stage Civilian Nuclear Programme faces an uncertain future. The Pressurised Heavy Water Reactors Programme has constraints of limited supply of uranium. The operational validity and commercial viability of the Fast Breeder Reactor Programme and the Advanced Heavy Water Reactor Programme remain uncertain. In the absence of this nuclear deal, the scaling up of nuclear energy production as per growing requirements would be doubtful which may restrict the pace of India's economic growth.

The DAE has been successful in making weapons but when it comes to producing electricity, its record is abysmal. It needs both finance and technology to rectify this deficit. The separation plan as Dr. Manmohan Singh has rightly agreed is the first step towards making India's nuclear power sector a genuine contributor to the economy as India's economic future is inextricably linked to its ability to produce power.

(iii) The pressure on India to burn its large reserves of coal which leads to rampant air pollution shall be reduced. The cause of environment shall be immensely helped.

Apprehensions

Despite widespread euphoria that followed the deal, serious apprehensions were expressed in some quarters. The scientists and officials at the headquarters of the Department of Economic Energy, Colaba and the Bhabha Atomic Research Centre (BARC), Trombay felt that the pact could mark the beginning of United States' domination of India's most important establishments and an attempt to downsize its nuclear military might. Placing as many as 14 reactors under international safeguards could have serious implications for our strategic programmes.

The deal could make the ongoing U.S. negotiations with North Korea and Iran to stall their nuclear programmes more difficult. Some American experts feel that this agreement may lead NPT signatories like South Africa and Brazil to seek nuclear weapons themselves.

It is also felt that a fierce political battle will be waged in Washington as well as within the Nuclear Suppliers Group over whether India has done enough to deserve a *de facto* nuclear power status. The obscure reasoning for keeping the breeders in the military list may also provide the dissidents a base to create an issue to sabotage the deal.

It is also apprehended that Washington shall be forced into entering a similar agreement with Pakistan at some stage which will be a dangerous development, given Islamabad's terrible record regarding WMD proliferation including A.Q. Khan's notorious activities. Though President Bush, on his visit to Pakistan, after completing his entourage to India refused to have a nuclear deal with Pakistan, in international politics equations change sooner than expected. Pakistan, viewed as a more useful ally to the U.S. than India may strike a bargain in this regard, at some opportune time, in return for actively assisting the U.S. in its policies regarding West Asia. If such a thing happens, the peace in the Indian subcontinent may be seriously disturbed.

Immediately after Bush's visit to Pakistan, General Pervez Musharraf said that Pakistan did not care about the U.S.-India nuclear deal. He urged his countrymen not to be India-centric. However, Pakistan's reaction since then has become more visceral. Pakistan's Foreign Minister Khurshid Kasuri has stated, "If the Indian deal goes through, there are some things we will do," hinting that Pakistan will cadge a similar deal from China. In fact in the days leading to the Bush's Pak visit, Musharraf went to Beijing but returned empty-handed. It appears that China has become cautious about transactions with Pakistan, given its increasing fundamentalism under military rule.

Pakistan is asking for a 'package nuclear deal' alongwith India despite rejection from Washington that Islamabad is not eligible for such an agreement, given its proliferation history. Pakistan's ambassador to the U.S. was quoted as saying, "Instead of a country specific deal on a subject as critical as nuclear technology, there should be a package for both India and Pakistan."

Pakistan's complaining has made no visible impact on the U.S. But, Islamabad has galvanised its lobby in Washington to derail the Indo-U.S. nuclear deal. Pakistan's reaction to U.S.-India nuclear deal has changed from feigned indifference to dismay and anger. This is not a good sign for peace and cooperation in the region. Only time will tell how President Bush beats the Pak lobby to see the deal through in Congress and how long he keeps Pakistan happy while still denying it a package nuclear deal.

China has voiced its misgivings over the U.S. offering nuclear fuel and technology to India. Qin Ganga, a spokesperson for China's Foreign Ministry, has asked India to abandon nuclear weapons and strengthen atomic safeguards. He said in a news briefing in Beijing that India should sign the NPT and dismantle its nuclear weapons.

It is pertinent to recall that NPT grants China, the U.S., Russia, France and Britain the status of nuclear weapons states but bars other signatory countries from having such weapons. Insisting India on signing NPT as sought by China may disturb the present arrangement and start fresh controversies.

The whole process of the deal, if it proceeds smoothly, shall take nearly two years to be formalised. In the meantime India will be under pressure from Washington to support its strategic objectives. One would recall that pressure started immediately after the Indo-U.S. Joint Statement of July 2005 that made India support U.S. and its European partners to seek punitive action against Iran for its nuclear fuel enrichment activities. Some circles believe that during his recent visit to India, Bush sought support for its position on the overthrow of military regime in Myanmar and a hardline towards Maoists of Nepal. This is the price that India seems to be willing to pay for the nuclear deal in utter disregard of neighbourhood diplomacy.

Scientists' Concern over the Indo-U.S. Nuclear Deal

Top Indian scientists have expressed four points to highlight their anxiety about the Indo-U.S. nuclear deal: (i) that India's nuclear weapons program should not come under any international security; (ii) facilities developed indigenously should not come under safeguads; (iii) indigenous research and development should remain autonomous; and (iv) the parliament should uphold national interest in this regard. The group included A.N.Prasad, M.R. Srinivasan, Placid Rodriguez, H.N. Sethna, P.K. Iyengar, S.L. Kati, A. Gopalakrishnan and Y.S.R. Prasad—scientists who have been directly involved with India's nuclear development at Bhabha Atomic Research Centre (BARC) and Department of Atomic Energy (DAE). They feel that on all four counts there is danger of crippling compromise. The statement issued by them says:

> It is important for our parliament to ensure that decisions taken today do not inhibit our future ability to develop and pursue nuclear technologies for the benefit of the nation. We therefore request you, the parliamentarians to discuss this deal and arrive at a unanimous decision recognizing the fundamental facts of India's indigenous nuclear science and technology achievements to date, the efforts made to overcome the unfair restrictions placed on us and the imaginative polices and planning enunciated and followed in the years after independence.

P.K. Iyengar—the retired Chairman of Atomic Energy Commission (AEC), and recipient of Padma Bhushan award said, "From the various testimonies being presented about this agreement in Washington, we feel that India's atomic autonomy is now under a serious threat." A nuclear expert at the Department of Atomic Energy said that the opinion expressed by the eight nuclear chiefs was indeed legitimate and the government should consider it before initiating any further step. The nuclear scientists said: "We have all worked in the field of atomic energy from the very early years after India's independence. From the very small beginnings, we have now reached a stage where we are in possession of all the technologies."

The scientists pointed out that India should accept safeguards only on civilian entities; "We have agreed to this before and we can continue to agree to this in the future too, but strictly restricted to those facilities and materials imported from external sources." They have reservations on the bill piloted through the

U.S. House of Representatives, saying it would hamper Indian research and development. The scientists are insisting that the parliament should set the ground rules for the Indo-U.S. nuclear deal.

The top level officials are doing their best to allay the fears of the scientists. A government spokesman said, "They are naturally anxious. Their insecurities have a lot to do with the experiences of the scientists who during the years that they were at the helm of India's nuclear affairs had to contend with a world busy tightening the nuclear noose around India. The current atmosphere of change is a difficult leap of faith for former nuclear denizens."

The scientists' objections about nuclear negotiations are dealt with in the Separation Plan that was agreed on March 2, 2006, the 123 Agreement and Safeguards Agreement currently being worked out. The essence of Separation Plan is that 14 of India's nuclear reactors were put in the civilian list and eight remained devoted to India's weapons program. This the officials said was intended to maintain India's minimum credible nuclear deterrence.

The government says that the perpetuity of safeguards is connected with the guaranteed fuel supplies including a strategic reserve for the lifetime of each nuclear reactor. The government officials said that Research and Development facilities had been kept out of the civilian list in the Separation Plan.

There are concerns in the U.S. legislation about provisions on end-user verification, reprocessing of spent fuel by India and annual certification by the U.S. President to the Congress. In this regard the government has told the U.S. that India should be able to reprocess imported spent fuel for civilian purposes without being hindered. The annual certification should be removed to the non-binding part of the legislation.

However, those who are in favour of the deal argue that the deal puts no curbs on fissile material production by India. In fact, it gives India the option of piling up fissile material and making as many military reactors as it wants and developing its breeder reactor. The actual cause of concern would rather be a disrupted nuclear fuel supply. That is why India is negotiating a safeguards agreement with the International Atomic Energy Agency to gain commitment from third parties to supply fuel in case the U.S. refuses to do so.

The deal does not stop India from conducting nuclear tests. Not even the fine print says so. What it says is that if India tests, the U.S. will break off all civil nuclear cooperation. This is nothing new, nor exclusively for India. This has been part of U.S. law since 1978 and applies to all countries including U.K. and Israel—ideologically, two closest countries to the United States.

Similarly, the idea of perpetuity is also not new. India first accepted the principle of perpetuity in 1978 when the Department of Atomic Energy let erstwhile USSR place Rana Pratap Sagar reactor in Rajasthan under safeguards. Thereafter, India also agreed to the same for its Koodankulam reactor in Tamil Nadu. Thus, India has been accepting perpetuity clauses in the past and that too for nothing. Through the deal it is required to do the same thing but getting international acceptance of its right to have both civilian and military nuclear programs in return. Without perpetual safeguards, no country will provide India with nuclear fuel or technology as it is a global norm. In the absence of regular supply of nuclear fuel, we may end up with many idle nuclear power plants. Even China, one of the five nuclear weapons states places many of its atomic installations under perpetual safeguards.

It has been argued that setting up nuclear reactors is a million dollars affair, and India with a shortage of capital cannot afford them. But India has a powerful and thriving private sector. That is why private players are being brought in. Reliance, Tata and others feel that they have the funds and are lining up to forage into the nuclear power sector. The critics are also ignoring the fact that once a reactor is up and running, the per unit cost of its electricity is among the lowest and least volatile in the industry.

In order to ensure that the concerns of the scientific community are addressed, the Prime Minister held an internal high level review of the deal. Those present at the meeting included Atomic Energy Commission Chief Anil Kakodkar, Principal Secretary to PM T.K.A. Nair, scientific advisor R. Chidambaram and Foreign Secretary Shyam Saran. However, there is no provision within the Constitution for Parliament to review an agreement that the government enters into with another government. Nevertheless, the Prime Minister tried to dispel the misgivings and gave a clear message that the government will not compromise on its strategic program. Discussing the issue in the Rajya Sabha, he said, "We will not accept any condition that goes beyond the parameters of July 18, 2005, joint statement and the March 2, 2006 Separation Plan agreed to between India and the U.S. The proposed U.S. legislation on nuclear cooperation with India will not be allowed to become an instrument to compromise India's sovereignty." Allaying the scientists' concern on the likely loss of autonomy in indigenous Research and Development, he said, "There will be no external supervision of our R&D work in the nuclear field." He continued that there was no question of India's foreign policy on autonomy becoming subservient to U.S. interests as a result of the deal. No legislation enacted in a foreign country can take away from us that sovereign right to solely determine what is in our national interest. Thus, there is no question of India being bound by a law passed by a foreign legislature. He assured the house that if the U.S. legislation or the Nuclear Suppliers Group imposes extraneous conditions, the government will draw the necessary conclusion consistent with the government's commitments to Parliament and the people. "In this uncertain and unpredictable world in which nuclear power provided security, the autonomy of India's nuclear program was the cardinal principal of our nuclear policy," he said.

Further Requirements

Though the deal has been done, many hurdles still need to be crossed before it is formalised and implemented; Bush has to seek the approval of the U.S. Congress. If it approves the deal, the Congress has to make amendments to American laws regarding non-proliferation. The support of the Congress and an early amendment of the laws cannot be taken for granted. It may in fact prove to be the biggest hurdle in coming the deal through as there is considerable opposition to the deal in the Capitol Hill.

The U.S. has to get the approval from the Nuclear Suppliers Group before the deal can be implemented. The Chinese opposition either at its own instance or to please Pakistan cannot be ruled out at this stage.

The International Atomic Energy Agency (IAEA) also needs to prepare India-specific safeguards so that nuclear rules and regulations that apply to NPT countries won't apply to India. The formalisation of the deal shall be based on India's acceptance of the principle of irreversibility of its decision irrespective of the future threats to its security.

Another roadblock that the implementation of the deal is likely to hit is the supply of uranium. Australia, the largest supplier of uranium, has made it clear that it would stick to its policy of not selling uranium to non-NPT countries like India. A committee is being set up to study India's specific position despite being a non-NPT country. Much will depend on the findings and final report of that committee.

The pro-Pakistan lobby will do its best to sabotage the deal. Many U.S. legislators find it contradictory that Bush is doing his best to deny nuclear capability to Iran which is an NPT signatory and favouring India which refused to sign the NPT.

Indo-U.S. Nuclear Deal—An Attempt to Create a New Balance of Power

The Indo-U.S. nuclear deal can be seen as an attempt by the United States to create a new balance of power in the world. It is America's third attempt. The first attempt was in the shape of formulation of the containment policy, creation of NATO and other alliance systems. The second attempt was through weaning away of China from communism and embracing the free market economy, following Henry Kissinger's visit to Beijing in 1989. And now, this third attempt is to focus on India as a balancer of power in Asia and the world.

The first two attempts were under the situation of a bipolar world order — an order that came to an end with the disintegration of the erstwhile Union of Soviet Socialist Republics (USSR) and collapse of the international communism.

Bush also accepted that the new policy towards India was necessary because of changes that have come about in the international system. The U.S. remains the foremost power in a world of balance of power which, besides the U.S., is comprised of the European Union, Russia, China and India. The U.S., however, is no longer an unchallenged superpower. Though it is militarily still indomitable, its dominance in many areas — economy, science and technology, industrial and agricultural production, etc. is declining. Other major countries no longer cower behind it to seek security protection in case of a perceived threat from another superpower. Four of the six balances of power are in Asia: the focal point of global economy is shifting from trans-Atlantic areas to Asia; the threat to the U.S. homeland is posed by terrorists hailing from West Asian countries; Asia holds most of the oil and gas reserves in the world; the region is the storehouse of cheap labour and a large manpower which is gaining in literacy rate and acquiring more and more technical skills. The two most important countries in Asia for geo-political reasons are China and India. Japan, though most developed of all Asian nations is politically not as influential as these two.

China vs India

In early 2005, America's National Intelligence Council, a think tank associated with the CIA noted in a report that China and India would emerge as major global forces by the year 2020 and that their impact on the world at large would be similar to that of the emergence of the U.S. in the early 20th century. The report observed that "the combination of high economic growth, expanding military capabilities and large population will be at the root of the expected rise in economic and political power for both the countries."

America played a significant role in China's economic development. During the latter half of the Cold War period,

China's economic growth was propelled by its closeness to the U.S. Without United States' help, influence and encouragement China would not have received flows of huge investment from other countries. The U.S. itself allowed China to have high trade relations with its chainstores, in high proportion.

Now China has embarked on such a stage of its economic development that it threatens to overtake U.S. in the next two to three decades in terms of GDP growth. The U.S. is afraid that unless a stable balance of power is promoted in Asia, it will be dominated by China. In order to counter the rising power of China, the U.S. is looking to establish India.

Promoting balance of power does not necessitate direct conflict with China. In the present-day world, violent fights between major powers are ruled out. The U.S. also cannot think of bringing about China's containment because the magnitude of China's annual trade with the U.S. and that with Japan is as high as $ 200 billion each. Moreover, the essence of balance of power lies in having a number of major nations competing with one another in peace and harmony and having a proper equation of power. Bush's announcement of issuing technology licence exemption for India, launching of Rs. 1000 crore Agriculture Knowledge Initiative, Indo-U.S. Space Cooperation for blast off, and initiatives to develop a bilateral business climate supportive of trade and investment encompassed in the Indo-U.S. CEO Forum Report are some of the measures that the U.S. is taking to bring India at par with China.

The U.S. has the experience of building up Germany, Japan and China. Now the U.S. is attempting to help India become a world class power. Just as building China helped the U.S. too, building India will be beneficial to the U.S. in terms of reviving the U.S. nuclear industry, providing it with opportunities for export of technology and services to the Indian nuclear market. India is a software giant. It has made rapid strides in Information & Communication Technology (ICT). The Indian software companies have since long been on the American radar. A large number of U.S. companies need to outsource their business through India to remain competitive. A stronger India will be more helpful for American software companies. These primarily are the reasons why Bush administration is tilted in favour of India. Moreover, building a balance of power in Asia is good both for Asia and the world stability.

Some people also believe that the balance of power that the United States is trying to create through this deal will only serve American interest. It is global dominance which is the underlying goal of the United States as elaborated in the various security documents and not what Condoleezza Rice may say of balance of power. Creating a regional balance of power through this "concession" will mean that there is no peer competitor for the U.S. America's building up of Pakistan's offensive capabilities against India bears testimony to this fact. While continuing to peddle superstardom dream to India, the United States has been regularly selling arms, aircraft and weapons worth billions of dollars to Pakistan. The latest arms package for Pakistan includes advanced targeting systems, satellite-guided bombs and the upgrading of 26 F-16s already in its arsenal. Besides, the U.S. has also announced the sale of 130 Harpoon anti-ship missiles with command launch systems and 10 P3C Orion dual purpose aircraft to Pakistan to monitor India's entire western flank and hunt down Indian submarines. It is thus quite clear that the U.S. wants to build and maintain Pakistan as a military counterweight to India. The challenge is, therefore, to preserve Indian interests in the context of global security and foreign policy objectives. Most of the concerns about the Indo-U.S. nuclear deal have been assuaged by those who favour it as a win-win situation for India and the world.

An Alternate Model — China-Russia-India Cooperation

Some experts have suggested an alternate model to the above equation for establishing a balance of power — that of China-Russia-India Cooperation. What goes against this model is China's nuclear proliferation to Pakistan. It is also difficult to imagine how India acquiesces into this partnership with countries having roots of communist ideology. India having a sizeable number of English-speaking people is naturally inclined towards the U.S. as its students approach American Universities for higher education; they get outsourced jobs and outsourced Research & Development centres from the U.S. Its noisy democracy that vows liberal values is in proximity with America which is another great democracy. It is, therefore, doubtful if India's relation similar to the U.S. is possible with either China or Russia.

The Global Energy Issue

Although the U.S. opposed the Kyoto Protocol which advocated that greenhouse gas emissions should be cut down, Bush continues to show concern towards environment and advocates the use of cleaner fuel. The U.S. realises that fast economic development in China has made it step up greenhouse gas emission. It has become the second major contributor to global warming with 18 per cent of world's greenhouse gas emissions after America with 25 per cent of world's emissions. India's emissions at present stand at 4 per cent. Pursuit of higher economic growth is likely to push this percentage much higher. The U.S. wants that India should not follow China's route of energy generation by excessive use of hydrocarbon fuels which will exacerbate the problem of environmental pollution. Bush feels that nuclear energy and other new technologies are the solution to the problem of excessive greenhouse gas emissions.

Rising Oil Prices and Nuclear Energy Option

The global prices of petrochemical products are fast increasing every year. The developing countries which cannot bear the burden of higher oil import bill have to cut down their imports and are facing energy crisis. The developed countries have also begun to feel the pressure due to limited supply, higher prices and diplomatic policies of the oil-exporting countries. It is apprehended that the persistent demand would raise the oil prices by $ 10 barrel or more per year, and the prices may reach $ 100 a barrel by 2008. Under these circumstances, nuclear energy has became an evocative article of faith — an obvious answer to the world's rapidly increasing energy demand.

The total quantities of crude oil and petroleum products imported by India during 2003-04 were 90.434 MMT and 7.897 MMT valued at Rs. 83,528 crore and Rs. 9,677 crore respectively. In the same period 14.620 MMT of petroleum products valued at Rs. 16,781 crore were exported.

During the first three-quarters of the financial year 2004-05, 71.818 MMT valued at Rs. 85,695 crore of crude oil and 5.610 MMT valued at Rs. 9,164 crore of petroleum products were imported and 13.025 MMT valued at Rs. 20,705 crore of petroleum products were exported.

There was an increase of 7.3 per cent in quantity and 41.8 per cent in value of crude oil imported during April-December 2004 over the preceding year. Crude oil imported during April-December 2003 amounted to 66.941 MMT valued at Rs. 60,450 crore vis-à-vis 71.818 MMT valued at Rs. 85,695 crore during the period April-December 2004.

During the year 2004-05, the public sector refineries purchased crude oil on term contract and spot basis. The countries from where term contract purchases were made included Saudi Arabia, Kuwait, UAE, Iran, etc.

The World Economic Forum organized in January 2006 in Davos focused on nuclear energy. Companies like Areva and GE gave several presentations to India and Chinese delegations sensing the two countries' massive energy requirements. India's power demand is projected to increase fivefold by 2030. The Government aims to increase production of nuclear energy from the present 3,000 MW to 20,000 MW in the next fifteen years. The Bush Government has taken an initiative in the form of Global Nuclear Energy Partnership with an allocation of $ 250 million for the year 2005-06.

World Nuclear Power Scenario

There is a revival of the nuclear industry worldwide. Rising energy demands, limited fossil fuel, increasing oil prices and environmental concerns have put back nuclear energy on the energy mix. The global installed capacity has increased since 1990 till now from 327 GW to 366 GW. Globally there are 439 reactors in operation in 31 countries and produce 16 per cent of the world's electricity. The nuclear energy industry, at present worth $ 125 billion, is growing. The nuclear energy as a percentage of total energy generated in some major countries of Europe, Asia and in the U.S. is shown in the following Table:

Nuclear Energy Generated in Major Countries

Country	Nuclear Energy as a Percentage of Total Energy Generated
France	78
Germany	32
Japan	29
U.S.	20
U.K.	19
Russia	16
India	2.8
China	2.2

Source: WNA

The data reveal that India produces only 2.8 per cent of its total energy generation through nuclear reactors. In this context the Indo-U.S. Civil Nuclear Cooperation assumes great significance in bringing India's nuclear energy production to a higher level to meet its increasing demand.

Disadvantages of Producing Nuclear Energy

Some people find India's euphoria over its nuclear deal puzzling, given that producing nuclear power is beset with several problems. The major such problems are discussed below:

Producing nuclear power involves high investment and long gestation period as compared to production through coal, gas or hydro sources. Building nuclear plants takes 10-15 years — the benefit come after about two decades after the operation of reactors. According to International Energy Association (IEA), the capital cost for nuclear power is around \$ 2,500 per kW while for coal it is \$ 1,000 per kW. Nuclear electricity proves 60 per cent costlier than power from gas-fired plants. Nuclear-generated power is so expensive that the Britain's Liberal Party has rejected it as uneconomic.

The public opinion in Europe is against nuclear plants because they generate radioactive waste whose storage can kill or injure future generations. About 20 per cent of Britain's electricity is nuclear. It has decommissioned nearly half its nuclear reactors and is not keen in replacing the ones whose life is ending.

If nuclear energy is good for India, so should it be for the U.S. But, the U.S. has not built a single nuclear plant since 1979. Ninety per cent of the electricity plants it is building are gas-fired. The West European countries are far more dependent on nuclear power than India. Only 3 per cent of our electricity is nuclear as compared to 52 per cent of Sweden's, 32 per cent of Germany's and 23 per cent of Spain's. All these nations are decommissioning their nuclear plants due to concerns of safety and economics. Why is India going overboard for developing nuclear energy while most other countries are denouncing it, needs to be looked into.

The experts have tried to find the reason in a mix of secrecy, patriotism and methods of discussion. The economics of nuclear power is not publicly discussed in India. There is an unspoken consent because it is considered unpatriotic to question the DAE's advocacy of nuclear-generated electricity.

Only about 3 per cent of our electricity is nuclear — it is understandable because huge coal reserves and large water resources make economic sense for us to produce thermal power and hydroelectric power which at present constitute 71 per cent and 26 per cent, respectively, of our total electricity. Yet, DAE has set for itself a goal of producing 20,000 MW of nuclear generated power by 2020 which is nearly seven times our current production of nuclear power. But nobody has questioned the wisdom of such a stiff target.

India's opacity is well contrasted with the transparency of the western world where opinion makers freely discuss the economics of producing electricity from different fuels like coal, oil, gas, uranium, etc. On the other hand, there was no open discussion on the relative merits and demerits of India producing nuclear electricity—before, during or after Bush's visit to India. We have failed to separate commerce from patriotism.

Handling nuclear waste is another big hazard connected with the production of nuclear power. India has chosen to ignore this significant aspect. In the UK, robotic arms safely handle nuclear waste inside the nuclear plants. India obviously lacks such technology, which is also very expensive. In America, the nuclear waste is stored deep inside a rocky mountain in Nevada. Some people feel that America is interested in setting up small nuclear reactors in the developing countries to dispose of its nuclear waste through them. We must guard ourselves against such a move.

However, producing nuclear power is not without arguments in favour:

The fuel cost in nuclear power is much lower at 15 per cent as compared to 60 per cent and 74 per cent in coal and gas respectively. India has abundant supply of coal but its technology of producing thermal power is outdated. Our coal is high on ash content and has to be mixed with imported low ash coal. The thermal plants are cheap to operate if they are near the mines which is not the case in India. A Nuclear Power Corporation reveals that if the thermal plant is more than 1,000 km away from the coal pithead, as most of our power plants are, then nuclear power may be a cheaper option.

Burning of coal remains a big environmental hazard. Release of tonnes of smoke in the atmosphere not only leads to various diseases in human beings and livestock but also contributes to global warming which in turn leads to fast melting of glaciers — the reservoirs of water; rise in the level of seas, submerging many costal areas and islands; change in the precipitation pattern, causing harm to natural ecosystems and hence species of flora and fauna. Nuclear energy, on the other hand, is clean and environment friendly. It produces no sulphuric acid or greenhouse gases. According to the Nuclear Energy Institute, in the year 2004, the U.S. nuclear power plants prevented 3.43 million tonnes of sulphur dioxide, 1.11 million tonnes of nitrogen oxide, and 696.6 million metric tonnes of carbon dioxide from entering the earth's atmosphere. The IAEA estimates that a 10,000 MM(e) coal burning plant produces about 3000,000 tonnes of radioactive ash annually, as compared to a similar nuclear plant producing 800 tonnes of low and medium level radioactive waste and about 30 tonnes of high-level waste that can be isolated from the biosphere.

Nuclear waste decays faster than chemical waste. Advanced countries like America are finding innovative solutions for its quick disposal. Finland will have an operational facility by 2010 for placing nuclear waste underground in a geological repository. Thus, the problem of storing disposable nuclear waste may not be as acute in future as it is today.

Gas plants with uninterrupted fuel supply have a cost advantage over coal and nuclear energy. These benefits, however, remain elusive to India as it imports 75 per cent of its gas without even a single pipeline in place.

Nuclear energy is therefore a viable option for India. The countries that are hesitant in setting up new nuclear plants have their own reasons. Many countries like France, Finland and Japan remain enthusiastic about nuclear energy after decades of use. Their economic growth has been greatly helped by nuclear power. They have been benefited by other applications of nuclear physics in medical sciences, agriculture and industry. Russia and China are also expanding their nuclear plans. In order to maintain a growth rate of 9-10 per cent on a consistent basis, India needs to produce much larger amount of power. The Indo-U.S. nuclear deal has provided us an opportunity to meet our energy requirements to pursue this high growth path. As the share of nuclear power is set to grow in India, it is necessary to ensure safety and efficiency by adopting best international practices and following security guidelines.

India and the NPT

India has remained outside of the Non-proliferation Treaty (NPT) which was signed in 1968. America and other leading nations have been putting pressure on India to sign the Treaty. NPT grants China, the U.S., Russia, France and Britain the status of nuclear weapons power. India's argument has been that if these countries are stockpiling nuclear weapons, how can they stop other countries who have their own security concerns, from acquiring such weapons. In the 1990s, the U.S. came up with some regional and global initiatives like Comprehensive Test Ban Treaty (CTBT) to stop India and Pakistan from pursuing their nuclear programmes, but the efforts failed when both these countries tested nuclear weapons in May 1998.

Through the nuclear deal, the U.S. aims to bring India into a modified non-proliferation regime. The move of India's exceptionalisation from NPT will virtually enforce non-proliferation norms through separation of its civilian nuclear reactors and placement of nearly three-fourths of India's hitherto unsafeguarded fissile material and facilities under International Atomic Energy Agency (IAEA) safeguards.

The gain for India is handsome in terms of power generation. In the 1970s we set a target of having 10,000 MW of nuclear power by 2000. As of now, the generation stands at 3,310 MW. The reason is U.S.-led embargo on India's nuclear programme which became tighter by the year. In 2001, Russia supplied fuel for the Tarapur nuclear power plant and agreed to construct two new reactors at Koodankulam but could not help further because of restrictions of Nuclear Suppliers Group. Though a non-signatory to the NPT, India has an impeccable record of 32 years since its first nuclear test in 1974, of behaving very responsibly and observing non-proliferation norms more rigorously than China which proliferated to Pakistan and West-European Companies. Pakistan, in turn, proliferated it to Iran, North Korea and Iraq, and also offered it to Libya. Out of the three countries which are non-signatories of NPT, i.e. Israel, India and Pakistan, the energy needs of India are many times more than those of the other two who also fail to match India's non-proliferation record.

India's Stand on Iran

According to a report by a UN agency, Iran has accelerated its nuclear fuel enrichment activities and rejected demands of international inspectors to explain evidence that had raised suspicions of nuclear weapons programme. The U.S. and its European partners have been seeking punitive action against Iran in the Security Council. IAEA, which customarily takes decisions by consensus, brought a resolution on Iran at Vienna which was adopted by vote. Out of the thirty-five countries on the board, twenty-two including India voted for the resolution. Apart from Russia and China, ten other countries belonging to the non-aligned movement, such as South Africa, Brazil, Mexico and Sri Lanka abstained.

The left allies of the ruling UPA criticized the Government for supporting the IAEA resolution on the following counts:

(i) It was thought to be an act taken under U.S. pressure and that the U.S. had given a blunt message that the nuclear cooperation agreement will not be ratified by the U.S. Congress if India takes an independent stand.

(ii) Till the eve of the vote, the Government was in favour of deciding the issue through discussions and consensus. By voting in favour of the resolution, the Government backed on its stand.

(iii) India has broken ranks with the non-aligned countries which had decided not to support the U.S. stand on Iran.

The Government set aside these allegations saying that the decision was based on 'very careful consideration' and aimed at averting 'a major confrontation' between Tehran and the International Community. Denying any U.S. pressure, Dr. Manmohan Singh said in the Parliament that 'India cannot turn a blind eye to the security implications of Iran's nuclear program. The resolution of the IAEA board states that, "the history of concealment" of nuclear activities and the "resulting absence of confidence that Iran's nuclear programme is exclusively for peaceful purposes have given rise to the questions that are within the competence of the Security Council." India feels that Iran, as a signatory of the NPT, should develop its nuclear technology only under international safeguards. The Indo-Asian News Service called India's 'stand on Iran issue difficult but principled.' The vote in Vienna has caused disquiet in some sections in both the countries. The two countries shared centuries of close cultural and civilizational affinities. The prospects of working together on Iran-Pakistan-India gas pipeline were an opportunity for greater and permanent interdependence. India ran the risk of this project being jeopardised by voting against Iran, though Dr. Singh remained hopeful that India's stand on Iran would not derail the Iran-India gas pipeline.

India's stand was also bold in the sense that it broke away from the non-aligned countries which had decided not to support the U.S. on the issue. Even Pakistan which is considered to be a close ally of the U.S. could not muster courage to vote against Iran and hence abstained.

India's stand on Iran expresses its concern over the proliferation of nuclear technology and the need to enforce IAEA safeguards in developing nuclear technologies. It also underlines India's firmness in taking important decisions as well as the confidence to withstand peer pressure from home and abroad. The U.S. must have taken cognizance of these qualities while deciding about entering into a nuclear deal of such magnitude with India.

Pakistan vis-à-vis India

The U.S. President's visit to India projected a sense of comfort and mutual understanding between Bush and Dr. Manmohan Singh which was not dimmed by demonstration from some quarters. But his visit to Pakistan presented a different mood.

Pervez Musharraf is regarded in Washington as a close ally in the fight against terrorism. Notwithstanding, the divergence between the U.S. and Pakistan on the key issues of democracy and proliferation was visible. Pakistan was viewed as a problem country — required for war on terror but also most prone to pass on nuclear secrets and material to al Qaida and other groups.

Refusing to extend the historic Indo-U.S. civil nuclear deal to Pakistan, President Bush clearly stated that India and Pakistan had different history — referring to Pakistan's clandestine nuclear proliferation to North Korea and India's unblemished non-proliferation credentials. Pakistan's contrast with India was obvious and heavily in India's favour. While Bush's visit to India was widely acclaimed and much celebrated, his visit to Pakistan was tense and censorious. This time there was also not much to encourage Pakistan to expect a more active U.S. role on Kashmir as it invariably seeks. The clearly differentiating American approach to the two South Asian countries shows that India has pulled away into a different orbit and is not to be linked with Pakistan.

The U.S. is not likely to find in India a military ally in the European or Japanese sense. But it will find it a country with largely similar views on global issues and common threat perceptions, a similar political and economic ethos despite the big asymmetry in their geographical positions.

Bonds of Democracy

Bush and his advisors have become aware that the hegemony they are seeking to establish could not be based on military power. After the Vietnam fiasco way back in the 1960s and the denouncement of almost the entire world for invasions of Afghanistan and Iraq in 2001 and 2003 respectively, there has been a progressive loss of the hegemony the U.S. enjoyed since the end of the World War-II. The findings of the Pew Research Center's survey of global attitudes towards the U.S. released recently confirm this view.

According to the survey: Ten out of seventeen countries surveyed had an overall unfavourable impression of the U.S.; fifteen expressed a lack of confidence in Bush and all seventeen believed that the U.S. made policy solely in its own interest. A majority ranging from 53 per cent in Canada to 70 per cent in France in eighteen of the twenty-one countries believed that removing Saddam Hussain from power had made the world a more dangerous place. The only way the U.S. administration has known of dealing with nations that confront its will is through unrelenting confrontation. But this policy has only brought disaster. Iraq is a case in example which was a staunch secular state run by Saddam Hussain before the U.S. invasion and now shows a fusion of religious fanaticism and nationalism against the U.S.

With these experiences and suffering after 9/11, the U.S. has started believing that the promotion of democracy is the only means to ensure liberty. Bush in one of his speeches, states:

> The survival of liberty in our land increasingly depends on the success of liberty in other lands. The best hope for peace in our world is the expansion of freedom in all the world. So, it is the policy of the U.S. to seek and support the growth of democratic movements and

institutions in every nation and culture with the ultimate goal of ending tyranny in our world.

This vision of a democratic peaceful world draws Bush to India like a magnet. His unstinted praise of India's multi-ethnic democracy reflects his realisation that the country is an example of the post-national global-State. India's proud self-image is of a country committed to peace, fairness and democracy. Bush feels that "India's leadership is needed in a world that is hungry for freedom."

Both India and the U.S. recognise that cooperation among the countries will lay the foundation for a peaceful political structure in future. This shared political interest is as important as other interests—security, energy and economic growth. During one of his speeches in India, Bush referred to Woodrow Wilson's liberal internationalism, which envisaged a democratic world, less prone to war. Bush also spoke of restoration of democracy in Nepal and the release of Aung San Suu Kyi — the Burmese leader fighting for democracy. As of now the approach to fighting terrorism is by replacing hatred with hope using the force of human freedom. Democracy is a great bond that ties India and the U.S. The U.S. President is excited most by India's democratic policy. In his Purana Qila speech, Bush declared, "India in the 21st century is a natural partner of the United States because we are brothers in the cause of human liberty."

Joining the U.S. in the cause of spreading democracy as a means of resolving ethnic conflicts and fundamentalism globally will bring high responsibilities on India. The following factors must be considered carefully in this regard:

- We must know what India will be required to do as a member of the Budapest-based International Centre for Democratic Transition following our agreement to cooperate in the promotion of democracy. This organisation which is an offshoot of the National Endowment of Democracy (NED) of the U.S., formed in 1983 to "support democratic institutions throughout the world", has a history of meddling in the internal affairs of other countries.

- As "a responsible major power", India might be required to provide foot soldiers to tackle *jehad* because the U.S. possesses the means but lacks manpower to deliver.

These factors reveal that we may be get caught in situations over which we have no control. So far, we are not a major target in the radar screen of international *jehadis*. One wrong step can attract the wrath of international terrorists towards India. In aligning with the U.S. in the spread of democracy, India therefore, must draw its limits so that our internal security is not threatened.

Shared Philosophy

Both India and the U.S. have shared the same philosophy. Bush acknowledged that Mahatma Gandhi moved generations of Americans with his non-violence. While Gandhi was himself influenced by the great American philosopher—Thoreau, Martin Luther King made the Gandhian thought of non-violence as 'the only logical moral approach' to fight prejudices. These values made India and the U.S. natural partners long ago. During the pre-independence period, India's freedom fighters were moved by American visionaries like Thomas Jefferson who stood against "every form of tyranny over the mind of man" and Abraham Lincoln who dedicated his life for the abolition of slavery.

Economic Cooperation between India and U.S.

Bush's visit to India has chalked out a new order of relationship between India and the U.S., not only in the nuclear area but also in business and economic relations. Both the countries have agreed on a bevy of initiatives regarding economic cooperation. The U.S. has shown a commitment to help India achieve the 10 per cent economic growth rate that Dr. Manmohan Singh thinks necessary to lift India from poverty. The initiatives announced by Bush government in this regard are:

Issuing of Technology License Exemption

Reversing years of a U.S. policy of technical denial, Bush has agreed to develop a positive list of Indian firms and agencies which would be given automatic access to U.S.

know-how. The U.S. Commerce Department has consented to create a license exemption for items that would otherwise require an export licence to end users in India enjoyed solely in civilian activities. The Indian officials have described the exemption as similar to the "green channel" in customs. The U.S. will also benefit in increased hi-tech exports to India.

Agriculture Knowledge Initiative

The U.S. has undertaken to launch a Rs. 1000 crore Agriculture Knowledge Initiative with a three year commitment to link our universities, technical institutions and businesses to support agriculture education, joint research, and capacity building projects including those in the area of biotechnology. Bush and Dr. Singh see this as an opportunity to launch a second Green Revolution to service India's agriculture which has been showing low and volatile growth rates.

The Agriculture Knowledge Initiative may prove to be the harbinger of the second Green Revolution that India is seeking. It may be recalled that it was the great American or Norman Borlang who was instrumental in launching the first Green Revolution in India through insect resistant high-yielding varieties of wheat and other foodgrain crops.

The first Green Revolution has left behind a legacy of increased irrigation and unrestrained fertiliser and pesticide usage-practices which being extremely harmful for the environment are no longer sustainable. The second Green Revolution requires a qualitative change in agricultural technology, like development of genetically modified crops. The Agriculture Knowledge Initiative may prove to be an important instrument of bringing the required technology change.

U.S.-India CEO Forum

The U.S.-India Chief Executive Officers' Forum was launched during the Indian Prime Minister's visit to Washington in July 2005. The Forum arose out of a recognition that in today's world, trade and investment were driven by the private sector. The top executives of both the countries were involved to outline how to accelerate the Indo-U.S. economic relationship.

The U.S.-India Joint Statement on Trade issued during President Bush's visit to India expressed the determination and readiness of both the countries to contribute in global trade keeping the development dimension in focus. Both the countries welcomed the report of the Forum and agreed to work on its recommendations through economic dialogue. They endorsed the efforts of the U.S.-India Trade Policy Forum to reduce barriers to trade and investment and agreed to hold a high-level public private investment summit in 2006. The dialogue continued on various issues including further liberalization of investment restrictions, regulatory transparency, dispute settlement and reducing tariff and non-tariff barriers to trade.

In the high powered U.S.-India CEO Forum co-chaired by Tata Sons Chairman Ratan Tata and William Harrison, Chairman and CEO of JP Morgan Chase, the SPC sectors including biotech and manufacturing were identified for strengthening Indo-U.S. economic relations. The CEOs from the two countries mooted the creation of a $ 5 billion fund to boost infrastructure development.

The Forum also endorsed the agreed workplan to promote bilateral trade in agriculture through agreements that keep open U.S. market to Indian mangoes, recognize India as having authority to certify shipments of Indian products to U.S., meet USDA standards and provide for discussions on current regulations affecting trade in fresh fruits, vegetables, poultry, dairy, and almonds.

Innovative and Advanced Technologies

The United States and India are also working together to support the creation of innovative, dynamic and knowledge-based economies. Realising the importance of knowledge partnerships, the two countries announced the establishment of the $ 30 million Bi-National Science and Technology Commission which the U.S. and India will co-fund. It will generate collaborative partnerships in science and technology and promote industrial research and development.

The two governments agreed to work together to promote innovation, creativity and technological advancement through the Intellectual Property Rights (IPR) regime — by taking up capacity building activities, human resource development and public awareness programmes. The U.S. is funding IPR training programmes to strengthen the enforcement and patent examination because the IPR regime is crucial for the promotion of a creative, technologically advanced economy.

India and the U.S. agree that trade is essential for promoting global economic growth, development, freedom and prosperity. They shared the goal of completing the WTO Doha Development Agenda before the end of 2006 and agreed to work in partnership to help achieve this goal.

Cooperation in Civil Space

India and the U.S. also agreed to continue to extend mutual cooperation in civil space, including space exploration, satellite navigation and earth science. The two countries entered into agreements that will permit the launch of U.S. satellites containing U.S. components by Indian Space Launch Vehicles, opening up new opportunities for commercial space cooperation between the two countries. India welcomed the inclusion of two U.S. instruments in the Indian lunar mission Chandrayaan-1. The memorandum of understanding to be signed between ISRO and NASA would be a significant step forward in this direction.

Public Health

The United States and India are also cooperating to expand efforts to combat and prevent HIV/AIDS by harnessing resources, knowledge and expertise. The following steps have been taken in this regard since then:

- The United States increased funding in the Financial Year 2005-06 for HIV/AIDS prevention, care and treatment program to $ 29.3 million.
- An Indo-U.S. Corporate Sector Fund for HIV/AIDS has been established. This is a partnership among U.S. and Indian businesses to fight AIDS. Six companies have already pledged a total of $ 1.2 million to the Fund.
- The U.S. Food and Drug Administration has given approval to 13 genetic antiretroviral drugs produced by

Indian pharmaceutical companies. These drugs can now be purchased as part of Bush's Emergency Plan for HIV/AIDS for use around the world.

The U.S. and India have also agreed to expand bilateral efforts to control Bird Flu which has emerged as a major threat to the poultry industry. The initiative includes: reaching out to the private sector, developing regional communications strategies and planning an in-region containment in case of outbreak of the epidemic and initiate quick response exercise. India will host the International Partnership on Avian and Pandemic Influenza meeting in 2007.

These initiatives will prove extremely helpful to India after the confirmed cases of Bird Flu in Nandurbar and Jalgaon in Maharashtra.

Divided Opinion

India is a democratic country where each individual group or party has the liberty to express their opinion on issues concerning India and Indian society. The majority feels that we must bandwagon with the U.S. and gain the benefits that go with joining the most powerful. A large number of people, however, feel that India should balance against what they perceive to be a unilateral and imperial U.S.

Some people feel that the Indo-U.S. nuclear agreement is an intrusion in India's strategic policy. There is an apprehension that the deal will lead us to the Non-Proliferation Treaty through the backdoor, cap our weapons potential and relegate India to a perpetual secondary status.

The U.S. House of Representatives bill of June 26, 2006 states that the President would have to submit yearly reports to the Congress from January 2007 onwards, describing in considerable detail India's nuclear-related activities in the previous year and the extent to which the U.S. has achieved its foreign policy objectives. Most of these objectives are such that have a direct bearing on India's defence strategies or foreign policies. They include: achieving a moratorium on the production of fissile material for nuclear explosion by India, China and Pakistan; adherence to Fissile Material Cut-off Treaty on which both the U.S. and India will be signatories; India's full participation in Proliferation Security Initiative and its interdiction principles; India's conforming to the convention and dual-use weapons under Wassennaar Arrangements and chemical and biological weapons under the Australia Group Policies; and India's full compliance in the U.S. policy on Iran's nuclear program. In the bill there is also a mendatory punitive clause, should India decide to test a nuclear device. The intention is clearly to control India's nuclear capabilities. It, therefore, appears that our foreign and strategic policies are being outsourced to the U.S. through this deal.

The deal which started with India's growing energy needs is now being used as a bait to gain a hold over the country's strategic asset—its nuclear weapons program. It has been argued that the non-proliferation regime has been central to United States strategic interests. It has always taken a serious note of India's actions that stood against the United States' established order centered on a five-nation nuclear monopoly. It has presented the deal to bury the hatchet but is compelling India to agree to shut down Cirus—the research reactor that provided the plutonium for the 1974 test and now produces one-third of India's weapons-grade plutonium. The intention is to stop India from emerging as a full-fledged weapons state. India has to accept perpetual, legally irrevocable international inspections on 35 identified, mostly indigenous facilities. In the guise of the deal, India is being drawn into more stringent obligations than the NPT and without any right to exit. Dr. Homi Sethna, India's top nuclear scientist expressed similar views when he said that it would be better off signing the Non-Proliferation Treaty (NPT) which permits the exit of any signatory nation, rather than the nuclear deal with the U.S. that will bind the country for perpetuity. Delivering a key-note address at the Forum of Integrated National Security (FINS) Dr. Sethna said:

> Therefore I prefer NPT...to signing the current deal with the U.S. India is supposed to get only uranium for its nuclear program to expand. Simply for this, so much compromising is uncalled for. The Americans were out

of the nuclear power reactor building business for the last 25 years. So where is the question of getting technology from them? Therefore, in order to end the current global sanctions on the nuclear program, we rather sign the NPT and it will give an escape route from going through all this trauma of separation and getting a special status agreement with IAEA under the additional protocol.

It is not easy to reach a consensus on the issue. To be allied with the U.S. is not only to join what appears to be the winning side but also to balance against an increasingly powerful and allegedly dangerous neighbour, China, which invaded us in 1962 and is still holding a large Indian territory under Boundary Dispute. Another grand strategy suggested for India is to work with like-minded countries to promote a multipolar balance of power. Such a strategy, it is suggested, would be in line with India's non-alignment policy during the Cold War era. It can be agrued in this regard that the countries within the group are governed by their economic compulsions, and their long-term allegiance to a single power or group cannot be taken for granted. While India's relations with Pakistan will always be under the microscopic eye, the differences exist with neighbours — Bangladesh, Myanmar, Nepal and Iran on many counts.

For many years, the United States and India were kept apart by the rivalries that divided the world. In the 21st century they are natural partners. Both these countries are linked by a deep commitment to freedom and democracy, a quest to expand prosperity and economic opportunity worldwide and to meet the common threats posed by terrorism, nuclear proliferation and environmental pollution. The strengthening of the U.S.-India relationship will have a decisive and positive influence on the future international system as it evolves in this new century.

The Indo-U.S. nuclear power deal is a historic break-through. It will enable both the countries to move forward towards their common objective of full civil energy cooperation. The partnership will enable India and the U.S. to work together with other countries to pursue sustainable development and meet increasing energy requirements through cleaner, cost-effective and more efficient technologies. The U.S.-India strategic partnership is rooted on shared values and is broad in nature and scope. The two countries will work together on global issues, expand economic freedom and ensure sufficient sources of clean energy. The nuclear deal has been made in mutual trust and a positive frame of mind. It is upto the Government of both the countries to nurture this trust and draw mutual benefits.

The Indo-U.S. Nuclear deal needs the approval of Congress to take effect. The hearings have started in the Senate Foreign Relations Committee (SFRC) and the House International Relations Committee (HIRC). The Committees will vote on whether to send it up to the full House and Senate which will debate the issue and vote on the bill, accepting or rejecting further amendments, if any. If there are differences between the House version of the bill and the Senate version, the two sides will meet in a 'conference' to reconcile the language. The bill must win majority in the full Senate and the House.

President Bush and the Secretary of State Condoleezza Rice are doing their best to muster support for the bill. People like Rice's pointman, Nicholas Burns and the Indian Ambassador to U.S. Ronén Sen worked the phones constantly, and personally met nearly 50 Congressmen. The two key interest groups are throwing their weight behind the deal. These also include the three million-strong U.S. Chamber of Commerce and the Indian American Community.

The detractors of the deal have brought forward the following issues during the debate:

It will break the NPT and trigger Arms Race

The detractors of the Indo-U.S. nuclear deal claim that the pact violates America's international obligations under the Non-Proliferation Treaty. According to them, India may not have to comply with the Treaty, but the U.S. as a signatory to it, has a solemn responsibility to discourage proliferation by others and to refrain from assisting other states' nuclear weapons program in any manner. The deal would breach this central provision of the NPT.

The war cry of the non-proliferation lobby is that if India, a non-NPT signatory, gets to have both civilian and military nuclear arsenals, the NPT could begin to unravel and the nuclear rogue states will spread. The deal will open the door for people to say 'is non-proliferation programme valid any longer?' and 'why is there different treatment for Iran and North Korea?' Some members echoed the views of China that India and the U.S. should implement the nuclear deal within the framework of global non-proliferation mechanism. Seeking Congressional support to the agreement, Condoleezza Rice tried to clear the above apprehensions, saying. "This agreement is a path-breaking and really very important agreement because India is an anomaly in international politics. It is a country that never signed Non-Proliferation Treaty, did develop nuclear weapons, but did so of course, having never signed the NPT. It has been cut-off as a result of those decisions, from any kind of civil nuclear cooperation with the rest of the world." Setting forth the reasons why Washington wants to change this anomaly, Rice said, "First of all, because the U.S. needs good strategic partners around the world who are democratic and India is a huge multi-ethnic, multi-religions democracy that is transparent and can play an extremely important role in the world as a strategic partner, a responsible strategic partner." Rice told lawmakers that there is a very big difference between the behaviour of India and that of Iran and North Korea, who callously signed the NPT and then did not remain in compliance with it. "India never signed the NPT," she said, "but we are asking India to adhere to many of the important elements of the guidelines that are making up the non-proliferation regime."

Even while seeing the Non-Proliferation Treaty as the cornerstone of its nuclear policy, the Bush administration is working on the rules that the Nuclear Suppliers Group has on certain standards of behaviour. Rice was firm in her belief that the deal would not trigger arms race saying that India's programme has been 'restrained' over the years and that the political situation in the subcontinent has improved. She also believed that those who signed the NPT and then violated it and disregard it are really the ones who come under punishment from the international system. Rice told the members that the civilian nuclear deal will not lead to an arms race in the South Asian region, nor will it complicate American policy with respect to North Korea or Iran. She maintained that it was simply 'not credible' to compare India to North Korea or Iran. She pointed to the fact that the civilian energy initiative had the backing of the Head of the International Atomic Energy Agency, Mohammad ElBaradei and countries like Britain, France and Russia. The Secretary of State said that the nuclear deal does strengthen international nuclear non-proliferation regime and that the path-breaking civil nuclear energy agreement with India deserves the thorough review of the U.S. Senate.

The senior Democrat, Lantos feels that the real threat to non-proliferation does not come from democratic India, but from non-democratic states such as Iran and North Korea, and how the great powers decide to handle them.

India must stop fissile production

The separation plan puts fourteen of India's twenty-two reactors as civilian and brings them under safeguards. Some quarters feel that this allows *too much freedom* to India to pursue its nuclear weapons programme and continue fissile production. Moreover, India's two developmental fast breeder reactors will remain unsafeguarded. With these facilities, India can produce enough nuclear weapons to significantly expand its nuclear arsenal. To quote Senator Richard Lugar, Chairman of SFRC whose endorsement and support is key to Congressional approval of the U.S.-India civil nuclear agreement, "In pursuing a nuclear relationship with India, we must deal with some fundamental facts. India has not signed the Nuclear Non-proliferation Treaty; it has built and tested nuclear weapons; and it has declared its intention to continue its nuclear weapons programs and the production of fissile material. Although the U.S.-India Civilian Nuclear Agreement would move India into a closer relationship with the International Atomic Energy Agency and would put more Indian reactors under safeguards, it would not prevent India from expanding its nuclear arsenal."

An editorial published in the April 2006 issue of *Arms Control Today* has urged lawmakers not to approve the U.S.-India nuclear deal unless India stops production of fissile material for weapons purposes. It has also been stated that the U.S. diplomats have failed to secure any new commitments from India to restrain its nuclear weapons programme as called for in a 1998 U.N. Security Council resolution. Daryl G. Kimball of the Arms Control Association (ACA) has suggested a fissile raw material production cut-off that would stop the production that the five original nuclear weapons states are understood to observe and also cap the growth of arsenals of India, Pakistan and Israel. Kimball is of the opinion that the controversial proposal for full civil nuclear assistance to India would inadvertently put the fissile material cut-off back in the spotlight. He added, "To leverage action on a Fissile Material Cut-off Treaty and begin to address the flawed proposal for nuclear assistance to India, Congress and Nuclear Suppliers Group member state should refuse to relax nuclear trade rules with India until it halts production of fissile material for weapons purposes." Raising objection to what he termed as Bush's "controversial proposal," Kimball pointed out that the deal would allow India to exclude from safeguards all of its military production facilities plus as many as eight additional power reactors and existing spent nuclear fuel. India's fast breeder reactors which are particularly well suited for weapons-grade plutonium production, would be kept off limits. As a result, a growing number of Congressional members and NSG states believe the administration gave up too much and got few non-proliferation benefits. They are concerned that the proposal would implicitly endorse, if not indirectly assist the growth of India's nuclear arsenal.

Seeking to allay the above apprehensions, the U.S. Embassy said it realises that India will continue to maintain its strategic programme but believed that majority of its future growth will be on the civilian side. The Embassy also stated that Washington believed that India will not join NPT as a non-nuclear weapon state.

Restrain India from detonating a nuclear device

The attempts to fast-track the India-U.S. civilian nuclear energy agreement have not been successful. On the contrary, there is a slowdown which is largely due to the controversy that has cropped up over the proposed U.S. text of the new bilateral cooperation accord that warns that the agreement would cease to exist if India were to detonate a nuclear device. The U.S. Assistant Secretary of State for South and Central Asian Affairs, Richard Boucher has declared that as far as the U.S. is concerned, India's public moratorium on further nuclear weapons testing is the linchpin of the U.S.-India civilian nuclear agreement. In the draft law introduced in the Congress and elsewhere, the fact that the Indian decision to have a moratorium on nuclear testing is one of the bases on which we can undertake this civilian nuclear cooperation. Washington has given New Delhi a draft of the legislation it had presented to the U.S. Congress incorporating some new suggestion—that the preliminary draft of the bilateral civilian nuclear cooperation agreement called for a cap on nuclear testing, warning that cooperation would be immediately suspended if India were to detonate a nuclear explosive device.

Immediately after the draft agreement containing this provision was handed over to the Foreign Secretary Shyam Saran by the U.S., when he visited the U.S. towards the end of March 2006 for discussions on the deal, New Delhi came to know of the provision. The External Affairs Ministry spokesman Navtej Sarna said, "In preliminary discussions on these elements, India has already conveyed to the U.S. that such a provision has no place in the proposed bilateral agreement and that India is bound only by what is contained in the July 18 Joint Statement, that is, continuing its commitment to a unilateral moratorium on nuclear testing." The Indian circles reacted sharply and categorically stated that such substantial changes or revisions were not acceptable to India. The deal was about India's civilian nuclear program, the sources said, and the strategic programme cannot be part of a bilateral treaty. The bilateral agreement will be prepared alongside the passage of the draft legislation to amend the U.S. Atomic Energy Act's Article 123 in the U.S.

Congress. The U.S. had shared with India a preliminary draft agreement on the Indo-U.S. civil nuclear cooperation under Article 123 of the U.S. Atomic Energy Act.

The Foreign Secretary Shyam Saran said he hoped that the new U.S. legislation to implement the agreement will be framed within already agreed parameters. "What we have at this point of time is an extremely carefully delicately balanced understanding. Whatever legislation that is passed must remain within those parameters", he said. Owing to the new provision, some internal sources have alleged that this is Washington's modus operandi to commit India to the Comprehensive Test Ban Treaty (CTBT) through the back-door.

Condoleezza Rice sought to allay the fears of Senators that by signing on to the changes in the Atomic Energy Act of 1954 to formalize the civilian nuclear deal, the United States is not encouraging an arms race in the region. "On the question of India's nuclear weapons program," she said, "first of all, the Indian programme we believe, just in terms of what India's incentives or disincentives are to grow its nuclear programs, its strategic program, are more related to the political-military conditions in the region, than to any quantity of available nuclear material." She emphasized that India's program has been restrained over the years; moreover, the region is one in which the political situation has improved and we hope it is going to continue to improve. She further said, "I think the assessment that we have, that India has some 50,000—give and take—tons of uranium available to it in its reserves and it would need a very small percentage of that on the military nuclear side."

The U.S. Assistant Secretary of State, Richard Boucher said that India has a moratorium on nuclear testing and has made a public commitment based on its own decision to continue that moratorium. He added that it was not surprising to find that encoded in various formats in documents and statements. Asked if there was any pressure by the U.S. to cajole India into making the commitment contained in the U.S. text of the bilateral agreement, now rejected by India, Boucher reiterated that the Indian decision to have moratorium on nuclear testing is one of the bases on which the civil nuclear cooperation can be undertaken. Boucher has acknowledged that the position on the text is not the same, but we have to talk about it which is normal part of diplomatic life, "It is not something complicated—You have to negotiate the agreement. It's going to be something that we have to negotiate, we have to discuss. We are not going to start posturing based on positions ascribed to us or pieces of paper that may have leaked. We look forward to hearing from the Indian government and sitting down with them to negotiate," said Boucher.

Back home, the additional provision was severely criticized. Former Prime Minister A.B. Vajpayee said that the obligations under the bill are far more stringent than those under the Comprehensive Test Ban Treaty. The proposed bill when passed, will convert a voluntary moratorium on further tests by India into a legally binding commitment for all times to come without any possibility of withdrawal under special circumstances, as provided for in the CTBT.

Prime Minister Manmohan Singh has ruled out placing all of India's nuclear reactors under safeguards and reaffirmed commitment on unilateral moratorium. Given the circumstances, India needs a strategic nuclear weapons program: "In our neighbourhood, we have China, which is a nuclear power and Pakistan that has developed its weapons through clandestine proliferation". Dr. Singh said, adding that he could not imagine the circumstances that would require India to resume its nuclear testing which many in India have said was the country's sovereign right. The Indian scientists have told the Prime Minister that they don't need further nuclear tests. But as for the distant future, a prediction cannot be made. India's commitment is to continue its unilateral moratorium.

Condoleezza Rice, who has presented India's case persuasively, is of the opinion that owing to the political-military conditions prevailing in the region, India needs its strategic program. She feels India would never accept a unilateral freeze or cap on its nuclear arsenal, though some Congress members have suggested that the U.S. should have negotiated that. The plans and policies of India take into account regional realities and no one can credibly assert that India would accept what would amount to an arms control agreement unilaterally that did not include other key countries, mainly China and Pakistan. The unilateral moratorium about which India has made a public commitment is no less important than that of the P5 which are the original weapons states—the U.S., Russia, and the U.K. France and China have decided not to test a nuclear weapon, but they have not signed any agreement or treaty in this regard.

India should define minimum nuclear deterrent

Amid efforts by the Bush administration to push the Indo-U.S. civil nuclear deal through the Congress, Richard Boucher created another controversy by asking India to "further define its credible minimum nuclear deterrent," saying it was absolutely necessary for alleviating tensions in Asia. He said that it has long been the position of the U.S. to think that all the parties in the region need to consider strategic stability. The U.S. has welcomed the discussions that the Indians and Pakistanis have had on the subject. The U.S. also had its own discussions with each of the parties on the questions of strategic stability in the region. This issue is "worth pursuing and important to talk about," said Richard Boucher.

The U.S. Assistant Secretary of State for South Asia said that New Delhi and Islamabad should work out mutual understanding to build confidence in both conventional and nuclear areas. "As in the past, we continue to look to India for leadership in stabilising nuclear and defence relations with its neighbours," Boucher said. He added that the previous U.S. governments have "pushed for India to further define its minimum credible deterrent in the nuclear field and we continue that today." He further said that Washington understood the complexity of this task having spent 40 years in discussions with the erstwhile Soviet Union over the nuclear programs of the two countries. The discussions are "complicated by China's intentions and by Iran's energetic pursuit of technologies that underlie nuclear weapons," said Boucher.

Following reports of Boucher's remarks, the Indian Foreign Secretary Shyam Saran asserted that India has no obligation to define its credible minimum nuclear deterrent to anybody, saying, "what our credible minimum deterrent would be is really for India to decide." He continued that India had on various occasions pointed out to the U.S. that there is no responsibility on the part of India to declare what its minimum deterrent is. Saran said, "We have a strategic dialogue with the U.S. where we have agreed to exchange views on our respective nuclear doctrines as well as issues like missile defence." On Bush administration's contention that it was pushing India and Pakistan for moratorium on missile tests, Saran said that New Delhi's position was that it would work with Washington in the conference on disarmament in Geneva on a multilateral Fissile Material Cut-off Treaty.

The U.S. is pushing for an Asian moratorium on nuclear weapons production in view of the relationship between India Pakistan and other countries of the region. To use the words of Condoleezza Rice: "We would obviously like to see, in the relationship between India, Pakistan and others, a regional moratorium on fissile material production. We have made it very clear that we would encourage that; we would encourage India and Pakistan to look at their nuclear relationship and the way that in some earlier days people were concerned about safety and security between the U.S. and the Soviet arsenals". To a question by Senator Kerry, Rice explained that earlier we could not achieve a restraint unilaterally by any one state. But the idea that has been pursued in today's arrangements and discussions is not just absolute levels but also safety, security and confidence-building measures which are so important.

Is India Giving Military Training to Iran?

The Indo-U.S. nuclear deal is floundering in the wake of American politics over Iran and the baseless accusals of U.S. lawmakers. As mentioned earlier, Iran, in utter disregard of NPT terms to which it is a signatory, has declared to pursue a nuclear weapons program—an act which has irked the U.S. and its allies which have referred it to the UN Security Council to take suitable action against Iran to deter it from making nuclear weapons.

Any positive gesture by India towards Iran is seen with suspicion and blown out of proportion. Many false stories are added to reality. According to Senator Barbara Boxer, two Iranian warships were docked in Kochi as part of a training programme under a 3-year old military cooperation agreement India has with Tehran. She goes on to say that this is not in the best interest of America when we are going to do this extraordinary special deal. At the SFRC hearing, Boxer stated that some lawmakers wanted India to end any such relationship with Iran as a precondition to the Indo-U.S. civilian nuclear deal.

Condoleezza Rice said that the Defence News report on a military to military relationship between Iran and India on which Senator Boxer made her statement was incorrect. "There have been Iranian ship port calls in India. The assertion that they train Iranian sailors is not right", she said. She also mentioned that the U.S. has made very clear to India its concerns about their relationship with Iran, about the pipeline and about their initial vote in IAEA. However, the Secretary of State's replies did not seem to satisfy Boxer who said that her remarks left a 'big hollow' and that the nuclear deal needed more 'checks and balances'.

Tom Lantos, the top Democrat in the HIRC, whose support is considered crucial to get the deal through Congress, said that India's military links with Iran could hinder the work of approving the Indo-U.S. nuclear deal. He also construed the report of two Iranian ships making a port call in Kochi, as India training Iranian forces. Lantos' spokeswoman told a wire service: "Congressman Lantos pointed out that episodes of conflict in relations between U.S. and India, such as India's early wavering in its commitment to refer Iran to the UN Security Council and more recent concerns raised about Iranian troops receiving training from India will only undermine Congressional support for the deal."

The Indian officials denied that there was any training programme with Iranians and said that the port call was a standard goodwill visit. Foreign Secretary Shyam Saran stated that he had alleviated the latest misplaced Iran-India obsession of Congressman Tom Lantos. In a press conference of the Indian Embassy following his three-day meetings with senior administration officials, Saran said, "The concern expressed was about a ship to one of the southern India ports and somehow, somebody had given the impression that India is engaged in training the Iranian navy or there were some exercises that took place, which is completely misleading.

It is quite obvious that the reports of India training the Iranian navy were misconceived. The presence of Iranian vessels in Indian ports was nothing more than ship visits involving cadets. This was a limited type of event and does not in any manner suggest Indian training or Indian contribution to Iranian military capabilities. Iranian naval ships visit a number of countries which have close relations with the U.S. A minor and a normal event of ship visits to its port should not call into question India's commitment to non-proliferation. It should be remembered that India voted to report Iran's safeguards agreements violations to the UN Security Council and has a very responsible record as an international actor.

The Iran issue came to haunt the deal when Democratic lawmaker, Tom Lantos, took exception to India's remarks about lending support to a statement by Non-Aligned Movement (NAM) that all countries including Iran had a right to nuclear research and production of energy. Lantos said that the statement issued by NAM was diametrically opposed to the approach taken by the five permanent members of the UN Security Council. Calling it a negative phenomenon, he warned that if India wants the nuclear deal to get through Congress and become reality, such things should not be repeated. He added that a blanket endorsement of NAM statements regarding Iran could be a deal breaker and have to be carefully avoided. The Indo-U.S. nuclear deal called for responsibility along political statements as against "signing mass statements of 117 countries who couldn't care less about the U.S.-India nuclear agreement except perhaps that some of them wanting to torpedo it."

Indo-Iran oil pipeline

India has oil and gas relationship with Iran. India and Iran signed a Memorandum of Understanding (MoU) in 1993 to get $ 6 billion (Rs. 28,200 crore) pipeline project off the ground. Under this project, gas will be transported from Assuliyeh fields in southern Iran to India via land and deep-sea routes. The pipeline which will traverse 707 km of Pakistan territory makes an economic sense to Pakistan as the country would earn between $ 200-400 million as transit fee. The project will not only alleviate energy problem in India but also emerge as an enduring symbol of peace in the subcontinent.

Some members of the Congress do not consider India's dependence on Iran for supply of natural gas as a positive sign and are seeking amendments to the Atomic Energy Act, 1954. Condoleezza Rice stressed before the lawmakers of the SFRC that even if the amendment goes through, the administration cannot give any guarantee that India's reliance on Iranian energy will go away or that the pipeline will not be built.

India is not the only country with an oil and gas relationship with Iran. One of the U.S.' closest allies, e.g. Japan has an oil and gas relationship with Iran. Italy is Iran's largest trading partner. Many European countries have trade relations with Iran. If India acquires access to civil nuclear energy, it does not mean that it will forgo other relationships. It may give India a better option for a more reliable energy supply, but breaking the energy association between India and Iran could not be accepted as the rationale behind the Indo-U.S. nuclear deal. Bush himself had remarked in a joint news conference, "Our beef with Iran is not the pipeline, our beef with Iran is in fact they want to develop a nuclear weapon... ." Reliable energy supply is a problem for countries like India that are growing at 8 per cent. They need energy supply and are looking for it anywhere they can. Some circles also believe that by voting in favour of referring Iran's nuclear weapons program to the UN Security

Council, India ran a great risk of its pipeline project being shelved by Iran. The Congress must appreciate India's spirit of siding with the international community against nuclear non-proliferation risking the pipeline project that would fulfil its energy needs and boost its economy.

Pakistan Tries Hard to Spoil Indo-U.S. Nuclear Deal

Pakistan has been trying hard to spoil the Indo-U.S. nuclear deal ever since President Bush visited India and Pakistan in March 2006, although it stated initially that its problems were not India-centric. Islamabad has said that a civilian nuclear energy deal between India and the U.S. would destroy international agreements to stop the spread of nuclear weapons. Pakistan's Foreign Minister Khursheed Mehmood Kasuri said that the United States' decision to give nuclear technology to India—which like Pakistan has a military nuclear program—would encourage other nations to follow suit. "The whole Nuclear Non-Proliferation Treaty will unravel. It is only a matter of time before other countries will act in the same way," Kasuri said. He added that nuclear weapons are currency of power and many countries would like to use it. If this deal goes through, the NPT will be finished. "It is not just Iran and North Korea. Brazil, Argentina and Pakistan will think differently," he continued to say.

Stepping up its campaign against the Indo-U.S. nuclear deal, Islamabad has sent a letter to all NSG members, urging them not to make an exception for India. This has been followed up with persuasive diplomacy in various world capitals against the agreement. The letter states that the deal with India would adversely affect the strategic stability and security environment of the region. This was re-emphasized by Khrushid when he visited Berlin in the wake of Manmohan Singh's visit to Germany. Despite Washington's continued rejections of its demand for parity in civil nuclear ties, Pakistan has claimed that it qualified for an arrangement similar to the Indo-U.S. nuclear deal, pleading that there still was time to rectify the situation. Prime Minister Shaukat Aziz has asked the U.S. to adopt 'a package approach' for India and Pakistan, saying that it would help prevent a nuclear arms race and promote restraint while ensuring that the legitimate needs of both the countries for power generation are met.

The Pakistan's letter to NSG members weighed heavily against the India agreement, stating that the NSG should instead consider a package deal which would include Pakistan. Kasuri also briefed the Dutch Foreign Minister on the latter's visit to Islamabad: "Pakistan merits the support of the international community, including the Nuclear Suppliers Group to acquire nuclear technology for peaceful purposes.

Pakistan, in the past had proposed a nuclear restraint regime to India, which did not show much interest, saying that its nuclear program was not Pakistan-centric.

Shaukat Aziz further pleaded his case by saying that Pakistan was determined to prevent terrorists and extremists from acquiring weapons of mass destruction or know-how. He claimed a major role for Islamabad in dismantling its former top scientist A.Q. Khan's network of international nuclear black market.

Pakistan's envoy to the U.S. has claimed that Islamabad's criticism of the U.S.-India deal does not amount to interference. He said, "We are not interfering, we are merely putting on the table that we also have an energy requirement and that we would very much like that the U.S. has a package approach to South Asia, so that Pakistan is not left out."

Despite all these claims, it is an open secret that Pakistan is trying hard to scuttle the Indo-U.S. nuclear deal due to sheer rivalry if nothing else. Special efforts are being made to exhort the Government of China to oppose this agreement at the Nuclear Suppliers Group just as it had in the past tried to sabotage India's claim for permanent membership of the UN Security Council when the issue of reforms of the United Nations came up. The U.S. has already rejected its demands for a similar deal or a package deal and for right reasons. Pakistan's nuclear proliferation, support to terrorism and suppression of democracy are too well known. International community including the Nuclear Suppliers Group fully understand Pakistan's intentions. The U.S. Congress would do well not succumb to pressure from these quarters.

NRI's Role in Indo-U.S. Nuclear Deal

The Indian American community is one of the wealthiest and best-educated minorities in the country. According to a Washington daily, it can play a pivotal role in pushing forward the Indo-U.S. nuclear deal. *The Washington Times* pointed out the manifold and multifaceted role it has come to play in the American political scene and said that the community's clout is being put to test as the Bush administration faces a tough fight in the Congress to pass the agreement.

New Delhi gave a clarion call to Indian Americans with political connections to reach Washington when U.S. Congress reconvened in the last week of April, 2006, and meet their Senators and Congressmen to firm up support for the bill on Indo-U.S. nuclear deal. The core group of 20 Indian Americans made a splash by giving a full page ad in the *Washington Post* costing upwards of one hundred thousand dollars, on why Congress must approve the pact. They have raised two and a half million dollars for this cause. The U.S.-India Political Action Committee—a formation having some clout in the Capitol Hill—brought together 20-odd Senators and Representatives for an event to turn the spotlight on the nuclear deal.

Both the groups have asked the Indian Americans across the country to virtually jam the e-mails and fax lines of lawmakers with their appeals for support. Many well-entrenched 'desi' outfits like the American Association of Physicians of Indian Origin (AAPI), and the Asian American Hotel Owners Association (AAHOA) having several well-known Indian American activists are garnering support for the deal.

Republican Senator John Cornyn from Texas took initiative to form the Friends of India Caucus at the behest of a Dallas-based influential NRI—Mr Ashok Mago. The latter is in touch with a dozen Congressmen from Texas, who are willing to co-sponsor the bill in the House of Representatives. The pro-India groups believe that the supportive announcements made by Senator Joseph Biden and John Kerry will make many skeptics to revise their stand.

Science and Technology Minister Kapil Sibal who visited Washington for a series of meetings with Senior Bush administration officials and U.S. lawmakers has said that the India American community's role is imperative to persuade Congress to approve Indo-U.S. civil nuclear agreement. Addressing the Overseas National Congress in Washington, he said that they had a very important role to play by convincing the American people as to how important this relationship is to the rest of the world.

The role of the Indian American community has attracted a lot of attention within Capitol Hill as well as from official Indian visitors who acknowledged that much depended on the community which is no longer seen as a political pygamy. The Indian Americans have been the fastest-growing ethnic group since the 1990s and remained one of the largest sources of legal immigration to the United States. Indian-American entrepreneurs own nearly 20 per cent of all Silicon Valley high-tech start-ups and an estimated 55 per cent of all U.S. motels are owned by Americans of South Asian ancestry. In 2000, one out of every nine Indian-Americans was a millionaire. Nearly 60 per cent of Indian-Americans over 25 have graduated from college. Politically, this has meant that the Congressional India Caucus, which began in 1992 with eight members, now has more than 180 members—among the largest on Capitol Hill. South Carolina Republican Congressman, Joe Wilson has been quoted as saying that many immigrant groups of the first generation of Indian-Americans tended to support Democrats. Once the Capitol Hill was heavily tilted towards Democratic members, but now the ratio is one to one.

As the Bush administration is seeking Congress support for the Indo-U.S. nuclear deal, several lawmakers have asked the Indian-American community to launch a massive effort to get the packet approved. Frank Pallone, the founder of the Congressional Caucus on India and Indian-Americans, has asked the Indian-American community to set up a 'war room' and launch a massive effort to get the draft legislation on the deal through Congress.

Nuclear Deal is in U.S. Interest

Despite opposition from some members, the Indo-U.S. nuclear deal is considered by many others to be in the U.S. interest. Some of them recounted the benefits during the SFRC debate.

In her speech before the House International Relations Committee, Secretary of State Condoleezza Rice said that American exports to India have doubled in only past four years. India is a rising global power and can be a pillar of stability in a rapidly changing Asia—it is a natural partner for the United States. In her speech before that Senate Foreign Relations Committee, Rice said that the initiative would benefit that environment.

Nuclear energy is clean energy. Providing India with an environmentally friendly energy source is an important goal of the deal. India's carbon emission increased 61 per cent between 1990 and 2001, next only to China. America's own energy problems will be exacerbated if it does not forge energy partnership with India, China and other nations experiencing rapid economic growth. The United States has an interest in expanding energy operation with India to develop new technologies, cushion supply disruptions and prepare for the declining global fossil fuel reserves.

The initiative will enhance energy security. India is a nation of over a billion people. Its economy is growing at approximately 8 per cent each year. It has a massive and growing requirement for energy which is expected to double by the year 2025. It is now the sixth largest consumer of energy in the world. Diversifying India's energy sector will help it meet its energy needs and also ease its dependence on hydrocarbons and the unstable sources of energy like oil, gas, coal and countries like Iran. This will be good for the United States as well as for India.

Senator Joseph R Biden, the ranking Democrat on the SFRC, also suggested that helping India to meet its energy needs will be in the interest of the United States. He pointed out to the fact that in the 1960s the U.S. helped bring the Green Revolution in India which boosted foodgrains production in India. "That was good for India and that was good for Americans' business. Now India faces a burgeoning need for energy, and so too, I believe, presents an opportunity for the U.S.," says Biden. He views the competition created by the phenomenal growth of India and China as a real opportunity for the United States. Richar Lugar, a Republican Senator also said that the SFRC is cognizant of the fact that a closer relationship with India is very valuable for the United States: "I believe that we will find little argument in Congress with the general premise that the national security and economic future of the United States would be enhanced by a strong and enduring partnership with India," he said.

The initiative will create opportunities for American jobs. Nuclear cooperation will provide a new market for American nuclear firms as well as assist India's economic growth. The initiative could add as many as five thousand new direct jobs and about fifteen thousand indirect jobs as America engages itself in nuclear commerce with India. By helping India's economy to grow, America will help its own.

The larger bilateral relationship is being viewed through the prism of Indo-U.S. nuclear deal. The HIRC sources say that if the law doesn't get passed, it will negatively impact bilateral relationships. Lantos asked the lawmakers to view all the benefits in the still larger and greater context of how this initiative elevates the U.S.-India relationship to a new strategic level.

Opinion of other Countries on Indo-U.S. Nuclear Deal

China

China remains non-committal on backing the Indo-U.S. nuclear deal. It feels that the international community is working on enhancing the authority and effectiveness of the international non-proliferation regime. China hopes that the cooperation of relevant countries can contribute to these efforts. A Chinese spokesperson said that the growing Indo-U.S. relations would be helpful for regional stability but insisted that the two countries should implement the historic deal within the framework of global non-proliferation mechanism.

China's stand on the Indo-U.S. nuclear agreement could be crucial as there should be consensus within the NSG members to amend its rules to clear the way for the implementation of the deal. Earlier, China, a member of the 44-nation Nuclear Suppliers Group, had critically questioned the U.S. efforts to push through the nuclear deal at a meeting of the NSG in Vienna.

The Chinese Foreign Ministry sources say that Beijing is of the view that the countries can develop nuclear cooperation for peaceful purposes while conforming to the regulations of the international non-proliferation regime.

Two major factors may cause China to work out a diplomacy against the Indo-U.S. nuclear deal: The first is its apprehension that a closer relationship between India and the U.S., cemented by the deal will weaken its position in Asia. If India is developed into a world power through U.S. help, China stands to suffer. With sufficient energy supply and latest technology provided by America, India might become a hub of manufacturing electronic goods and capture bulk of the trade which is currently flowing to China. The second factor is that China and Pakistan have been partners in nuclear proliferation. China being close to Pakistan, the former is likely to go against the Indo-U.S. deal under latter's pressure.

Russia

India has important strategic and economic relations with Russia. In fact, our relations with Russia have the strength of tradition and content of mutual cooperation. Recognizing India's energy needs, Russia has called for making an exception for the country in the Nuclear Non-Proliferation Treaty to give it access to civilian nuclear technology. Anatoly Antonov, Director of Russia's Foreign Ministry's Security and Disarmament Department says: "We cannot ignore India's energy requirements. It is a rapidly developing country with good non-proliferation record. We should probably make an exception in this case without adopting new norms that may erode the non-proliferation regime." Antonov is of the opinion that NPT is an important element of international security and stability. However, it must be used to deal with new challenges and threats to non-proliferation regime.

Russia has played a significant role in India's establishing nuclear reactors to harness nuclear energy. It has been supplying fuel for our Tarapur plant. India has received the first part of a promised supply of 60 MT of enriched uranium fuel from Russia for two units of Tarapur Atomic Power Plants in the first week of April 2006. The first consignment of about 25 MT of uranium which arrived from Russia at the Nuclear Fuel Complex of the Department of Atomic Energy has been delivered to Nuclear Power Corporation of India Ltd. The current fuel supply to Units I and II of the U.S.-built reactors would last for 8 months in one unit and 18 months at the other. The Russian Prime Minister has said that the supply was within the international framework and Russia had informed the Nuclear Suppliers' Group about it. However, Washington has expressed reservations to the move saying such a step should be taken only after India fulfils its obligations under the Indo-U.S. civil nuclear deal.

Apart from its tilt towards India because of decades of friendly relations, Russia plays an important part in solving global problems even in the unipolar world. It is using its influence to find out a mutually acceptable solution to Iran imbroglio. In view of the above, it can be expected that Russia would remain positive about Indo-U.S. nuclear deal.

U.K.

India has historical relations with the U.K. Both the countries have a mutual desire to deepen and diversify bilateral relations. U.K. has warmly welcomed the Indo-U.S. civil nuclear cooperation initiative. It has indicated that on the basis of Joint Statement, it was "ready to discuss with our international partners the basis for the cooperation in civil nuclear matters with India."

France

France is one of the countries that are coordinating diplomatic moves at the NSG to make an exemption for India. In fact, India is banking on French support to deliver the European Nations' support on the India exemption issue.

For France, piloting the India deal is important because it underscores their belief from the 1990s that a nuclear exemption should be made for India. The French officials feel that since India has already announced its separation plan, the India debate should continue as a positive gesture and India should be given emergency fuel for Tarapur. France has not incorporated a specific termination clause with India in the bilateral nuclear cooperation pact, signed during President Chirac's visit to India in February 2006. However, the French officials hold that any testing by India would have a very negative impact and could jeopardise the NSG's acceptance of the deal. Yet, France remains a key supporter of India's ambitions to emerge from decades of nuclear outcast status.

Australia

The Australian Prime Minister John Howard has stated that there are a lot of good things about the Indo-U.S. nuclear deal in particular the fact that for the first time India's civil nuclear facilities will come under international inspections. However, he refused that Australia will be selling nuclear fuel to India. "We do have a long-standing policy of selling uranium only to countries that are part of the NPT regime...." Howard said.

Prime Minister Manmohan Singh hopes that Australia, as a member of the Nuclear Suppliers' Group, would endorse what India and America have worked out—an arrangement that would help the cause of nuclear non-proliferation. He reminded that India has an impeccable record of not entering into any unauthorized arms proliferation.

Australia, with 29 per cent of the world's medium cost uranium reserves, operates three mines and is a big exporter of uranium to non-nuclear weapons states and the NPT signatories. India does not fit into either category. For nuclear weapons states, Australian uranium must be covered under a safeguards agreement with the International Atomic Energy Agency.

John Howard, during his visit to India in March 2006 had detailed discussion with his Indian counterpart. Both the countries agreed that a group of officials will discuss a possible supply of uranium to India.

There have been positive signals from Australia about the Indo-U.S. nuclear deal. The Australia's Minister for Foreign Affairs Alexander Downer has stated that some of the proposals put forward by India, even if they don't amount to signing the NPT but only adhering to the transparency of the regime, may not be optimal but it is a step in the right direction.

Although India and Australia share a common colonial history and a common language, yet their strategic interest have rarely converged. They also lack high-level approval for joint military exercises, military and technical cooperation and regular service to service contacts and intelligence cooperation.

A report on India by the Australian Strategic Policy Institute in Canberra reveals that the Howard administration continues to treat terrorism in India more as a "recessionist and ethnic conflict rather than part of a so-called jehadist and global Islamic struggle." Australia was once called by Howard as U.S. "deputy" in the Asia Pacific region, but it departs from Washington where it is in its own interest to do so. While the U.S. is focusing on using India as a possible means of containing China which it views as a strategic threat, Australia is less inclined to look at India from the same angle.

The European Union

The European Union is of the opinion that the India-U.S. nuclear issue should address the basic issue of non-proliferation. Andris Piebalgs, the European Commissioner for Energy, said on his visit to New Delhi, "We are looking with interest at the debate on the India-U.S. nuclear deal in the U.S. Congress. We want the basic issue of non-proliferation answered." He added however that, "we should be extremely ambitious about nuclear fusion." Till we get a sustainable answer to energy security, coal has an important potential for supplying energy resources. But a lot of research and development is necessary in the coal sector so that the disadvantage in the form of carbon dioxide emissions are mitigated. Energy efficiency, renewable energies, clean conversion technologies and fusion energy are therefore extremely important.

Germany

Initially, Germany was a non-believer in the Indo-U.S. civil nuclear cooperation. It was not in favour of making an exemption for India at the NSG. Thanks to Indian diplomacy, particularly to Prime Minister Manmohan Singh who visited Germany in April 2006, Germany has become more open on the issue and is likely to support the deal.

Scandinavian Countries

Norway, Sweden, Denmark, Iceland, Finland and Faroe Islands comprise Scandinavian countries. They have their non-proliferation agenda and are likely to remain the last holdouts at the NSG discussions. They have expressed substantial doubts about the Indo-U.S. nuclear deal for fear of inadvertent damage to the nuclear non-proliferation regime.

New Agenda Coalition

A group including countries like Brazil, Egypt, Ireland, Mexico, New Zealand, Slovenia, South Africa and Sweden have formed a New Agenda Coalition which has raised "NPT concerns"—asking for fullscope safeguards from India, in line with the 1995 declaration during the NPT extensions.

Cyprus

Cyprus, a member of the Nuclear Suppliers Group, has backed the Indo-U.S. civil nuclear deal lending a boost to efforts to achieve a mandatory endorsement of the agreement by the U.S. nation world body. As a member of the NSG, Cyprus welcomed the Indo-U.S. civil nuclear cooperation declared on March 2 during the visit of President George W. Bush. Cypriot President Tassos Padadopoulos has stated that such cooperation would be helpful in addressing concerns relating to global energy security and environmental protection.

International Atomic Energy Agency

It is pertinent to remember that IAEA Director General, Mohamed ElBaradei had welcomed the announcement of nuclear cooperation agreement saying that it was an important step towards satisfying India's growing need for energy, including nuclear technology and fuel as an engine for development. Later, the IAEA Director General gave the deal a shot in the arm by giving some compelling arguments in its support. He said that it would be illogical to deny civil nuclear technology to India—a country that has not violated any legal commitment and never encouraged proliferation of nuclear weapons.

ElBaradei commented that the U.S. has come to treat India as a valued partner and a trusted contributor to international peace and security. It is, therefore, difficult to understand "the logic that would continue to carve out civil nuclear energy as the single area of non-cooperation." Setting forth his views in a *Washington Post* Op-Ed piece, the IAEA Chief termed the deal as a creative break with the past, making India a part of international effort to combat nuclear terrorism and rid the world of nuclear weapons.

Replying some critics, ElBaradei clarified that there was no such thing as a 'legitimate' or 'illegitimate' nuclear weapons state. The fact that five states, i.e. the U.S., U.K., Russia, France and China, are recognized in the Non-Proliferation Treaty as holders of the nuclear weapons was regarded as a matter of transition. The Treaty does not in any sense confer permanent status on those states as nuclear weapons holders. He said that it was also important to consider the implications of denying peaceful nuclear energy to India—a country with one-sixth of world's population and an enormous energy demand.

U.S. Non-Proliferation Laws and the Nuclear Deal

The U.S. has undertaken an obligation to "seek agreement from the Congress to adjust the existing U.S. laws and policies to achieve full civilian nuclear energy cooperation." Therefore, the historic Indo-U.S. nuclear agreement should, *inter alia*, bring some changes in the legal regime governing nuclear proliferation in the United States.

The primary legislation involved in the initiative is the Atomic Energy Act, 1954. A civil nuclear cooperation between the two countries took place in the 1950s and 1960s. Following a nuclear test conducted by India in 1974, the U.S. amended this Act by the Nuclear Non-Proliferation Act (NNPA) in 1978. The main condition imposed by this amending legislation was that it barred nuclear exports to non-nuclear weapon countries that did not sign the so-called "fullscope safeguard agreement" with the International Atomic Energy Agency. This blocked fuel supplies to the Tarapur Reactors which, though safeguarded, were barred from receiving fuel supplies because India's entire nuclear program was not under safeguards subject to international inspections.

Section 123 of the Atomic Energy Act states that an agreement of cooperation must exist between the U.S. and the importing country as a precondition for any significant nuclear cooperation. The Section further specifies that there are nine criteria that such an agreement has to fulfill. Out of these, the following three are relevant for India:

(i) IAEA safeguards have to be maintained by non-nuclear weapons states;

(ii) Safeguards continue in perpetuity, irrespective of termination or suspension of the agreement; and

(iii) There should be no enriching or reprocessing of nuclear fuel without prior approval.

If an agreement falls short of these criteria, the President can grant exemption—if imposition of this requirement would be "seriously prejudicial to U.S. non-proliferation objectives or otherwise jeopardise the common defence and security." However, the Export Administration Amendment Act, 1985 brought an amendment which introduced a further requirement that the Presidential exemption would only be effective if both chambers of Congress adopt a joint resolution stating that it favours such an agreement.

Section 129 provides for stopping nuclear exports to non-nuclear weapon states that have indulged in nuclear proliferation activities after March 10, 1978. India falls under the provisions of this Section, having conducted its nuclear test series in 1998. However, the President has again been empowered to waive this termination on the basis of Section 123. This determination must be submitted to Congress from where it would be referred to the Senate Foreign Relations Committee and the House International Relations Committee for a 60 days' continuous session. Moreover, the President is required to report annually to Congress under Section 601 of NNPA, on federal efforts to prevent proliferation.

Due to these complications, multiple approvals, annual Congressional review and annual reports to Congress, accommodating the Indo-U.S. Nuclear Agreement under the existing provisions of law appears difficult.

The other option that is being resorted to in this case is to bring about amendments in the IAEA and the NNPA to relax the criteria for cooperation and make the process of approval from Congress of a Presidential determination less stringent. It is apprehended that such amendment would bring about a general relaxation in non-proliferation rules and regulations and may result in similar agreements being signed by the administration with countries like Pakistan and Israel. The best option would therefore be to enact another law which would state that the relevant provisions of the Atomic Energy Act and the Nuclear Non-Proliferation Act would not apply to India, while providing for adequate safeguards at the same time.

Lantos' Twist to Nuclear Legislation

In an attempt to prompt a divided U.S. Congress to support the Indo-U.S. nuclear deal, Senator Congressman Tom Lantos has announced his plan to introduce a compromise legislative proposal. He said however that he would forward his proposal only after the U.S.-India agreement and India's safeguards pact with the International Atomic Energy Agency are submitted to the Congress.

However, with both the agreements still under negotiation, analysts feel that Lantos' proposal could lead to further delays in the Congress' disposal of the nuclear deal. Hinting at the possible delay of the whole exercise, Lantos says that the final vote of the Congress on the U.S.-India nuclear deal would occur only after the bilateral agreement is completed—whether it takes "a week, six months or a year." He says that the deal does not have the wide and bipartisan backing it needs. Moreover, very few legislative days are left in the Congressional year which is stacked with many agenda. Hence, there is not enough time to develop the consensus necessary to achieve all the objectives of the administration. He says, "we need to come up with a legistlative compromise that will keep the momentum for this important agreement moving forward." Lantos fully supports the nuclear deal and feels his legislations will put Congress on record, explicitly welcoming the proposed nuclear accord and its positive impact on America's relations with India. He, however, concedes that it would not immediately make all of the major legislative changes to the Atomic Energy Act sought by the administration and necessary to complement the agreement.

Lantos said that his draft legislation will also express "the sense of the Congress"—that while non-proliferation and NPT are the cornerstones of the U.S. foreign policy, peaceful nuclear cooperation with countries that are not parties to NPT may still be in the interest of the U.S. foreign policy and non-proliferation of such countries to meet certain criteria.

The Senior Democrat leader's compromise legislation has, however, evoked a lukewarm response from the Bush administration. It is felt that the legislation would create more hurdles. The state department is confident that the legislation that is already in place and being debated by the key committees of both Houses of the Congress can win approval.

Reacting to Lantos' compromise proposal, the state department's counsellor Philip Zelikow said that the deal be put to vote only after a formal U.S.-India agreement on civil nuclear cooperation and a safeguards pact with the International Atomic Energy Agency are submitted to the Congress. "The objectives that Congressman Lantos is seeking, we think, can be obtained in the framework of the existing legislation without delaying action and creating still more legislative hurdles," said Zelikow. Lantos has claimed that his proposal would put the deal on the fast track but analysts have pointed out that it might be quite a while before the two agreements that Lantos wants to be submitted to Congress are negotiated and finalised.

The former chief weapons inspector in Iraq, Hans Blix showed guarded optimism regarding the Indo-U.S. nuclear deal. He pointed out that competition over oil and gas is generating conflict among nations. Therefore, cooperation on the aspect of energy is welcome. The Nuclear Non-Proliferation Treaty does not prohibit nuclear cooperation between a signatory and a non-signatory unless such cooperation facilitates the production of more nuclear weapons. According to Blix, this can be ensured by means of a treaty to facilitate verification of a country's enriched uranium stockpile. The International Atomic Energy Agency can do the verification as a second stream of intelligence, in addition to national intelligence agencies as it has the right to go into sensitive facilities and interrogate people. Blix also advocated the setting up of an international bank of enriched uranium which could lend fuel to users who would then not have to set up their own enrichment facilities.

Nuclear Deal and the Nuclear Suppliers Group

The U.S. and India prepared the ground to make the nuclear deal more attractive to the Nuclear Suppliers Group even as NSG prepared to hold the Plenary scheduled at Rio de Janeiro from May 29 to June 2, 2006. They took the G-8 route to woo the members of Nuclear Suppliers Group. India was engaged in some high level diplomacy—through Manmohan Singh's visit to Germany, Foreign Secretary Shyam Saran's lobbying hard with Japan and diplomatic engagements with Canada. The U.S. pushed the G-8 summit in St. Petersburg to issue a statement supporting the deal. Ensuring G-8 support was considered a big boost before NSG took a call on the deal.

As the deal made it to the top of agenda at the Plenary of NSG in Brazil, New Delhi planned to brief each of the 45 NSG countries on various advantages of allowing nuclear trade with India—one of the world's fastest growing economies.

India started with countries like Brazil and South Africa who have given up their nuclear options, before activating dialogue with powerful countries like Japan and Germany where nuclear energy continues to be a divisive issue. The Minister of State for External Affairs, Anand Sharma visited Brazil and South Africa to discuss the nuclear issue with the respective governments. Germany and Japan indicated a softening of their stand following diplomatic parlays through G-8. New Delhi then turned to the Scandinavian countries, which are known for their extreme nuclear non-proliferation sensitivities, and tried to convince them that relaxing NSG rules to facilitate nuclear trade with India—a non-signatory to Nuclear Non-Proliferation Treaty—will "substantially strengthen the global non-nuclear proliferation regime". At a meeting in London, India fine-tuned a strategy with the U.S., France and Britain to take the agreement forward with the NSG.

The NSG countries seemed to have concerns about the nature of safeguards for the 14 civilian reactors India has agreed to place under UN scrutiny. In this regard, the final blueprint of India's safeguards agreement with the International Atomic Energy Agency would be a crucial factor in swinging opinion in NSG in its favour. Some NSG members wanted an assurance that the nuclear fuel obtained from the NSG countries shall not be diverted to India's strategic programs. In this regard, India's impeccable non-proliferation record provided the answer. The issue of a permanent ban on India's nuclear testing also came under close scrutiny at the Rio de Janeiro Plenary. On this count, India had already made it clear that it was committed to stand by its obligations under the July 18 Indo-U.S. Joint Statement.

The Nuclear Suppliers Group is roughly divided into three groups on the issue whether India should get a free pass on dual-use technology without signing the Non-Proliferation Treaty. The most supportive of the Indo-U.S. nuclear deal are the four western nuclear powers—the United States, France, U.K. and Russia. The only P-5 member not to endorse the nuclear deal is China. However, Beijing has maintained a neutrality and it is assumed that it will hold out for some sort of wording about future exemptions—something that can be passed on to Pakistan as a face-saver. Although it has called India a friendly neighbor and said that it does not object to India's developing nuclear energy for peaceful purposes, yet it has taken the position that relevant parties should honour the obligations they have undertaken as signatories to the NPT.

Ireland and New Zealand are among the most unflexible NSG members. Sweden, Norway and Austria also hold the orthodox view of strict compliance of NPT. However, the NSG's hardliners on non-proliferation have been weakened with the softening of stance by Canada.

In between the supporters and the detractors are over twenty countries who are sitting on the fence. They range from an officially negative South Africa to a vocally supportive Spain.

Getting an exemption for India from the Nuclear Suppliers Group is vital for ending nearly three decades of technology discrimination against India. As said earlier, the Bush administration as well as the Indian government are doing their best to woo the NSG members to pass an exemption in favour of India. Only time will tell whether this comes off or not.

The final Congressional approval to the Indo-U.S. nuclear deal will come after the signing of an additional protocol with the Nuclear Suppliers Group and successful India-IAEA negotiations on a safeguards agreement.

Two-vote Strategy

In an attempt to ensure early passage of the civil nuclear deal by the Congress, the U.S. is contemplating a two-vote strategy which will entail tagging of the proposed bilateral agreement to change the legislation. The U.S. Ambassador to India, David Mulford explained, "Basically, the Congress understands it is going to act upfront on the legislation on civil nuclear deal... . They (Congress members) are wrestling with the idea of the moment as to how they do that so that they have a final say on whether or not other pieces should be coming or not." There is a move towards possible two-vote solution where there can be upfront vote which will address the law change and subsequently a second vote on 123 agreement or bilateral agreement when it has been negotiated. Mulford said that it will be specified in the legislative process on nuclear deal that the bilateral agreement will have to take place within a specific time frame.

Conclusion

The Indo-U.S. Nuclear Deal is a historic agreement waiting for the approval of the U.S. Congress. By applying the most advanced technology and international standards to Indian civil nuclear program, the U.S. aims to increase safety and reduce the risk of proliferation. India receives much needed help to meet its energy needs at the threshold of the fast economic development. At the same time, the deal will take the pressure off the petroleum products and reduce the prices thereof for consumers in India, America and around the world. It will also help the cause of environment by bringing about a reduction in the use of hydrocarbons.

However, the road is not all that smooth for the deal to be finalized and negotiated. Besides the divided opinion of Congressmen, main issue bedeviling the deal is one relating to the added proposal that India should commit not to conduct further nuclear tests. The Bush administration is insisting that the no-test proviso be a part of the bilateral agreement. Under Secretary Nicholas Burns reminds that there was a reference about India's moratorium on nuclear testing. According to him, "that was a very important commitment made to our government by the Indian government and it provided some of the backdrop to the negotiations that subsequently took place towards the separation plan that India engaged in. It is a very significant commitment... ."

New Delhi believes that it is a general commitment and there is no necessity to codify it in a bilateral agreement and make the deal conditional upon such codification.

Despite all the euphoria about the deal, there are sections that are against it. They argue that allowing India access to U.S. nuclear material and equipment would make New Delhi further only American strategic goals in the region. It would buttress

India's utility as a hedge against China and encourage it to pursue economic and strategic policies aligned with American interests. They feel that India will be under considerable pressure from Washington to support its strategic objectives.

It is being felt that with every round of negotiations with the U.S., India has ended up giving more and more concessions. Some people find the proposed new clause that if India explodes a nuclear device, the U.S. President would be empowered to terminate the deal, quite shocking. The obligations under the Bill, they say, are even more stringent than those under the Comprehensive Test Ban Treaty.

India's interest in global energy stability are not in alignment with those of the U.S. The U.S. has a history of intervening militarily in other countries to supervise their energy sources according to its interests. India has no such history nor intentions. The U.S. itself has not built a new reactor since 1979 and has a gap of two generations in terms of hands on experience of running a nuclear power plant from the start.

There are doubts about the costs associated with India's strategic program with the U.S. import of latest technology, setting up of new reactors and nuclear fuel is likely to cost millions of dollars, which may prove to be a heavy burden on the India's capital resources.

Indo-U.S. Nuclear Deal should be seen in the light of bilateral cooperation in a number of fields—production of clean energy to mitigate the shortage of energy and help the cause of environment at the same time, increase agriculture production, facilitate trade, fight global terrorism, spread democracy to establish enduring peace and check nuclear proliferation. The world community particularly the Nuclear Suppliers' Group should realise the global benefits of the deal. America should not insist on stringent clauses like asking India to ban nuclear tests permanently and appreciate India's geo-political compulsions to build or acquire nuclear weapons. India's unilateral moratorium and an impeccable record should be sufficient to maintain the trust required in the agreement.

India is unlikely to acquiesce into the test ban issue. There have been calls from the U.S. establishment and senior French officials for India to commit itself to "peaceful, non-explosive" uses for the nuclear assistance it will receive. This is something that New Delhi will not agree to in bilateral agreements, either with the U.S. or with France. New Delhi is insisting that India will do what it committed itself to in July 18 statement and that there is a voluntary moratorium on testing and a commitment to enter into a universal non-discriminatory fissile materials cut off treaty—these two commitments remain.

Some circles feel that India needs to be more generous and do more on its plan, separating its civilian and strategic nuclear reactors if it sees smooth passage of waiver permitting nuclear commerce with countries of Nuclear Suppliers' Group. The NSG countries appear to be dissatisfied with the India's separation plan and getting the deal through would be easier with a more generous Indian approach.

The agreement is very delicately poised and there should not be any mistake. It can be put off if India sticks to the separation plan. However, the deal is feasible though it requires fine technological and diplomatic engineering before it can be cleared by the NSG where the U.S. and France are its most positive supporters.

The problem is how to spell out the moratorium, which is in the form of self-commitment by the government of India, in the text of the deal in such a manner that it satisfies America's non-proliferation lobby and lawmakers and at the same time does not give the impression that India has succumbed to U.S. pressure.

5

China Warms to Indo-U.S. Nuclear Deal

—Siddharth Srivastava

Chinese Premier Wen Jiabao said he had no objection to India cooperating with other countries to develop nuclear power, provided nuclear non-proliferation protocols were followed.

In a significant turnaround, China has for the first time backed the Indo-U.S. nuclear deal.

Chinese Premier Wen Jiabao was quoted by a newspaper in Australia as saying: "India is a friendly neighbor of China and we do not object to its developing nuclear energy for peaceful purposes and co-operating with other countries in nuclear power generation."

"At the same time, we take the position that relevant parties should honor their obligations they have undertaken as parties to the non-proliferation treaty," Jiabao said in an interview ahead of his visit to the country.

So far, Beijing has been sufficiently ambiguous in its reaction to the New Delhi nuclear deal. The language that has been used is negative and forewarning of deep apprehensions. Wen's interview is the first in which a top Chinese leader has spoken positively about the deal. India, is a non-signatory of the Non-Proliferation Treaty (NPT), which it feels is biased in favor of the top nuclear five United States, Russia, United Kingdom, France, and China.

In the past, Beijing has spoken aloud about its misgivings. Following the New Delhi pact, a spokesman for China's foreign ministry said that the current international safeguards on nuclear weapons were the hard-won product of many countries' efforts and should not be weakened by exceptions. "China hopes that concerned countries developing cooperation in peaceful nuclear uses will pay attention to these efforts. The cooperation should conform with the rules of international non-proliferation mechanisms," he said.

Earlier this month, Vice-Foreign Minister, Dai Bingguo in India for the seventh round of boundary talks stayed away from making any comment. "We have taken note of it, but we have primarily come here for border talks and that is our agenda," he said, on being asked by reporters.

The state run Chinese media has been openly critical of the deal. "There are concerns that the move will set a bad example for other countries as India has refused to sign the Non-Proliferation Treaty after it conducted nuclear tests in 1998," the official Xinhua news agency noted.

After a studied silence, following the Indo-U.S. nuclear pact in July 2005, *Renmin Ribao,* China's leading political daily, had accused Washington of being soft on India and deriding the NPT. Reproving the U.S. of "double standards" on nuclear proliferation, the *Renmin Ribao* said if the U.S. makes a "nuclear exception" for India, other powers could do the same with their friends and weaken the global non-proliferation regime.

Beijing's considerable dilution to the Indo-U.S. nuclear deal that was ratified earlier this month comes in the wake of Russia and China calling for setting up an institutional framework for trilateral cooperation with India.

The call was made in a joint declaration adopted by President Vladimir Putin and Chairman Hu Jintao during their summit meeting in Beijing on March 21-22 two weeks after U.S. embraced India as its crucial strategic partner in the region. A trilateral meeting of businessmen from India, Russia and China has been scheduled in Delhi for end of March, and the Foreign Ministers of the three countries are to meet in India later this year.

Last year, India joined as observer in the Shanghai Cooperation Organization (SCO). Earlier this month, Russia decided to supply nuclear fuel strapped nuclear reactors at Tarapur, following the Indo-U.S. pact. Low enriched uranium has since been delivered.

The U.S., meanwhile, is pushing for India to be accepted as a nuclear exception given its record as a responsible nation. In what is being seen as the biggest Indian push on Capitol Hill, this week India's Foreign Secretary Shyam Saran has been dispatched to launch a charm offensive on U.S. Congressmen, who have begun deliberations on the pact. Saran is seeking meetings with the big names of the Senate and House committees, including Senators Richard Lugar and Joseph Biden, and Representatives Henry Hyde and Tom Lantos.

New Delhi has been apprehensive about China's reaction to the nuclear deal.

Even as Washington seems to have finally de-hyphenated its approach towards India and Pakistan, New Delhi does not want Sino-Indian relationship to be pegged to India and U.S. An important reason for Washington to closely engage India has been the strategic need to balance the growing economic and military might of Beijing, a notion that New Delhi has been keen to dispel. New Delhi has also been trying to keep Beijing away from the tendency to seek Islamabad each time it feels insecure about India.

Analysts have also been talking about Beijing's fears about firming up of deeper security relations between India and U.S. Beijing has been rapidly strengthening its entry to the Indian Ocean region and component sea-lanes of trade, has been wary of the near conclusion of the Indo-U.S. Maritime Security Framework announced during the Bush visit. Beijing will also be not happy with the U.S. defense department statement during the Bush visit that Washington has agreed to sell India more sophisticated fighter aircrafts and other high-tech arms.

However, it seems that the momentum of good relations between India and China has prevailed. Sino-Indian relations are currently at their best phase with talks underway on the boundary issue and business flourishing. India's President APJ Abdul Kalam's recently remarked that the "wound" of the

1962 conflict with China had "healed" and India's "national aim" was the coming together of the two Asian powers. Commerce Minister Kamal Nath said recently that Sino-India bilateral trade pegged at over $ 15 billion this fiscal could overtake Indo-U.S. trade in the near future. India and China concluded the seventh round of border talks this month on "a constructive and friendly" note.

Indeed, there will be plenty of opportunity for New Delhi to build on Jiabao's latest utterances.

The year 2006 has been declared the India-China friendship year with more than 40 events and meetings to celebrate the occasion. Following up on the Jiabao's visit to India last year, both countries are firming up another round of high-level visits with Jintao to arrive soon, and Prime Minister Manmohan Singh likely to visit Beijing later in the year. Earlier this month, Manmohan met Bingguo for over 30 minutes and is said to have impressed New Delhi's nuclear imperatives, apart from an early resolution of the boundary question.

In hindsight, Jiabao had perhaps given a hint of a re-think in Beijing's mindset regarding the pact.

Earlier in April 06, Jiabao said Beijing valued relations with India, saying strong bilateral ties would "usher in a true Asian century". This year marks the year of friendship between China and India, Wen said, adding, "cultural exchanges will be high on the agenda".

"Now China-India relations have entered a new historical stage," he said, hoping that the "fraternal friendship will become vibrant and strong" and remain in the hearts of the two Asian states. Wen was speaking at a press conference, shortly after the end of the national legislature's annual session.

India can now hope for Beijing's support at the Nuclear Suppliers Group that will soon take up India's case as the nuclear exception.

Beijing Blusters over India's Nuclear Deal

6

—Siddharth Srivastava

Will the goodwill that has been built between India and China in the recent past end up being sacrificed at the altar of improved India-U.S. relations? In another indication that there may be trouble brewing between Beijing and New Delhi, the official Chinese media have made a frontal assault on the landmark India-U.S. nuclear pact and cautioned of its "negative impact" on the global nuclear order.

This is the first instance of a direct and open criticism of a crucial aspect of India-U.S. relations that has been picked up by the official Chinese machinery/organs, which previously chose to be quiet about the nuclear deal inked between Prime Minister Manmohan Singh and President George W. Bush in July.

The latest fusillade runs the risk of opening up other niggling issues between India and China, such as the border questions that have been set aside in the interest of building trade and business between the two countries.

In the past few months, Beijing has found itself ranged against India at the International Atomic Energy Agency (IAEA) on Iran and the Nuclear Suppliers Group (NSG). However, China has never publicly criticized the India-U.S. nuclear agreement that aims to recognize India as the sixth nuclear power of the world as well as open up civilian nuclear supplies, despite being a non-signatory of the nuclear Non-Proliferation Treaty (NPT).

There have been niggling issues between India and Beijing recently. Beijing's involvement in Nepal has upset New Delhi, with it conveying its strong displeasure on the issue. Beijing has sought to explain its lack of support to India's quest for a seat in the UN Security Council due to the bracketing with Japan in the G-4 (Brazil, India, Japan and Germany).

However, there have been no such exchanges about the India-U.S. nuclear agreement, until this frontal attack.

The *Renmin Ribao,* China's leading political daily, has accused Washington of being soft on India and deriding the NPT. Reproving the U.S. of "double standards" on nuclear proliferation, the *Renmin Ribao* said if the U.S. made a "nuclear exception" for India, other powers could do the same with their friends and weaken the global non-proliferation regime.

"Now that the United States buys another country in with nuclear technologies in defiance of international treaty, other nuclear suppliers also have their own partners of interest as well as good reasons to copy what the United States did," *Renmin Ribao* said.

"A domino effect of nuclear proliferation, once turned into reality, will definitely lead to global nuclear proliferation and competition," the paper added. The Chinese criticism of the India-U.S. nuclear pact is in contrast to the solid support for the deal from Russia, France, Britain and Canada.

Commenting on the shift in U.S. nuclear policy toward India, *Renmin Ribao* questioned: "U.S. acts leave people more and more dubious: is it striving to prevent nuclear proliferation or actively pushing in the opposite direction?"

"Always calling itself a 'guard' for nuclear proliferation prevention, the United States often condemns other countries for irresponsible transfers but this time, it hesitates not a bit in revising laws, taking the lead in 'making an exception', for India," *Renmin Ribao* wrote, warning "this will bring about a series of negative impacts".

With China aggressively and openly joining the voices against the India-U.S. nuclear deal, New Delhi's quest for nuclear technology is turning knottier by the day. A reflection of Chinese thinking comes in the face of last month's meeting of the 45-nation NSG in Vienna that put off action on the U.S. proposal to lift restraints on transferring nuclear technology to

India. According to reports, there was positive feedback to the proposal at the group's meeting, but a "decision was deferred until the future".

At the meeting, Britain, France, Germany, Russia, Czech Republic and Canada were generally supportive, but Sweden and New Zealand asked "hard questions", while Japan seemed wary of the India deal, officials have been quoted. These countries want a permanent regime change rather than making an exception for India.

According to reports, China, Brazil, South Korea and Austria were among the countries that opposed any nuclear supplies to India. Countries such as South Africa, Brazil and Argentina that voluntarily dismantled their nuclear weapons program to join the non-proliferation regime are against any move to grant a special status to India.

Commenting on the *Renmin Ribao* piece, foreign policy analyst C. Raja Mohan said, "India might be willing to countenance the talk of nuclear 'double standards' from the White Knights of the Western world like Sweden or Ireland. India, however, will be deeply troubled by at similar rhetoric from Beijing."

New Delhi, which bitterly complained about China's support for Pakistan's nuclear weapons program in the 1980s and Islamabad's missile capabilities in the 1990s, will find it a bit rich if Beijing now opposes international civilian nuclear energy cooperation with India in the name of double standards.

"India has been willing to overlook the extraordinary campaign by Beijing to defeat the attempt by the G-4—India, Japan, Germany and Brazil—to expand the permanent membership of the UN Security Council earlier this year," Raja Mohan said. "China explained away this campaign by saying that the target was Japan and not India. A similar campaign on denying the benefits of civilian nuclear energy cooperation to India could reopen New Delhi's many past grievances against Beijing," he added.

Indeed, New Delhi does understand that there are vexed issues to be addressed that are going to take some time before the nuclear supplies open up. The NSG is scheduled to meet only in May unless a special meeting (there is one to discuss Iran) is called to change the rules.

There will be other tricky areas to cover, including the number of nuclear facilities India agrees to place under IAEA safeguards (by separating civilian and military installations) and how quickly it does so.

Hearings at the U.S. Congress are going to be tough, where India's proximity with Tehran will be scrutinized. India's stand on the November 24 vote of the IAEA, that will decide whether Tehran will be referred to the UN for sanctions, will be crucial as far as support from the U.S. is concerned.

New Delhi will also like to ensure that any exception in its case will not be used by Pakistan, which is also aiming for some nuclear leeway in the NSG. New Delhi has never been comfortable with Beijing's proximity with Islamabad.

Pakistan in turn is looking to leapfrog on a U.S. promise to open civilian nuclear interactions with India, despite the allegations of proliferation in the past. Pakistan has formally approached the NSG seeking a deal similar to the one between the U.S. and India to produce nuclear power, saying that it needed more atomic power plants to meet future energy requirements.

Given that Pakistan continues to be a crucial ally in Washington's "war on terror", Islamabad's concerns cannot be completely ignored. The U.S. has been trying to mollify Pakistan through military sops. In the past, President George W. Bush has spoken to President General Pervez Musharraf and assured him that the India-U.S. nuclear pact was not directed against Pakistan and would not in any way tilt the "balance of power" in South Asia. Some observers say that ultimately U.S. will end up supplying nuclear reactors to Pakistan as well.

However, analysts agree that the nuclear deal will come through given the lucrative market that India offers, though nobody hazards a time frame. India will hope that the hurdles will be overcome at the U.S. Congress before May when the NSG is likely to look to change the rules.

Several powerful nations do not want to lose out on the nuclear contracts that are likely to follow. Russia sees India as a major market and has been keen on expanding nuclear links with India. French President Jacques Chirac has been the first international leader to speak of the need to accommodate India into the global nuclear order. British Prime Minister Tony Blair has endorsed the U.S. decision, while Canada's move to renew civil nuclear energy cooperation following India's vote against Iran at the IAEA has been a big bonus.

India has been closely watching China, which has recently become a member of the NSG. By launching such a strong criticism, India's aspirations have turned that much more difficult.

India-U.S. Nuclear Deal: The Benefits

7

—Hari Sud

Ultimately the India-U.S. Nuclear Deal has to translate into economics, commerce, trade, development and FDI.

At the moment, Indian Opposition politicians think that the country's independence and prestige have been sold out. Many U.S. politicians are thinking that a gaping hole has been punched into the NPT regime. Yes, both are right, although the Indian side is stretching it a bit. In U.S., the Nuclear Lobby Group has gained an upper hand. When Manmohan–Bush finalized this deal in July of 2005, the Lobby Group mounted an instantaneous opposition. Unable to persuade the Bush administration to renege the deal, they changed tactics and have started a campaign against it with the U.S. Congress (the elected body). This resulted in U.S. sending a tough negotiator in Nicholas Burns to negotiate further details and possible concessions to salvage the deal in the U.S. Congress. He did well and ended up in getting ironclad concessions prior to President Bush's visit to India.

The opposition to this agreement is not dead yet. The Nuclear Lobby Group is making a last ditch effort to scuttle the deal in the Congress. But full backing of the President Bush and his able Secretary of State Condi Rice will ultimately help to get this deal through. On the other hand, most of the analysts and politicians opposing the deal in India are now lying low.

How does US Benefit with This Deal?

President Bush is looking forward to the changing times. From 1970-78 when U.S. sponsored NPT (Non-Proliferation Treaty) and its subsequent laws, it was their intent to punish

India for exploding a nuclear bomb in 1974. They set a date of 1967 as criteria for inclusion in the select group. China was gleeful; as they had exploded their bomb in 1964, hence found their berth in this group automatically. So did France. To exclude India with a fifth of humanity and a bomb was a mistake. India at that time was economically weak.

For 25 years India endured its exclusion for not signing the NPT and was barred from any civilian use nuclear technology and materials. Later, U.S. politicians, to placate Pakistan, even blamed India for starting a nuclear arms race. In short, India was ignored. Although China was no better economically then, yet it was welcomed as one of the world powers.

Economic Benefits to U.S.

If India sets up 10 large size nuclear power plants, which is its intent in next 15 years, India will import technology and hardware from U.S. for at least half of these projects (technology for the remaining may come from elsewhere). Each of these plants at a Greenfield site will cost about $4 billion. In short, orders worth $15-20 billion could be placed with the U.S. companies in next 6 to 8 years. Remaining orders may go to France, Germany, Canada and U.K. Fund for these installations will come to India either in the form of FDI or soft & commercial loans. Banks and equipment manufacturers abroad will be delighted to make this amount available to India. In return, India will pay it back with export of goods and services, in the same way China did it for the past 25 years. It is a win-win situation for the U.S. lenders and U.S. suppliers. Further expansion of business dealings on both sides will follow.

Another example of emerging Indo-U.S. co-operation is in the area of aerospace industry. Order for $8 billion worth of commercial airplanes has been placed with Boeing of Seattle. Another big order for 125 military planes is on the way. U.S. parliamentarians have to work these big business deals in their thinking prior to their vote.

The high tech manufacturing industry is at a take-off stage in India. In last three months, announcements by big U.S. companies about investments totaling $7 billion dollars have been made. This has gone far beyond India's expectations. This sector together with IT services and BPO will power the U.S. industry and businesses into higher profitability and help India accelerate its growth.

Co-operation in auto parts, pharmaceuticals, R&D and defense industry cannot be ruled out. For each of these, U.S. is looking for a low-cost supplier, that could be alternative to China.

Political Benefits to U.S.

With a few strokes of pen, President Bush eliminated a major Cold War irritant from the scene. India is not politically and diplomatically aligned with U.S. as Europe is, but India as a strategic partner in ensuring safety of sea-lanes of the Indian Ocean is very valuable. At the moment, as long as U.S. stays in Iraq and Afghanistan, the world will perceive U.S. as a big bully. A major regional power, with a different outlook than the European and the U.S. is needed to cool the tempers off. India has to step in to prevent further sliding of the Middle East into anarchy.

Military Benefits to the U.S.

U.S. benefits immensely with India as a major military power. Forty per cent of world's oil and commerce passes through the Indian Ocean sea-lanes. These today are unprotected. Pirates in the Red Sea and at the Malacca Straits prey on commerce. Indian cooperation will be helpful in keeping the sea-lanes free.

Another unstated benefit for U.S. appears to be their assessment that India could be a counter weight to a "rising China" in the region. This is not the view of Indian policy-makers who believe that a constructive engagement with China is more beneficial and not linked to any military or strategic relationship with U.S.

Future military expansion in India to take up its role as a regional player bids well for the U.S. military hardware suppliers. They will gain immensely over next 20 years.

What does India Get out of the Deal?

Benefits to India are immense with this deal. First and foremost is the *de facto* recognition of India as a nuclear power. It is not clearly stated in the deal, but it's an implicit understanding. India missed this opportunity in 1970-78. It is unlikely that this opportunity is to be missed again. Second is future recognition of India as a permanent UN Security Council member. India has tried this in last three years. It has not succeeded. It is unlikely to succeed in next 10 years. But with a trillion and a half dollar economy (8% growth over ten years), India will make this grade. When UN reform movement gains strength in the future, India will be right there and waiting for this opportunity.

Economic Benefits to India

There is an urgent need in India for capital to build its infrastructure and manufacturing base. And there is only one source to get it, i.e. U.S. & Europe. U.S. and Europe at this moment are content with sending capital to China to supply them with consumer goods. The former very cleverly had avoided exporting manufacturing technology to supply high-priced, high technology capital goods to China. This component together with auto-parts, pharmaceuticals and computer hardware could herald India into big leagues and beyond in ten years. Commercial Aircraft manufacture, shipbuilding, factories to make giant power plants, steel making plants, mining & drilling hardware, petroleum & petrochemical plant building facilities could be ultimately shared with India. The latter within ten years will have a workforce sufficiently skilled to undertake all the foregoing. It will be beneficial to U.S. Labor costs in India will always stay a third of U.S., and European costs. That will make India an ideal candidate for this technology transfer.

Opportunity of the KPO (Knowledge Process Off-shoring) is knocking at India's door. Indian graduates of Science and Engineering will play a major role in this expansion. In about 5 years KPO Off-shoring will grow immensely. India stands to benefit most from it. Thanks to the edge, Indian science & technology graduates have established.

Political Benefits to India

After 50 years of isolation, India will have the opportunity to say something, in world forums like UN, WTO and world monetary lending institutions, and be heard. This was not the case previously. Reasons – India had no clout. With western economies in the future, tied more and more with India, the latter's clout will improve. There will be frequent inter-government exchanges on matters of mutual interest. India could become a full member of the select group of G-8 members. Gone will be the days that U.S. politicians will heap scorn on India, the way they are doing it today. The Indo-U.S. nuclear deal is in fact dumping the past and unlocking the hidden potential of the future. In addition, Pakistan may get the cue and begin a rethink of its policies towards India.

Military Benefits to India

Indian military is in need to diversify its sourcing of military hardware. Russia has been a very reliable source for the past 40 years. This source has to be diversified. Ultimately, all military hardware will have to be produced in India. But development time in India is too long and success factor is low. This has to be speeded up. The only way at India's disposal is buy its immediate needs and import technology to develop its own weapon system. It is a bit expensive up front but pays dividend later as India joins the select group of countries as a source of military hardware.

Technological Leapfrog

The immediate benefit would be in getting the latest technology for nuclear power generation. Current progress in India on building its own nuclear power plants at best has a failing grade. Most of nuclear power plants in India are of other country's design. The Indian Department of Atomic Energy falsely clings to the view that Fast Breeder Reactors will allow India to bridge the nuclear gap in the future. That future may be difficult to arrive. It may be too distant. This will hold economic development as hostage. Moreover, developing nuclear technology is one thing, implementing it is another. For even homegrown technology, India will have to import critical components.

U.S. Congress and its Support

The support of U.S. Congress is crucial to the deal. This is a major headache, Bush Administration has to deal with. Currently, U.S. Nuclear Lobby Group has the ear of the U.S. Congress. The latter has become hostage to its past fallacies. They enacted bad laws in the past and are having difficulty modifying them. Now it is for the U.S. Congress to redeem itself by changing the bad laws.

Conclusion

Thanks to diplomatic and political skills of President Bush and Prime Minister Manmohan Singh, we have a deal which could lift India into the trillion-dollar club, faster. They both have worked hard. Ten years from now when electricity supply situation in India's households, industry and farms is significantly better, we have to thank them both. Thank God, we are not struck within one-sided, Iran-Pakistan-India pipeline deal. This would have held India permanently hostage to Pakistan.